*Brazilian Adventure*

# Brazilian Adventure

Peter Fleming

 THE MARLBORO PRESS / NORTHWESTERN
NORTHWESTERN UNIVERSITY PRESS
EVANSTON, ILLINOIS

The Marlboro Press/Northwestern
Northwestern University Press
Evanston, Illinois 60208-4210

Originally published in 1933 by J. Cape, London. Copyright © 1933 by Charles
Scribner's Sons; copyright renewed 1961 by Peter Fleming. The Marlboro
Press/Northwestern edition published 1999 by arrangement with Random House UK
Ltd./Jonathan Cape. All rights reserved.

Printed in the United States of America
10  9  8  7  6  5  4  3  2
ISBN 0-8101-6065-X

Library of Congress Cataloging-in-Publication Data

Fleming, Peter, 1907–1971.
    Brazilian adventure / Peter Fleming.
        p.   cm.
    Reprint. Originally published: London : J. Cape, 1933.
    ISBN 0-8101-6065-X (pbk. : alk. paper)
    1. Brazil—Description and travel. 2. Mato Grosso (Brazil : State)—Description
and travel. 3. Indians of South America—Brazil. 4. Fawcett, Percy Harrison,
1867–1925? 5. Fleming, Peter, 1907–1971. I. Title.
F2515.F742 1999
918.1'720461—dc21
                                                                99-36759
                                                                     CIP

The paper used in this publication meets the minimum requirements of the American
National Standard for Information Sciences—Permanence of Paper for Printed
Library Materials, ANSI Z39.48-1984.

# CONTENTS

# CONTENTS

## PART THREE

### THE RACE TO THE AMAZON

## EPILOGUE

### HOME SWEET HOME

8

# FOREWORD

MOST expeditions have serious, scientific, non-committal books written about them. But ours was not that sort of expedition, and mine is not that sort of book. Only an alienist could have chronicled our activities either seriously or scientifically. I have, however, been as non-committal as I could.

Differing as it does from most books about expeditions, this book differs also from most books about the interior of Brazil. It differs in being throughout strictly truthful. I had meant, when I started, to pile on the agony a good deal; I felt it would be expected of me. In treating of the Great Unknown one has a free hand, and my few predecessors in this particular field had made great play with the Terrors of the Jungle. The alligators, the snakes, the man-eating fish, the lurking savages, those dreadful insects — all the paraphernalia of tropical mumbo jumbo lay ready to my hand. But when the time came I found that I had not the face to make the most of them. So the reader must forgive me if my picture of Matto Grosso does not tally with his lurid preconceptions.

The hardships and privations which we were called on to endure were of a very minor order, the dangers which we ran were considerably less than those to be encountered on any arterial road during a heat wave; and if, in any part of this book, I have given a contrary impression, I have done so unwittingly.

The expedition may claim to have thrown a little (but not much) light, of a confirmatory nature, on the mystery surrounding Colonel Fawcett's disappearance. Otherwise, beyond the completion of a 3000 mile journey, mostly under amusing conditions, through a little-known part of the world, and the discovery of one new tributary to a tributary to a tributary of the Amazon, nothing of importance was achieved. But I should like to take this opportunity of expressing my profound appreciation of the parts played in the incidents herein narrated by all members of the expedition, and our gratitude to Capt. J. G. Holman, of São Paulo, for the invaluable services rendered by him to the expedition in Brazil; and in particular I should like to thank Mr. Roger Pettiward, who always saw the joke.

PETER FLEMING

Nettlebed,
   Oxfordshire
*March,* 1933

*To C.*

# PART ONE

## THROUGH THE LOOKING GLASS

# CHAPTER I

## SIGNING ON

It began with an advertisement in the Agony Column of *The Times*.

I always read the Agony Column first, and the news (if there is time) afterwards. This is a practice which most people will deplore, saying that it argues, not only disrespect to a great journal, but an almost impudent lack of curiosity with regard to what are called World Events.

I suppose they are right. But this is a dull life, and the only excuse for the existence of newspapers is that they should make it less dull. It is popularly supposed to be a good thing to know what happened in the world yesterday; but for my part I find it at least equally important to know what may be happening in the world to-day. I fail to see how anyone who has the industry to acquire, and the fortitude to assimilate without panic, a working knowledge of the morning's news can find life any easier to face for the assurance that there is deadlock at Geneva, vacillation at Westminster, foot-and-mouth in Leicestershire, sabotage in Poland, and a slump in Kaffirs. I, on the other hand, without burdening my memory with a lot of facts of uncertain value and ephemeral validity — without even opening the paper — can start the day equipped with several agreeable and stimulating subjects for speculation. What strange kind of a creature can it be whose wolf-hound — now lost in Battersea Park — answers to the name of Effie? How will the Jolly Winter Sports Party ('only sahibs need apply') be finally constituted? Why is Bingo heart-broken? And what possible use can Box A have for a horned toad?

It will be objected that these are frivolous and unprofitable topics for thought: that in these distressful times one ought to be concentrating on graver matters — on War Debts, and on find-ing fresh excuses for Japan. Theoretically, I know, there is a great deal in this. But at heart I am impenitent. At heart I prefer — and I am afraid I always shall prefer — the world of the Agony Column to that great stage of fools to which the editorial pages of *The Times* so faithfully hold up a mirror. The world of the Agony Column is a world of romance, across which sundered lovers are for ever hurrying to familiar rendezvous ('same time, same place'): a world in which jewellery is con-stantly being left in taxi-cabs with destinations which must surely be compromising: a world of faded and rather desperate gentility, peopled largely by Old Etonians and ladies of title: a world of the most tremendous enterprise, in which Oxford B.A.s, though equipped only with five European languages, medium height and the ability to drive a car, are ready to 'go anywhere, do anything': a world of sudden and heroic sacrifices ('owner going abroad'): a world in which every object has a sentimental value, every young man a good appearance, and only the highest references are exchanged: an anxious, urgent, cryptic world: a world in which anything may happen. . . .

'Exploring and sporting expedition, under experienced guidance, leaving England June, to explore rivers Central Brazil, if possible ascertain fate Colonel Fawcett; abundance game, big and small; exceptional fishing; ROOM TWO MORE GUNS; highest references expected and given.— Write Box X, *The Times*, E.C.4.'

This is my favourite sort of advertisement. It had the right improbable ring to it. As I gazed, with all possible detachment, at a map of South America, I seemed to hear the glib and rapid voice of Munchausen, the clink of gold bricks. I had a curiously distinct vision (I don't know why) of two men with red faces deciding, in the bar of the Royal Automobile Club, that what they wanted was a couple of suckers to put up a thou. So wisdom prevailed; and for ten days, though I thought quite often about the interior of Brazil, I did nothing to increase my chances of exploring it.

But on the tenth day, or thereabouts, I found myself reading a long article on the middle page of *The Times* which was clearly about this expedition. Its plans were outlined, its itinerary indicated, and the latest theories about Colonel Fawcett's fate were discussed with that almost medieval disregard for the geographical facts involved of which I was shortly to become a leading exponent. So the thing really existed. The project was genuine. There was an expedition leaving England in June. And *The Times* took it seriously.

This was altogether too much for me. I was still careful to pretend to myself that it would be out of the question for me to go to Brazil. It would cost too much and take too long; and it would be the act of a madman to throw up the literary editorship of the most august of weekly journals in favour of a wild-goose chase. All the same, I argued, it will do no harm to find out a little more about it. . . .

So I wrote to Box X asking for particulars, and presently got an answer from which it appeared that neither the time nor the money involved were as far beyond my means as I had expected. From that moment I gave up struggling with the inevitable. I wrote back and applied for an option on one of the vacancies in the expedition, which, I explained, I would not be in a position to take up definitely for another fortnight or so. In this letter I had meant to rehearse at considerable length my qualifications to take part in an enterprise of this sort, but when the time came these proved curiously indefinable. So I only put down my age (which was 24) and where I had been educated. As a regular reader of the Agony Column, I knew that this latter piece of information, though seemingly irrelevant, might well prove of the first importance; for by Agony Column standards an Old Boy is worth two young men.

This verbal economy I have always believed was good policy. Surfeited with the self-portraiture of applicants who appeared, almost to a man, to be as strong as a horse, as brave as a lion, and to have some knowledge of commercial Spanish, Box X was instantly attracted by my laconic method of approach. More letters were exchanged, a meeting took place, and before long I found myself committed — in the capacity of special correspondent to *The Times* — to a venture for which Rider Haggard might have written the plot and Conrad designed the scenery.

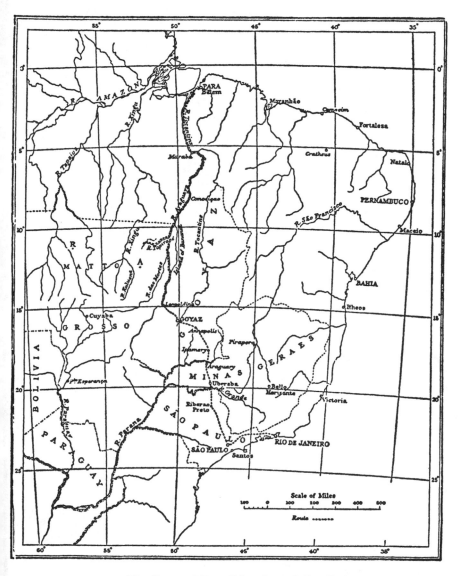

The Route of Expedition through Brazil

# CHAPTER II

# THE MYSTERY OF COLONEL FAWCETT

THE story of Colonel Fawcett is a curious and romantic one, and appears to have acquired in the eyes of editors an imperishable news value, on which the passage of time produces little or no effect. To judge by the press cuttings which I still receive, hardly a week passes in which some English newspaper does not make an apocryphal reference to the lost explorer. Fresh rumours are always coming in, fresh expeditions are always on the point of starting. The press has manufactured out of Colonel Fawcett's fate one of the most popular of contemporary mysteries.

The press had first class material to work on. In the early summer of 1925, Colonel Fawcett, accompanied by his son Jack and another young Englishman called Raleigh Rimell — both in the early twenties — left the last outpost of civilization on the edge of an almost entirely unexplored region in the Central Brazilian Plateau. None of them has ever been heard of since.

In more respects than one this was not an ordinary expedition. Its aims alone (in so far as they are known) were sufficient to invest it with a glamour even greater than that which normally attaches to the penetration of unknown and dangerous country. Fawcett was after a Lost World.

Less, probably, is known about the interior of Matto Grosso than about any other inhabited area of equal size in the world. It was in 1925, it is to-day, and it is likely to remain for some time very largely virgin territory. Between the headwaters of the great northward-flowing tributaries of the Amazon —

between the Araguaya and the Xingú, between the Xingú and the Tapajos — there are huge tracts of jungle which no white man has even attempted to enter. You can believe what you like about those regions: no one has authority to contradict you. You can postulate the existence in them of prehistoric monsters, of white Indians, of ruined cities, of enormous lakes. Fawcett plumped for ruined cities.

'It is certain,' he wrote, not long before his disappearance, 'that amazing ruins of ancient cities — ruins incomparably older than those in Egypt — exist in the far interior of Matto Grosso.' He had long held this theory, which was based specifically on a document[1] discovered in the archives at Rio de Janeiro. This document was the log of a Portuguese expedition, and it told the following story:

In 1743 a small party consisting of six Portuguese and a dozen negro slaves, with a train of 20 to 30 Indians, set out in quest of some half fabulous silver and gold mines, the secret of which had perished in 1622 with their original discoverer, a half-Portuguese, half-Indian soldier of fortune. The expedition went north from Minas Geraes. Eleven years later the survivors were heard of in the coastal regions of Bahia; but they never reappeared.

In the heart of the Central Plateau they came on a sudden jagged range of mountains. Climbing up a crevice in the precipitous sides, they emerged on a rich table-land and saw before them the outlines of a city — a city massively built with huge blocks of stone and absolutely deserted; it appeared to have been devastated by an earthquake. The expedition's report describes at some length its buildings and monuments, which seem to have been chiefly remarkable for the fact that they were just the sort of thing you would expect to find in a ruined city of terrific antiquity. But it describes them in considerable detail, and appends copies of the hieroglyphic inscriptions seen on some of them; so there is some foundation

[1] Manuscript No. 512, Biblioteca Nacional, Rio de Janeiro.

for Fawcett's contention that the story is too circumstantial to be dismissed, and that 'its details are beyond the imagination of more or less illiterate people'.

The expedition found a few gold coins and a number of mine shafts, and gold could be panned in large quantities in the local river. But their leader was anxious to return to civilization and organize a party sufficiently large and well-equipped to exploit their discovery; so they left the city and headed for the distant Atlantic coast, though not before they had caught sight of two of those men with white skins and long black hair to whose existence somewhere in the Central Plateau so many early reports testify. From the River Paraguassú the expedition sent on its report by Indian runner to the Viceroy at Bahia; and that was the last that anybody heard of them. Whether they got lost, or whether their Indians deserted them, they never reached the coast. Their report was pigeon-holed, to be unearthed in the middle of the nineteenth century, when the Brazilian Government made a half-hearted and unsuccessful attempt to find this exceptionally well-appointed cradle of a lost civilization.

Its whereabouts, wrote Fawcett in 1925, were known — 'so far as the general location and surrounding topography are concerned' — to only three men. 'One was a Frenchman, whose last attempt to get there cost him an eye, and it is probable he will make no more; the second is an Englishman who before he left the country was suffering from an advanced stage of cancer, and is probably no longer alive; the third is the writer.'

The writer was peculiarly well qualified to make the most of his exclusive knowledge. Lt.-Col. P. H. Fawcett, D.S.O., had a remarkable record. He was a rare combination of the mystic and the man of action. As a subaltern in the Royal Artillery (on the list of whose officers his name still appears), he served for seven or eight years at Trincomalee, where he became deeply interested in Buddhism, and where he spent all his available leave and money on a fruitless search, carried out with the aid of a cryptic map, for the buried treasure of the Kandyan Kings. He was a Founder's Medallist of the Royal Geographical Society, and from 1906 to 1909 he was lent to the Bolivian Government, for whom he surveyed a long and excessively unhealthy sector of the Brazilian-Bolivian frontier. He made several other expeditions in those parts of South America, and was out there when the war broke out; he returned to serve with distinction on the Western Front. As soon as he was demobilized he went back to Brazil, and until the time of his disappearance concentrated all his energies on the quest for his Lost City. In 1920 he made an abortive attempt to penetrate the regions north of Cuyabá, the capital of the state of Matto Grosso; but the expedition was held up by floods, and his companions broke down. Fawcett had to turn back.

It was not a thing he was accustomed to doing. He was a man of indomitable courage, and his powers of endurance were extraordinary. Insects, fever, and privation had no effect on him; time and again in his travels he outlasted the men who were with him. The problem of personnel was accordingly one to which he had given the closest attention, and the way in which he solved it in 1925 was not the least remarkable feature of his desperate venture.

'All exploration across, as opposed to expeditions into these regions depends for its success on the selection of a limited personnel, able, if need be, to do without transport under extremely trying conditions,' Fawcett wrote. Pack animals were out of the question; water was too unreliable, the cover too dense, and the various insect pests too ubiquitous and too destructive for horses, mules, or oxen to survive a long journey. Nor could you depend on the obvious alternative — porters; for most of the tribes fear and hate their neighbours, and Indians will rarely accompany you beyond the limits of their own territory. Moreover, there was the food problem; 'game', wrote Fawcett, 'is nowhere plentiful in this country; there is usually enough to feed a small party, but never a large one'. So he took with him, as I have said, only his son and one other young Englishman. They carried their own provisions and equipment, and even when they started they must have been travelling dangerously light.

Fawcett kept very quiet about his plans, which to this day are known only in their general and exceedingly ambitious outline; he did not want to blaze the trail to his private Atlantis. It appears that he hoped to travel north from Cuyabá to somewhere about lat. 10 south, and then turn east through the heart of that huge stretch of unknown country between the Xingú and the Araguaya. Here, in the Serra do Roncador, or Snoring Mountains (an entirely imaginary range of hills, as is now known), he expected to find his Lost City. I am convinced that his journey, as contemplated, was not impossible; but it would be hard to find one that was much more difficult and dangerous. It is easy enough — as you will learn, if you manage to read this book — to penetrate those regions by water. It is when you leave the rivers and strike across country that the trouble begins.

On April 20th, 1925, Fawcett and his two companions set off from Cuyabá with two guides. They went north over the same trail that Fawcett had followed in 1920, and on May 29th they reached a place called Dead Horse Camp, where one of Fawcett's animals had died on his previous expedition. From Dead Horse Camp Fawcett sent back his last despatch to the North American Newspaper Alliance, which had helped to finance him. It is dated May 30th, and it ends:

'Our two guides go back from here. They are more and more nervous as we push further into the Indian country . . . I shall continue to prepare despatches from time to time, in hopes of being able to get them out eventually through some friendly tribe of Indians. But I doubt if this will be possible.'

It was not possible. Since that day there has been no authentic news of Fawcett. He had warned his friends that he expected to be out of touch for at least two years, and that a prolonged absence was more likely to mean success than failure. But by 1927 it was obvious that there was cause for grave anxiety, and enquiries were addressed to the Brazilian Government through H.M. Ambassador at Rio de Janeiro. Two or three months later the Brazilian Government replied that their officials in the interior had failed to trace Colonel Fawcett, and that it was to be feared that his party had perished.

It was to be feared . . .; but it was not certain. Here was the most universally attractive kind of mystery, and the public pounced on it. Fawcett's wife gallantly proclaimed her faith in her husband's survival: a faith which the passage of eight years has not shaken, and which is strengthened from time to time by telepathic communications through various intermediaries. (According to many of these messages, the explorer is not only safe, but has reached his Lost City, of which the residential amenities are considerable.)

In 1927 the Colonel's fate offered a fascinating field for speculation. Was he alive? Was he the captive of an Indian tribe? Had he been made a god? Had he voluntarily renounced civilization in favour of the jungle? These and many other alternatives were debated hotly. They are still being debated to-day; before me lies an article from a Sunday paper of recent date, headed 'Is Jack Fawcett Buddha?'

In a good year you will get as many as three or four travellers who claim to have met and spoken to Colonel Fawcett at some not very precisely indicated spot in the Brazilian interior. The first in the field was a Frenchman, who shared with Shakespeare both the habit of spelling his name in a number of different ways and a tendency to underrate the value of plausibility. The press gave a great deal of prominence to his story, of which the final version was that the Frenchman had been shooting alligators near Cuyabá with a friend, when his attention had been momentarily distracted from this manly pastime by the sight of an old bearded man sitting by the side of the road being bitten by mosquitoes. They exchanged a few remarks in English on the subject of insect life in the tropics (the old man revealing a rather pleasant vein of irony) and then they parted. Nobody seriously supposed that they would ever see each other again, and before long the Frenchman and his story were forgotten.

The first important development in the Fawcett case was a full-blown relief expedition. It was led by Commander George Dyott, and was largely financed by an American newspaper syndicate. In May 1928 the expedition followed Fawcett's three-year-old trail northward from Cuyabá;[1] but it did not follow his precepts in the matter of equipment. Dyott started with 64 bullocks, 10 mules, and 26 men; his companions were two camera-men and two wireless operators. This well-provided but cumbrous party accomplished a great deal. Dyott traced Fawcett from Dead Horse Camp down the Rio Kuliseu to a village of the Anauqua Indians, where the chief's son had a small brass plate hanging round his neck, stamped with the name of a firm in the City which had supplied Fawcett with some airtight cases in 1924. Aloique, the chief in question, guided Dyott on the three days' journey across country to the Rio Kuluene, the banks of which are inhabited at that point by the Kalapalos Indians.

Here Dyott was told — in sign-language — both by Aloique and by the Kalapalos that Fawcett and his two companions had reached the Kuluene in 1925, and that although both young men were lame and exhausted Fawcett had taken them on, after a short rest, into the unknown country lying east of the river. For five days the watching Indians had seen smoke from their fires, as they blazed their way through the tall grass of the campo; on the sixth there had been no smoke, and Dyott's informants described in pantomime the tragedy which its absence indicated. They were convinced that the party had been massacred, and their evidence differed only

[1] See the map on p. 19.

in that Aloique named as Fawcett's murderers the Suyá Indians, while the Kalapalos suspected Aloique's own people, the Anauquas.

Dyott was then within four or five days' march of the place where Fawcett met his death, and Aloique said that the bones were still there. The main body of the expedition had continued down the Kuliseu to its point of confluence with the Kuluene, and Dyott, who mistrusted Aloique's motives, decided to rejoin them before returning with his companions to visit the scene of the tragedy. This, as it turned out, he was never able to do. He found the camp at the junction of the two rivers full of Indians, importunate in their demands for the knives and trinkets which he had distributed at first with perhaps too lavish a generosity, and he did not like their attitude. Moreover, he was running short of food. So under cover of night he slipped off down the Xingù in light canoes, jettisoning many hundreds of feet of film to facilitate his escape, and pausing only (when he was out of reach) to announce to the world by wireless that he was surrounded by Indians.

So Dyott, if the information given him was reliable, cleared up all the stages of Fawcett's journey except the last; he narrowed down the area in which it would be profitable (for those who find a profit in such things) to investigate the circumstances of what must clearly be regarded as a tragedy. I remember that in London I was inclined to be scornful of Dyott's failure to bring back final and conclusive proof of Fawcett's fate when it was so nearly in his grasp; I am not scornful now that I have seen something of the difficulties with which he had to contend.

After Dyott's return to civilization in the autumn of 1928 no further light was thrown on the Fawcett mystery for some time, and as the years passed the chances of Fawcett being alive became more and more remote. Then, suddenly, in March 1932, a month before I saw that advertisement in the Agony Column, a Swiss called Stephan Rattin turned up at the

British Consulate at São Paulo with a very curious story. He said that he was a trapper (though what he trapped, and where he sold the skins, was never made clear) and that in the preceding year he had made a prodigious journey into the heart of Matto Grosso, in a direction roughly NNW. of Cuyabá, along the Rio Arinos. Somewhere near the point marked R on the map he had found a white man in an Indian village; a tall man, advanced in years, with blue eyes and a long beard. He was a captive, and very disconsolate. Under cover of a drinking bout in which the Indians were indulging, Rattin got a few words with the prisoner, who was dressed (in the approved style) in skins.

They conversed in English; and although this was a language in which Rattin was by no means proficient he did not explain why they did not use Spanish or Portuguese. The old man opened the conversation by announcing that he was a colonel in the English army, and implored Rattin to inform a friend of his in São Paulo, called Paget, of his plight. (It subsequently transpired that a Major J. B. Paget had helped to finance Fawcett's last expedition.) The old man showed Rattin a signet ring, the description of which, according to Mrs. Fawcett, corresponds to a ring which her husband always wore; and he made some reference — showing signs of great distress — to his son, who he said was 'asleep'. Rattin promised to go to São Paulo and deliver the message to Major Paget; and at dawn he departed on a journey which was to take him five months. The Indians made no attempt to detain him.

The verbatim report of Rattin's statement to the British Consul-General at São Paulo is a curious document, full of discrepancies and inconsistencies, yet stamped with that rather dream-like inconsequence which is often the hall-mark of reality. Why did the white man disclose only his rank, and not his name? Why did they talk in English? Why did Rattin — who used a pencil and paper to copy some meaningless carvings which the white man had made on a tree — bring back no written message? If Rattin's story was a fabrication, these are points at which he could hardly have overlooked the necessity for strengthening its verisimilitude. The more one looked at it, the more surely one was forced to the conclusion that if Rattin was a liar, he was a very bad liar.

Yet there are other details in his statement which, if they had no foundation in fact, were brilliant inventions: notably the bit about the iodine. Rattin said that the backs of the old man's hands were badly scratched, and that he took out some iodine and dabbed it on them; when the Indians saw him doing this, they crowded round and tried to paint their faces with the stuff. If that never happened, how could one reconcile such a subtle piece of circumstantial decoration with the fundamental improbabilities of Rattin's story? The mind that so cunningly evolved the one could hardly have bungled the other so sadly.

Besides, if the whole thing was an invention, what did Rattin hope to gain by it? He made out that he had never heard of Fawcett before; and now, finding himself acclaimed on all sides as the discoverer of the lost explorer, he hardly made the most of his opportunities for acquiring fame and wealth. He said that he was prepared, and indeed determined to lead an expedition back to the Indian village and bring the prisoner out. But it must be a small expedition, and its members of his own choosing. He asked only for a little money to defray expenses; and if that was not forthcoming he would effect the rescue on his own.

His story received world-wide publicity. But in May, two months after his appearance in São Paulo, no one in England knew what its sequel was going to be. Interest in Fawcett had suddenly been re-awakened, and the odds against the explorer's survival had shortened dramatically. It looked as if our expedition was a timely phenomenon.

# CHAPTER III

## NO NONSENSE

I KNOW of few keener intellectual pleasures than that which can be derived from listening to two old men talking about Modern Youth and the Spirit of Adventure.

They always take the same line. For the first time in our rough island story, they complain, young men have ceased to be adventurous.

What do they mean by adventure? They mean what popular historians of the Elizabethan age have taught them to mean. They mean the *Wide World Magazine*, slightly lyricized by a Muse who seems to have had something to do with both Rudyard Kipling and Rupert Brooke. They mean travelling steerage, and topees, and stockades, and husbanding every drop of the precious fluid, and planting the Union Jack, and going down with fever, and at the end of it all a sheaf of assegais over the sideboard and a slight limp. You don't find young men doing that sort of thing nowadays; they mutter gloomily, shaking their heads and staring with horrified fascination at photographs of the latest fancy dress party in the *Tatler*.

They are quite right. You don't. For adventure — adventure in the grand old manner — is obsolete, having been either exalted to a specialist's job or degraded to a stunt. It is all very well to cheapen us against the Elizabethans, for whom every other landfall meant a colony. In those days all you needed was an enquiring turn of mind and a profound contempt for scurvy and Spaniards. A passage on any boat with a sufficiently conjectural destination was almost certain to make an Empire builder of you. And since on those journeys every able-bodied man was useful, you were entitled to feel that you were doing something worth doing. Nobody accused you of wanting balance, or said that it was time you settled down. The community capitalized your wanderlust. Restlessness was good citizenship.

But the age of geographical discovery has gone, and so has the age of territorial annexation. Experts are quietly consolidating the gains of spectacular amateurs. In Darien to-day a pair of eagle eyes is not much good unless you have also a theodolite. A wild surmise will not do. As for planting the Union Jack, those portions of the earth's surface where such an action could have any lasting political significance are very few and (I strongly suspect) entirely valueless from the economic, the strategic, and the residential point of view.

Of course there is still plenty of adventure of a sort to be had. You can even make it pay, with a little care; for it is easy to attract public attention to any exploit which is at once highly improbable and absolutely useless. You can lay the foundations of a brief but glorious career on the Music Halls by being the First Girl Mother To Swim Twice Round The Isle Of Man; and anyone who successfully undertakes to drive a well known make of car along the Great Wall of China in reverse will hardly fail of his reward. And then there are always records to be broken. Here you can make some show of keeping within the best traditions, and set out to take the Illustrious Dead down a peg by repeating their exploits with a difference. Rivers which they ascended in small boats you can ascend in smaller; if they took five months to cross a desert, go and see if you can do it in four. Where they went in litters, you can ride; where they went on mules, you can go on foot: and where they went on foot, you can go (for all I care) on roller-skates. It is a silly business, this statistical eye-wiping. These spurious and calculated feats bear about as much relation to adventure as a giant gooseberry does to agriculture.

The old men who grumble that modern youth is not adventurous make two cardinal mistakes. They fail to appreciate the facts, and they have got their values all wrong.

The facts are that four male children out of five start life predisposed in favour of adventure. This has always been so, and it is so to-day. Young men are just as adventurous in 1933 as they ever were. But they can see with one eye that chances of any form of useful or profitable adventure are very rare indeed. If they have the time and the money to equip themselves with a more than ordinary knowledge of surveying, or tropical hygiene, or marine zoology, or (of course) aviation, they can put themselves in a position to take one of these rare chances. Or, again, if they have the time and the money, they can take as much adventure of the picaresque, irresponsible kind as their stomachs and the far-flung consulates will stand. But few of them can afford either the time or the money. So they give up all thoughts of a topee, buy a bowler, and start working at jobs which are almost always, at first, drab and uncongenial. This is a very good thing for the country and everyone else concerned; and it reflects great credit on the young men.

For (and this is where clubland gets its values wrong) adventure is really a soft option. Adventure has always been a selfish business. Men who set out to find it may — like men who go and get married — feel reasonably confident that a successful issue to their project will be of service to the world. But the desire to benefit the community is never their principal motive, any more than it is the principal motive of people who marry each other. They do it because they want to. It suits them; it is their cup of tea.

So it requires far less courage to be an explorer than to be a chartered accountant. The courage which enables you to face the prospect of sitting on a high stool in a smoky town and adding up figures over a period of years is definitely a higher, as well as a more useful, sort of courage than any which the explorer may be called on to display. For the explorer is living under natural conditions, and the difficulties he meets with are the sort of difficulties which Nature equipped man to face: whereas the chartered accountant is living under unnatural conditions, to which a great deal of his equipment is dangerously ill-suited. Moreover, and finally, the chartered accountant is doing an essential job, and the explorer (in these days) is not.

All this must sound as if, at one time or another, I had done a good deal of exploring, filling in the intervals with strenuous bouts of research into the Psychology of Chartered Accountancy. Alas, neither of these deductions would be correct. I had not meant to theorize so abominably. I only wanted to make it clear that, in my view, to sign on to an expedition bound for the interior of Brazil is neither laudable nor extraordinary, but rather the reverse. Most people of my age would do it like a shot, if they had the chance. But they don't have the chance, and they have wisely given up hoping for the chance. In many cases, indeed, they have schooled themselves with almost too complete a success to eschew the coloured dreams of boyhood. By quite forgoing those dreams, they have all but forgotten that they ever had them. At least, that is how I explain the fact that, in those six fantastic weeks before I sailed to Brazil, the people to whom I told my plans showed less envy and more amazement than I had expected.

I kept as quiet about the whole thing as I reasonably could, for it is unpleasant to be regarded as either a lunatic or a hero when you know perfectly well that you are merely going to take an exceptionally long holiday. All the same, it was amusing and instructive to watch people's reactions.

There were the Prudent, who said: 'This is an extraordinarily foolish thing to do.' There were the Wise, who said: 'This is an extraordinarily foolish thing to do; but at least you will know better next time.' There were the Very Wise, who said: 'This is a foolish thing to do, but not nearly so foolish as it sounds.' There were the Romantic, who appeared to believe that if everyone did this sort of thing all the time the world's troubles would soon be over. There were the Envious, who thanked God they were not coming; and there were the other sort, who said with varying degrees of insincerity that they would give anything to come. There were the Correct, who asked me if I knew any of the people at the Embassy. There were the Practical, who spoke at length of inoculations and calibres. There were the people whose geography was not their strong point, and who either offered me letters of introduction to their cousins in Buenos Aires or supposed that I would find a good many Aztec ruins. There were the Apprehensive, who asked me if I had made my will. There were the Men Who Had Done A Certain Amount of That Sort of Thing In Their Time, You Know, and these imparted to me elaborate stratagems for getting the better of ants and told me that monkeys made excellent eating, and so for that matter did lizards, and parrots; they all tasted rather like chicken. (The only person in this category whose advice proved valuable was Mr. Siemel, better known to the reading public as Tiger Man: we had an interview with him in London and I retain memories of a charming and impressive personality.)

Then there were the numerous and kindly people who wrote to me after I had given a talk for the B.B.C. about our projected search for Fawcett. Most of these wanted to come too. One of them offered his services as cook, adding that he had a fair knowledge of Arabic; another sent me a sword-stick. One lady asked me to have a look for her nephew, while I was about it; he had disappeared in Bolivia several years ago. 'In appearance he resembles the Duke of York, with beautifully shaped hands and feet . . . I am a steady reviewer of fiction (two books per day),' she wrote: and added, rather surprisingly, 'This does not encourage illusions, nor blind one's eyes to Life in the raw.' I wrote back and said that I would keep a sharp look-out for her nephew.

# CHAPTER IV

## OUTLOOK UNSETTLED

THERE are, I suppose, expeditions and expeditions. I must say that during those six weeks in London it looked as if ours was not going to qualify for either category. Our official leader (hereinafter referred to as Bob) had just the right air of intrepidity. Our Organizer, on the other hand, appeared to have been miscast, in spite of his professional-looking beard. A man of great charm, he was nevertheless a little imprecise. He had once done some shooting in Brazil, and we used to gaze with respect at his photographs of unimaginable fish and the corpses (or, as it turned out later, corpse) of the jaguars he had killed. But when pressed for details of our own itinerary he could only refer us to a huge, brightly-coloured, and obsolete map of South America, on which the railway line between Rio and São Paulo had been heavily marked in ink. 'From São Paulo,' he would say, 'we shall go up-country by lorry. It is cheaper and quicker than the train.' Or, alternatively: 'The railway will take us right into the interior. It costs less than going by road, and we shall save time, too.' It was clear that Bob, for all his intrepidity, viewed our Organizer's vagueness with apprehension.

At the other end — in Brazil, that is to say — the expedition's interests were said to be in capable hands. Captain John Holman, a British resident of São Paulo whose knowledge of the interior is equalled by few Europeans, had expressed his willingness to do all in his power to assist us. On our arrival in Brazil, as you will hear, this gentleman proved a powerful, indeed an indispensable ally; but at this early stage of the expedition's history our Organizer hardly made the most of him, and Captain Holman was handicapped by the scanty

36

information which he received with regard to our intentions. In London we were given to understand that the man who really mattered was a Major Pingle — George Lewy Pingle. (That is not his name. You can regard him as an imaginary character, if you like. He is no longer quite real to me.)

Major Pingle is an American citizen, holding — or claiming to hold — a commission in the Peruvian army. He has had an active and a varied career. According to his own story, he ran away from his home in Kentucky at the age of 15; joined a circus which was touring the Southern States: found his way across the Mexican border: worked for some time on a ranch near Monterey: accompanied an archaeological expedition into Yucatan, where he nearly died of fever: went north to convalesce in California: joined the ground staff of an aerodrome there and became (of all things) a professional parachutist: went into partnership with a German, whose ambition it was to start an air-line in South America: and since then had travelled widely in Colombia, Peru, Chile, and Brazil. All this, of course, we found out later. All we knew, or thought we knew, in London was that Major Pingle was a man of wide experience and sterling worth who had once accompanied our Organizer on a sporting expedition in Brazil, and who was even now preparing for our arrival in Brazil — buying stores, hiring guides, and doing everything possible to facilitate our journey. A great deal, obviously, was going to depend on Major Pingle. 'This Major Pingle,' I used to tell people, 'is going to be the Key Man.'

It was difficult to visualize Major Pingle, all those miles away. The only thing we knew for certain about him was that he was not very good at answering cables. This, we were told, was because he must have gone up-country already, to get things ready. Whatever the cause, however, very imperfect liaison existed between his headquarters in São Paulo and ours in London; and when a letter did at last reach London from Brazil, our Organizer lost it. So it was impossible to find out definitely whether Major Pingle's preparations were being made in the light of our plans, or whether our plans were being made to fit his preparations, or neither, or both. It was all rather uncertain.

Before we left London, however, we did eventually evolve a plan of operations, which was (unfortunately) announced at some length in *The Times* on the eve of our departure. We decided to rely on Dyott's rather than on Rattin's evidence, and to make our objective the area marked A on the map on page 19. (The spot where Rattin claimed to have seen his white man is roughly indicated by R.) None of us believed for a moment that Fawcett was alive, and we were careful to stress the fact that the solution of the mystery surrounding his disappearance was only our secondary object. Our primary purpose, we said, was to survey and map the Rio das Mortes, freely translated by *The Times* as 'The River of Death'. (It was not until we reached Brazil that we discovered that perfectly satisfactory maps of this river already existed.)

'The River of Death', I wrote in *The Times*, 'got its name in the old slave-trading days. A Portuguese explorer found good gold up the river and, returning to the coast, formed an exploration company to work the deposit. A party of Brazilians followed the prospectors and attempted to jump the claim. A fight took place, in which both sides suffered severely; but the issue must remain a matter for conjecture, since the Indians massacred all the survivors. But the river's name, although a survival, is not an anomaly. The River of Death flows through the heart of a region inhabited by the Chavantes, a tribe of Indians whose uncompromising hostility and whose mastery of the arts of jungle warfare have won them an unenviable reputation in Matto Grosso.'

The expedition, I continued, would go up-country from São Paulo by train and motor lorry; would embark on the Araguaya at Leopoldina; and would travel down it in canoes as far as the mouth of the Rio das Mortes. We should then push as far up that river as possible, and form a standing camp on its banks. With this camp as base, we hoped that it would be possible for some of us to strike westwards across unknown country to the point near the Kuluene where Dyott believed Fawcett to have perished. There followed a summary of the theories about Fawcett, and an imaginative but restrained description of the country and its ferocious inhabitants. Our chief obstacle, I said (and believed), was going to lie in the unreasonable prejudices of the aboriginal population.

The observant reader will have noticed that the writer of *The Times* article from which I have quoted shows a healthy respect for the tribes of the interior. I hope his anticipations have not been unduly aroused. What with these early indications of an Indian menace, and what with all my dogmatizing about adventure, the observant reader is probably relying on me to curdle his blood for him before we go much further. As chapter gives place to chapter, and still no arrows stick quivering in the tent-pole, and still no tomtoms throb their beastly summons to the night assault, the observant reader will get pretty fed up. 'This chap', he will say, 'led me to suppose that, once in the interior of Brazil, he would be under almost continuous fire from his dusky brethren. And now here he is in the last chapter proposing to lay down his pen without having sustained so much as a flesh wound from their primitive weapons.'

I see the observant reader's point. Perhaps I had better meet it in advance by explaining one of the more fundamental misapprehensions which existed, in London, with regard to the expedition's activities.

It was our Organizer who started it. Our Organizer was one of those people who have the most tremendous difficulty in distinguishing between the real and the ideal. In his accounts of Brazil the actual was inextricably confused with the apocryphal. Fact and fancy presented a united and imposing front, with truth, a closely-guarded hostage, far back in reserve. Now it is common knowledge that a great many of the tribes in Matto Grosso are hostile to white men; and it does so happen that the Chavantes, who are as bad as the worst of them, command about 100 miles of the west bank of the Araguaya. When we got to know him better, we saw how inevitable it was that our Organizer should have got it into his head that one morning, before breakfast, he had been called on to repel an attack by these savages, of whom he had killed no less than sixteen. Naturally, he said, one didn't talk much about these things, and we said, No, naturally one didn't.

But a manly reticence was not enough. Deeds were our trouble, not words. All purchases of equipment were made on the assumption that a Brush with the Natives was the first — and must not be the last — item on our programme. Three automatic shotguns — one with a sawn-off barrel — were to be the spearhead of our defence. According to our Organizer, tests carried out during the War (though it was not quite clear on whom) had proved these weapons to be of unrivalled efficacy in Stopping a Rush at Close Quarters. Cartridges specially loaded with buckshot increased our chances of survival, if not of solvency.[1] Our last acquisition before leaving England was a quantity of tear-gas bombs. These, as far as I can remember, were thrown overboard before we reached Rio, to avoid trouble with the Customs.

Then there was the question of The Films. It had somehow been assumed from the start that we should have at least one, and probably two camera-men with us. Since we were going into an unknown part of the world, and on a quest which, if successful, would automatically attract a good deal of attention, this seemed a fairly reasonable assumption. When I signed on, I was put in charge of negotiations with the film companies.

[1] I should explain here that the expedition was financed by the members. Each of us paid £400 into the expeditionary funds.

This was my own fault. I often find myself — among people who know nothing about the cinema at all — giving the impression that I know rather a lot, and have indeed, at some period not specified and in a capacity which it would perhaps be difficult to define, been connected with the industry. In a sense, this second impression is correct; but only in a sense. At the age of eleven, on the Dorset coast, I acted in a film which (had it ever been released) would have depicted the life of the English schoolboy to an expectant — and I hope a credulous — world. I had two parts in it, neither of them very big ones. In the first I had to dive off a rock into the sea, registering pleasure. About 60 or 70 of my fellow-pupils had to do the same thing at the same time; it was a difficult scene to steal. All the same, I believe that I gave as sensitive a performance as any, and I can well remember the chagrin and resentment with which we learnt that this scene would have to be cut, owing to our not having worn bathing-dresses. My other part I felt less at home in. A particular enemy of mine happened to have won a scholarship somewhere that term, and in the film about thirty of us had to carry him in triumph round the school grounds, cheering. This ridiculous ceremony was extremely distasteful to me, and to represent it as a traditional feature of our school life exceeded, in my opinion, the bounds of dramatic licence. I was reluctant, naturally and healthily reluctant, that the world should see me paying extravagant homage to a purely intellectual achievement. I am convinced that I did myself scant justice in the part. Luckily no one, as far as I know, ever saw the film, which was taken on a very hot half-holiday by a man in a Guards tie and a leather overcoat.

After that my film career lapsed for several years, only to be taken up again at Oxford, where an ineffectual British film company attempted the difficult task of translating University life into terms of the cinema. In their genteel though turgid drama I played the part of five undergraduates (or 'undergrads.', as they were called) and one Anglo-Saxon knight, or thane. This film was not released either: mercifully. About a year later I spent a week in Paramount's studios on Long Island. Here, however, I did nothing except apologize to people for getting in their way, and marvel at Miss Claudette Colbert's ability, through a score of retakes, to say, 'My, you're looking fine!' with unabated conviction to a man with a primrose-coloured face. That was the end of my connection with the cinema, unless of course you imagine that the writing of film-criticism implies, because it requires, an understanding of the art: which is as silly as to suppose that a small boy has to be something of a glazier before he can use his catapult.

But to return to Brazil, or at any rate to the road thither. I mentioned this matter of the films because — although, providentially, nothing came of it — it added another element of the fantastic and the problematical to the comedy of our preparations in London. Our Organizer's original theory that the more powerful magnates would stop at nothing in the scramble for the film rights of the expedition may have been psychologically sound: for everyone knows what an unscrupulous lot these magnates are. But unfortunately no scramble took place. Any insight which I might have hoped to acquire into the competitive methods of magnates was denied me. Approached, the magnates showed a tendency to have just gone out to lunch. It was Their Mr. So and So who received me: Their Mr. So and So who, when our interview was early interrupted by an entrancing creature in an aquascutum and a ballet skirt, was clearly bent on keeping his promise to 'be along in a tick': Their Mr. So and So whose faith in the dramatic possibilities of virgin jungle could be gauged, only too easily, by his far from covert glances at a startling wrist watch: Their Mr. So and So who, with a warmth only to be explained by my imminent departure, wished me an interesting trip.

Nothing came of the film idea.

The best thing that happened to the expedition during this

period was the acquisition of Roger. This took place in the following way:

Roger was walking along Gower Street. He had passed the School of Tropical Hygiene. He had passed the Royal Academy of Dramatic Art. In one minute, in less than one minute, he would have reached the Slade: would have spent the afternoon mixing blue and yellow and making green (or whatever it is that artists do): would never have heard of the expedition, for Roger is an inconstant reader of *The Times*.

By one of those coincidences which (as novelists are always careful to say) would hardly pass muster in a work of fiction, I came out in a great hurry from my office on the other side of Gower Street just as Roger passed. At Eton and at Oxford I had known him only by sight. In the last three years I had met him three times. But here was a fine large chap with an eye for comedy: so I called across the street: 'Roger, come to Brazil.'

'What?' said Roger: playing, I dare say, for time.

'You'd better come to Brazil,' I said, getting into a car.

'Why?' said Roger cautiously (or perhaps incautiously), also getting into the car. We set off down Gower Street: past the Royal Academy of Dramatic Art: past the School of Tropical Hygiene. I talked rapidly. At the end of Gower Street Roger got out.

'I'll let you know for certain on Monday,' he said. But his fate was sealed.

Pure coincidence is a rare commodity. About three months later I was sitting over a fire in the middle of a chill night without a moon. A small river brushed quietly past our sandbank. Trees — too many trees — stood up all round us. No white man had ever been to this place before, and probably none would ever come there again. Broadly speaking, we were as far as it was possible to be from anywhere. In his burrow, roofed over with branches against the mosquitoes, a one-eyed Brazilian snored with all the passion of the south. Roger was the only other person present. He also was asleep. As I watched him, it suddenly occurred to me that here was the perfect, the flawless example of a pure coincidence.

If the Recording Angel, collecting advance data for his dossiers, had suddenly swooped down between the drought-sapped branches, woken Roger up, and said to him: 'Explain your conduct, please. I observe that you are sleeping — not at all soundly, on account of the mosquitoes — beside a river which is marked on no map, inside one of the biggest tracts of unexplored territory in the world. I understand that you are looking for traces of a complete stranger whom you believe to have perished more than seven years ago. Would you mind telling me why you are doing this — what is the prime and fundamental cause of your being in so improbable a situation?' — If this question had been put to him, Roger could have given only one answer. He must have said: 'I am here, in the last analysis, because on the 20th of May last I walked down Gower Street at precisely the time I did. If I had been a minute earlier or a minute later — if I had not stopped to buy an evening paper, or if my shoe-lace had broken — I should not be here. You can't have anything much more fundamental than that. I hope you are satisfied.' And the Recording Angel, too often embarrassed with a wealth of motive, a luxuriance of contributory circumstances, would have flown off well pleased with a case thus simple and explicit. Or so I figured, while the mosquitoes exulted over the victim of coincidence.

For me, the enrolment of Roger made the whole expedition at once more and less plausible. More, because here at last was a member with some technical qualification for the task in hand (Roger had some knowledge of surveying, which he proceeded forthwith to increase at the Royal Geographical Society). Less, because two heads were better able than one to appreciate the hare-brained nature of our enterprise, and the childish inadequacy (so far) of our methods. For, in spite of our official plan, it was clear by this time that no one really knew where we were going or why we were going there, or whether it wouldn't perhaps be better to go somewhere else instead.

In our more rational moments we fell back on a kind of lackadaisical fatalism; when we got out there, Roger and I used to remind each other, the possible and the impossible, the probable and the improbable, would sort themselves out automatically. But our laissez-faire broke down whenever we looked at a map of Brazil. This never failed to throw us into a sort of frenzy. At that time there was no map available in London which was either sufficiently accurate or sufficiently detailed to be of the slightest use to us; and this fact, after a comparison of the best we could find, we had the sense to suspect. Even so, at the sight of a map we would go into a species of trance or fit. Our manner would become judicious, calculating, alert. We would bandy place-names which we afterwards found meant even less to the inhabitants of those parts than they did to us. We would gauge the navigability of non-existent rivers, and wrangle over the height of ranges with which the cartographers (those visionaries, those humorists) had arbitrarily embossed the plateau which was to be our goal.

Perhaps the best moment of all was when we learnt, from a paragraph in a Sunday newspaper, that Rattin had started once more for the interior. He was on his way back to rescue his white man, and he had with him two or three companions, one of whom was acting as correspondent for an American news agency. For three successive weeks the same paper recorded their progress across the last frontiers of civilization; and after that a silence fell which has not been broken, so far as I know, up to the time of writing.

But before it fell Roger and I had become feverishly excited. All the convincing aspects of Rattin's story presented themselves to us with overwhelming force; its inconsistencies were forgotten. Rattin *must* be on to something, we argued; and if it was not Fawcett, one lost colonel was as good as another, after all. We followed Rattin across the map with frantic guesswork, as one follows a flea across a counterpane. I remember well the faces of the editorial staff of *The Times* as I outlined a scheme (which was at the time very dear to me) for flying up to Cuyabá with a cage of carrier pigeons and following Rattin down the Rio Arinos by canoe: the theory being that, even if he found his man before we caught him, those pigeons of ours would get the news back first. *The Times* declined to use its influence to alter the nature of the expedition. But it declined with ill-concealed reluctance; there was a wistful, a hankering look in its august official eye.

*The Times* did however assist and even encourage the concoction of a code in which despatches were to be transmitted. Based on the tragedy of *Othello* (with which I happen to be particularly familiar) its genesis was due to the theory, then prevalent, that we should find ourselves involved in some kind of a race with rival journalistic interests. Othello was to stand for Fawcett, Iago for Rattin; and there were endless permutations and combinations deriving from the text of the play.

In the end, of course, hardly any of the hopes and fears which I have outlined in the preceding pages came anywhere near to being realized. But I should have done wrong to omit all mention of them. They make a colourful and ironic background for the things that really happened; and the fantastic preliminaries in London are an integral part of that curious comedy which the expedition was destined to provide.

# CHAPTER V

# GETAWAY

THE liner wore an air of dignified but slightly impatient resignation, like a horse on whose back small and clutching children are being allowed a moment's ride. All liners on the point of departure have this air. They resent the clutter of farewell, the influx of irrelevant landsmen. Some of these — notably the porters and the journalists — give offence by the initiate, the even proprietary bearing with which they tread corridors specially carpeted for this emergency. They seem hardly to be aware that they are afloat in salt water, and to regard the stately ship as an ephemeral and inconvenient place of resort: as it might be a marquee.

But the main body of the invaders err in the other extreme. These (while their talk of 'going upstairs', their unforgivable cries of 'waiter', broadcast their unseaworthiness) display a childish and exclamatory delight in the most commonplace adjuncts of ocean travel. 'Look!' they ejaculate, 'a *library*! *And* a gymnasium. . . .' They turn on taps. They price the dolls and dressing-gowns in the shop. To hear them enthuse, they might have supposed that their friends would be travelling in an eighteenth-century slaver. No self-respecting modern ship can stand much of this sort of thing.

Even the conduct of the passengers leaves something to be desired. Once at sea they will be meek and malleable: attending boat drill, trying to be punctual for dinner, perhaps even calling the captain Sir. But now, in harbour, with a sheaf of envious or sympathetic telegrams in their hand, they are above themselves. Anxious to appear at home in this milieu which so excites the wonder of their friends, they give an immense amount of trouble by asking whether they can have vases to put their flowers in, and why their porthole won't open, and where the swimming bath is, and which is the cool side of the ship, and by ordering monstrous rounds of drinks at the very last moment. When at last the time comes for visitors to go ashore, it is with a certain petulance that the siren issues its deafening ultimatum. And who shall blame it?

The expedition came on board six strong. All appeared bemused but resolute. A gigantic bull mastiff — which could hardly have survived a week in tropical jungle — had been added to the party. This pleased the photographers, but made us feel more spurious than ever. 'I wish I was coming with you,' said a little spotted man from a provincial paper, shaking my hand with some emotion. It was rather a pathetic remark, so inconceivable was it that any of us should share his wish. Incidentally, that was the last time anyone made it.

At last the boat began to move, sidling slowly out towards midstream. Figures on the quayside dwindled with a horrible deliberation; we parted by inches. Between ship and shore emotions were stretched unfairly, and for too long. The band played 'Good night, Sweetheart,' with considerable briskness. A few gulls wheeled over the shining water. Kent looked bright and busy under the summer sun. We had started; we were away.

Certain people, of whom I am one, thrive in an atmosphere of uncertainty. It is not that we have the gambler's spirit, that we challenge chance for the sake of the game. We are not so dashing. If we take risks, we take them because we are lazy. We delegate our responsibilities to fate. In any situation, the more you are obliged to leave to chance, the less you are obliged to do yourself. Being for the most part inefficient, incapable of foresight, and rather irresponsible, we like best those situations in which a great deal has to be left to chance.

This (I reflected, as the docile fields were left behind) was just such a situation. Reviewing it, I decided that the immediate future had rarely appeared less cut and dried. My only fear was that there was too much uncertainty: that the situation would have no chance of developing: that our enterprise, if not exactly still-born, would be exposed at birth on the chill uplands of the impracticable: and that I should be home again in time to shoot grouse and criticize Mr. Shaw's new play at Malvern. A most lame and impotent conclusion, as the lady said to Iago.

But not a very unlikely one. Only that morning I had received an urgent letter from the Foreign Office, in which was transmitted a warning from His Majesty's Ambassador at Rio de Janeiro to the effect that:

'General Rondon has been publishing in the press the severest strictures on foreign explorers in Brazil, whose intentions he considers suspect, especially in connection with attempts to search for Colonel Fawcett. The Ambassador gravely doubts whether General Rondon will give any facilities to expeditions of this kind and fears that he may even cause special legislation to be passed in order to hinder them.'

This was scarcely encouraging. Everyone knows how fiery these South American legislators can be. I visualized a gun-boat intercepting the liner, and our manacled transhipment; anti-foreign demonstrations in the streets leading to the jail; an International Incident (with, of course, what they call Repercussions)....

Uncertainty existed with regard to more things than our official reception. The question of the films, which I thought had died a natural death, had been unexpectedly revived. Before he said good-bye, our Organizer had assured us repeatedly that two expert camera-men were even now flying south from Hollywood (sometimes it was from New York) at the bidding of America's most powerful film concern; they would meet us at Rio. This suggested untold complications, and made it harder than ever to visualize the future. Not that I seriously expected to see those camera-men....

But what was there (when you came to think of it) that one

could seriously expect to see? The exotic unrealities of our intentions — till now a decorative and amusing background to the familiar flurry of a London life — would henceforth supply the pattern of our whole existence. We were through the looking-glass. The time had come to stop talking about what we were going to do and do it. We were bound for Brazil, a distant country. Before we could even fail honourably in our enterprise (which was the best outcome I ever hoped for) we had to reach a part of that country of which the Brazilians themselves did not trouble to conceal their ignorance and fear. None of us could speak Portuguese. None of us had any relevant experience of the tropics. All arrangements for our transport were in the hands of Major Pingle, that experienced but uncommunicative man, that by now semi-legendary figure: whom none of us had ever seen, whose very existence we had to take on trust. Foreign explorers, it seemed, were suspect, however bona fide. What would they think of us, who could hardly pass for explorers at a cocktail party? What would they think of us, with our tongues in our cheeks and tear-gas bombs in our trunks? . . .

The bugle went for lunch. England was out of sight. There was nothing to do but wait, for a fortnight, and see.

# CHAPTER VI

# ROLLING DOWN

A FORTNIGHT passed: so many blue, null days. I do not like ships. We called at Lisbon. From fishing boats gaily and affectionately painted, men throw up brimming baskets of sardines to other men on the quay. No sardines are spilt. It must be very difficult to do. Women wearing funny little black hats, coloured handkerchiefs, and cavalry moustaches carry huge fish in baskets on their heads. I wonder whether it affects the character always having a dead fish so near one's brain? Roger and I bathed at Estoril and nearly missed the boat. The expedition was photographed at Lisbon.

We called at Funchal. Madeira rises out of the dark blue water, an unconvincing, an overstated island. Her gorges and terraces are arbitrarily and improbably disposed. Wisps of cloud pose self-consciously about her peaks. From a grey prosaic beach land soars straight up like a backcloth: a backcloth in the old, the anxiously romantic manner. In the steep and extortionate town oxen pull sledges through the cobbled streets, deliberately quaint. Morris Cowleys are also to be seen. Indeed, the place has a slightly colonial atmosphere: one feels the need for a Residency. The inhabitants wear buskins, and for the most part carry in their hands a long, black, demonic-looking fish, curled in a loop, its tail stuck through its mouth. Madeira contrives to be at once drab and gaudy, at once matter of fact and artificial: like a musical comedy in rehearsal. The expedition was photographed at Funchal.

We called at Teneriffe. This island is more stark and more credible than Madeira: something like Corsica. Spanish policemen rode fine horses meditatively up and down the quay. Their hats — absurdly impractical, shading neither the eyes nor the neck — gave them the air of highwaymen stylized in the Cochran manner. The expedition was not photographed at Teneriffe, I don't know why.

After that there were nine empty days. We lived in that state of suspended animation in which oceans are crossed in the twentieth century. I find it irksome. I do not like ship life, even in the balmiest of tropic seas. Flying fish always remind me of French dictation; I find myself murmuring 'Ouvrez les guillemets' as each shoal scuds out from beneath our bows. Why this should be so I cannot explain; nor have I any means of telling whether the fauna of other seas would affect me in similar ways — whether, for instance, my subconscious mind connects the albatross with Greek composition, or the auk with logarithms. The point is in any case immaterial.

Roger and I lent precarious purpose to our lives by wrestling dutifully with the theodolite. We took readings on the masthead, on both the mast-heads. In an endeavour to get fit — how ill-timed, how premature an endeavour we happily could not know — we pedalled many miles every day on a stationary bicycle. For the rest we behaved much as if we were ordinary passengers with sane, accessible destinations and no revolvers in our sponge-bags. We sat in the sun. We dived, rather ostentatiously, for counters in the swimming bath. We entered for the manlier deck sports, and scratched, and were always being dunned for our subscriptions. We carried about with us good, long, worth-while books: books which we had never really had a chance of reading before: books which we still mean to read one day. We became adept at evading the. Ship's Bore, whose college blazer — like the peacock which warns the jungle of the tiger's passage — flamboyantly betrayed him. We played simple and as far as possible silent games with the two little French girls, aloof, precocious, and disconcertingly idiomatic. We listened with respect to the General's solutions of the world's problems, in which the phrases To Open Up (used of unspecified areas within the British Empire) and To Go Under (the hideous

alternative to Making Good in the Opening Up business)
bulked largely. We were facetious about the charming family
of political exiles from Brazil. We postponed writing letters.
We ate. We slept. We were bored.

We came into Rio at sunset. This must surely be the best
time to do it.

For some hours Brazil had been in sight, a dark-green
formidable outline, a coast (as far as we could see) almost unscathed by man. The huge cliffs slanted a little backwards, as if
the land had been reined in sharply on the brink of salt perdition.
The charging jungle stopped short only at the sea. I got the
impression of a sub-continent with imperfect self-control.

We were passing a little island in the harbour's mouth.
Against a tawny sunset the hills behind the city stood up fiercely.
On their crests the tiny black silhouettes of trees showed with
more than their share of detail and prominence. Some frigate
birds went out past us to the darkening sea, flying low. The
water front, still some way ahead of us, flaunted a solitary sky-
scraper. All sky-scrapers look foolish and unnatural when
isolated from their kind. It is only in the mass, huddled and
strenuously craning, that they achieve a sort of quaint crude
dignity. Alone, cut off from their native background of com-
petition and emergency, they appear gauche and rather forlorn.
With this one it was particularly so. Ridiculously at variance
with all that we could see, hopelessly irrelevant to all that we
imagined, it had the pathos of the boor. It domineered without
conviction, the totem of another tribe. It knew itself for a
mistake, an oversight, an intrusion. It was like a bag of tools
left behind, when the curtain rises, on a stage set for romance.

Later I was told that during the last revolution they threw
a full-sized billiard table out of a window on its fourteenth floor.
Then I forgave it. Where that sort of thing can happen to them,
there is a place for sky-scrapers.

As we came closer the city evaded us. The hills drew in with

53

the darkness, and Rio merged into her bodyguard. Between their shoulders we saw under a furled bank of cloud a strip of lemon-coloured sky, level and straight-edged like a wainscot. A little covey of rockets went up from somewhere in the town. They burst in a chorus of inoffensive plopping noises and left surprised balls of smoke hanging in the air. There are always rockets in Brazil. The birth of a saint or the death of a patriot, the outbreak or suppression of revolt, the rise or fall of a government — if there is none of these things to commemorate to-day, there was yesterday. There are sure to be some fireworks left over. Rockets are to the Brazilian calendar what exclamation marks are to the correspondence of a débutante.

In the twilight — yes, in the swift tropical twilight of which you have all read — the political exiles, no longer able to control their emotion, pointed out to us again and again the Sugar Loaf and Corcovado, those astonishing peaks. We duly marvelled. Our aesthetic susceptibilities were on their mettle. Two people were heard to say that the scene, if reproduced on canvas, would fail to command belief. The ship buzzed with ecstasy.

It had indeed been very gorgeous, that sunset harbour, those sudden hills. But the Ship's Bore had warned us of another treat to come, and now we saw what it was. The lights began to go on. The works of Nature were succeeded on the stage by the public utilities of Neon. Hundreds and thousands of points of light sprang out of the darkness to guide our guesses, to betray the evading city. Windows burned in unforeseen clusters high up on the shadowed hills. A gay and disorderly phalanx of lights triumphed in the body of the city. The famous *perlas*, a spaced resplendent string, blazoned faithfully all the convolutions of the water front. The dome which had housed their 1922 Exhibition held the centre of the stage and glittered with a will, as vulgar as a gilded cabbage. The harbour, almost still, juggled gently with reflections. 'Fairy-like', said everyone. And so it was. I allowed the General to dismiss the rival merits of Hong-Kong without a protest.

And now we were almost alongside. We had edged our way round two or three warships, the nucleus of the Brazilian navy. It is so long since these craft left their moorings that they are said not to be afloat at all, but fast aground on the accumulation of their daily refuse. Be that as it may, they are a feature of the harbour no less embarrassing then permanent. For in time of revolution those hooded guns may speak for either side with results equally unwelcome to the capital's non-combatants; and your true patriot — in a revolution both parties answer to this description — would need to think twice before retaliating on a target so important and expensive.

There had meanwhile come on board our ship a number of brutal and (for all I know) licentious minor officials, of whom the more obviously disillusioned formed a quorum and examined our passports. There now ensued a scene familiar and distasteful to every traveller. I have seen it played out in China, in Mexico, in Russia. I will reproduce it in full.

The root of the trouble is the Anglo-Saxon habit of writing our names backwards on all official documents. On Mr. George Beowulf Smith's certificate of vaccination the prudent fellow appears, not as George Beowulf Smith, but as Smith, George Beowulf; and in every quorum of officials you are almost certain to find one to whom Mr. G. B. Smith is for documentary purposes Senhor (or Monsieur, or Tovarisch) S. G. Beowulf. No sensible person blames him; the man is doing his best, and since the whole business is unnecessary anyhow it is no part of our duty to correct his misapprehensions. One after another, we wisely submit to being entered in the archives of a foreign power by names which, since our early schooldays, we have been at pains to keep secret from our closest friends.

But here at last is one of us who cannot stand by and see error thus perpetrated: a Mr. Sidney Peregrine Brown. No man shall take his name down inverted and (consequently) in vain. He has seen how things are going. He will stop the rot. While his papers are examined, he waits his chance.

The papers are in order. To the list of those who have complied with his government's regulations the official adds, in a spikily ornate script, the name of Senhor Brown Sidney Peregrine.

The man whose identity it partially conceals steps forward.

'No,' he says; his voice is firm, confidential, helpful. 'No. Not like that. The name is Brown. Sidney Peregrine Brown.' He taps the official's list, that monument of error.

The official looks up. He does not understand.

Brown (*slowly and very loud, for he has remembered that he is talking to a foreigner*): You have got my name THE WRONG WAY ROUND. My name is BROWN: *not* Peregrine. (*He taps the list again.*)

The Official (*still not understanding*): You are Senhor Peregrine? Yes?

Brown: No. That's just what . . .

The Official (*in a terrible voice, his eyes narrowing with suspicion*): You are not Peregrine? (*He snatches up Brown's papers.*) These are papers of another? No?

Brown (*beginning to perspire*): No. I mean, Yes, I am. You don't understand. (*Drawing a deep breath.*) Peregrine is my Christian name . . . Mon nom chrétien, Pérégrine. BROWN is — I mean Brown est . . .

A voice from among the Passengers (*eagerly, with pride*): Try him with German, sir. My wife speaks German. Here, Helen, come and . . .

Another Voice: What does it matter?

A Third Voice: It doesn't matter.

A Fourth Voice: Tell him it doesn't matter.

A Fifth Voice (*snarling*): How much *longer* . . .

Brown (*desperately*): *Would* you mind waiting a minute, please? This man has made a mistake with regard to my identity. I have no wish to . . .

The Official (*aware that there is an ugly feeling abroad and determined not to be put upon*): Senhor Peregrine, faz favor . . . (*He twitches Brown by the sleeve and thrusts the list of names before his eyes.*) Brown Sidney Peregrine. 'Sta claro? O nome do Senhor, não é?

> (*Cries of 'Si', 'Oui', 'That's him', and 'Who cares?' from among the passengers.*)

The Official (*confused*): O qué?

A Resourceful Passenger: He says it's all right, Brown.

Brown (*puce and defiant*): But it's not all right. Un moment, Signor. You've made the same mistake all the way along. Vous avez trompé avec toutes les noms. You've got everyone THE WRONG WAY ROUND. Look, I'll show you. (*He seizes a pen.*) This is how we write our names in England. Voici l'ordre propre des noms. . . .

But everyone feels that things have gone far enough. The official grabs the list which Brown is preparing to amend; while from those passengers — like S. G. Beowulf and Fleming Robert Peter — who have connived at its misnomers arises an outcry so formidable that the traitor Brown is only too glad to let the Lounge Steward explain away his objections in glib and Cockney-flavoured Portuguese. In a minute or two all is going on as before. Only the official, more ostentatiously lynx-eyed now, takes his revenge by copying out our names very slowly indeed; though still in the wrong order.

And now we realized that the engines had stopped. We were there; we had reached Brazil. In a language distantly related, through Eton and Guatemala, to the Spanish tongue I did my best to satisfy a sudden flush of journalists. And there, coming up the gangway at their heels, was Major Pingle.

Major Pingle you must visualize for yourselves. I shall give you only the minimum of help. He is a tall, thin man of about forty, with a ragged moustache and phenomenally small ears. There is something of the camel in his gait, and he has that short, mouse-coloured hair which looks as if it never grows. His appearance is in no sense attractive. But you would, I think, have been intrigued rather than repelled by that scarecrow figure: a Rough Diamond, you would have said, a Character. His eyes, his flickering and rather defiant eyes, you would perhaps not have liked. In his tendency to digress you would have foreseen a source of irritation. But you would have been reassured by his blunt, uncompromising manner, his scepticism, and his obvious effectiveness. It would surprise me if after your first meeting you had not concluded that beneath that rugged exterior there beat a heart of gold: if only because Major Pingle himself had so repeatedly implied that this was so.

At last the expedition, heavily photographed, went ashore. Everyone was in high spirits. It was said that we were leaving for São Paulo the next day.

# CHAPTER VII

# RIO

It is curious, now, to recall that when on the next day we failed to leave for São Paulo I was surprised as well as annoyed. I never, as a matter of fact, got really broken in to Brazil. Procrastination on principle — procrastination for procrastination's sake — I learnt quite quickly to expect. I learnt the necessity of resignation, the value of resignation, the psychology of resignation: everything except resignation itself. To the very end I went on struggling unhappily: to the very end, against my better judgment, knowing it to be futile, I continued to cajole, insult, threaten, and bribe the dilatory with a view to reducing delay. It was never any good.

Delay in Brazil is a climate. You live in it. You can't get away from it. There is nothing to be done about it. It should, I think, be a source of pride to the Brazilians that they possess a national characteristic which it is absolutely impossible to ignore. No other people can make this boast. The English are a race of shopkeepers; but it is possible to live in England without being seriously inconvenienced by the process of barter which rages round you. A tendency on the part of the traveller to melancholy or extravagance need not be curbed among the gay and thrifty French. Self-revelation may be practised among the inscrutable Chinese, and generosity among the Scots. You don't have to be a bigamist to go to Turkey, and a coward can find contentment in plucky little Belgium. But a man in a hurry will be miserable in Brazil.

We were six days in Rio, having what is known as Trouble With The Customs. A certain amount of this was inevitable, for no attempt had been made in London to get a special permit for our heavy and elaborate armament. We easily managed, however, to make matters worse than they need have been. I vividly remember the scene in the Customs shed on the night we landed. Major Pingle had disappeared. Roger and I and Captain Holman (a heaven-sent ally) danced feverishly round a mountain of luggage, perjuring ourselves now wilfully, now in ignorance, and always with poor success. We knew nothing about the contents or ownership of anything besides our own suit-cases. Some of the expedition, on their declaration forms, had confessed in full to all their weapons; others admitted nothing, but hid revolvers in their boots. In the absence of labels it was impossible to tell to which pieces of luggage the declaration forms referred; so that Roger and I had no idea how much, or what, was hidden where. We cursed the absentees and watched with resignation a comprehensive and fruitful search.

Looking back, I cannot remember very clearly what I expected from Rio, or why I was disappointed. It is, as they say, a fine city. Make no mistake about that. It is one of the places (for all I know, one of the several places) where Brazil's national motto, Order and Progress, has not that rich flavour of irony which is too often, alas, the chief recommendation of public watchwords. Its streets are clean and wide and (when possible) straight. Its taxi-cabs purr majestically and go like the wind. Its tram service is indefatigable. Its cinemas are numerous, its gardens a delight, and all the male inhabitants wear collars. Its buildings boast — and in Brazil this is something to boast about — the usual offices. But above all I should like to praise its statuary.

I know nothing of sculpture. But there are plinths in some of Rio's public places before which even the Philistine must bow; he may even go back to his hotel and lie down for a bit. There really is something alarming about these turgid and pullulating groups. A great gout — a three-dimensional and lapidary gout — of legend, history, symbolism, religion, and political philosophy soars upwards and outwards from a base no bigger than your dining-table. 'But this cannot be going on all the time,' you gasp, overcome by the contrast between the permanence, the immobility, of the sculptured stone and the painfully gramatic luxuriance of the artist's fancy.

Victory has got a half-Nelson on Liberty from behind. Liberty is giving away about half a ton, and also carrying weight in the shape of a dying President and a brace of cherubs. (One of the cherubs is doing a cartwheel on the dying President's head, while the other, scarcely less considerate, attempts to pull his trousers off.) Meanwhile an unclothed male figure, probably symbolical, unquestionably winged, and carrying in one hand a model railway, is in the very act of delivering a running kick at the two struggling ladies, from whose drapery on the opposite side an eagle is escaping, apparently unnoticed. Around the feet of these gigantic principals all is bustle and confusion. Cavalry are charging, aboriginals are being emancipated, and liners launched. Farmers, liberators, nuns, firemen, and a poet pick their way with benign insouciance over a subsoil thickly carpeted with corpses, cannon-balls, and scrolls. So vehement a confusion of thought, so arbitrary an alliance of ideas, takes the reason captive and paralyses criticism. But you cannot help feeling that such vigour of conception is hardly calculated to make for stability in execution; the thing *must* be top-heavy. You flinch. You tend to cower. It is with a feeling of relief that you turn the corner of the square.

When you look down on Peking from the chipped and flaking terraces of the Winter Palace, you see as many tree-tops as roofs. The city walls seem to enclose as much park as town. *Rus in urbe;* the palaces and temples are approached, like the palaces and temples of legend, through glades where the grass is uncut and carries dew. You may find a broken magpie's egg in the forecourt. Rio has not this charm; in the tropics such a gentleman's agreement with nature is rarely possible. Looking down on the city from the Sugar Loaf, you are aware of conflict. Rio has edged in between the hills and the sea, and on that boldly chosen strip of land has met and trounced the jungle. She gleams up at you complacently, a successful opportunist.

But the jungle is still there. You can reach it easily by tram, or through suburban backdoors. It has been driven back into impregnable positions on the steep hill-sides, and there it waits, conceding no more ground than it must. Somehow you feel that there ought to be a no-man's-land between the houses and trees, that there must be something embarrassing in having so old an enemy for so close a neighbour. But Rio is not embarrassed. I suspect her of relishing the sharp and inescapable flavour of contrast, of flaunting her civic amenities rather provocatively at those glum and climbing walls of green. This is the right attitude, and as long as she maintains it there will be at least one big city in the world who has not surrounded herself with an area devastated by that process known as Development. On Rio's outskirts no bowler-hatted contractors carve Paradise into Desirable Building Sites; her inhabitants can enjoy a green thought in a green shade on the shores of that harbour which must surely have been described before now as God's gift to the picture-postcard industry.

But no place has the power to charm when you are kept there against your will. Negotiations with the Customs for the release of our fire-arms went forward slowly. Contact with a foreign bureaucracy is almost always instructive and amusing if not, at the time, congenial; but we were denied this contact, for Major Pingle conducted all the negotiations himself.

In this, and in many other matters connected with the expedition's preparations, he was ably assisted by Captain Holman. To the good offices of this gentleman the expedition in its early stages owed a great deal. In Rio and in São Paulo he worked indefatigably in our behalf, and had it not been for his kindly and experienced aid our departure for the interior might have been indefinitely delayed. He accompanied us on the first stages of our journey, and it is with gratitude that I remember his invaluable services. But for Captain Holman, the expedition might have been a very different affair.

There was nothing to do. We bathed. We rode incalculable distances in trams. We drank beer in the Avenida and watched the strolling, the perpetually strolling crowds. We read the articles about us in the newspapers, noting with indignation their suspicion of our motives, with trepidation their scepticism about our scientific attainments, and with admiration their ingenuity in misprinting our names. We visited a music hall whose posters announced 'The 100 Most Beautiful Women of this World or the Next', an advertisement, as it turned out, nicely calculated to destroy hope as well as illusion. We went to night clubs and watched the *maxixe*, a dance the nature of which can perhaps best be indicated by saying that its purpose appears to be to get St. Vitus decanonized. We ate. We slept. We were bored.

But there is an end to all things, even to delays in Brazil (though that will not prevent me from always referring to them as interminable). On July 8th we caught the night train for São Paulo. 'We really have started at last,' we told each other.

We were wrong.

# CHAPTER VIII

# GETTING WARMER

ALMOST the first thing that Major Pingle had told us was that he had some entirely new, secret, and reliable information about Fawcett. We were given to understand that it greatly increased our chances of success, but would necessitate some change of route. Major Pingle seemed, however, curiously reluctant to divulge this information in Rio. He was busy. His maps were in São Paulo. He didn't want the journalists to get wind of his secret; and he confessed to each of us in turn that some of the others could not be trusted not to talk. His behaviour, in a word, was enigmatic.

This, however, was the only matter in which he failed to impress us favourably. In all other respects his handling of the expedition's affairs was reasonably prompt and unquestionably able. He had lived many years in Brazil, and it was clear that he knew how to deal with the inhabitants.

Moreover, if by his secrecy, his reticence, he failed to win our confidence, it must be remembered that we had done nothing to deserve his. Since its inception in London, the conduct of the expedition as a whole had been, to put it mildly, grotesquely unprofessional. Reviewing our progress up to date, Roger and I decided that he would be a rash man indeed who did not treat us, over important matters, like a pack of children. And to Major Pingle this question of secrecy was an important matter. He had a horror of journalists. He was an uneducated man, and his views on the Press were lurid and fantastic. This phobia was one of his blind spots. When he spoke of newspapers his shrewd, sceptical outlook deserted him, and he became credulous and chimerical, crediting all newspapers with diabolical motives and supernatural powers. We looked upon him, remember, as a character; and this was one of his foibles: not a very difficult one — when I remembered the Foreign Office warning about Rondon's campaign in the Press and the marked coolness of our own reception — to make allowances for.

There were, however, those maps in São Paulo; and we had been promised that in São Paulo this new, this breath-taking information would be revealed. At the earliest opportunity, therefore, I bearded Major Pingle and reminded him of his promise, pointing out that before we started up-country I must inform *The Times* of any change in our plans, and of the reason for it. Major Pingle gave way, though not with a very good grace; and in the unromantic surroundings of his hotel bedroom unfurled with a mysterious air a thick wad of largely irrelevant maps. He then produced a sheet of paper, grimy and rather crumpled. On it was type-written the new and secret clue to Fawcett's fate.

I can see now how important that grimy sheet of paper was to Major Pingle, and also why he was so reluctant to produce it. It was important because it roused my hopes of getting a decent story for *The Times* and thus gave Roger and me an excuse for continuing on an enterprise which otherwise, under the gathering shadows of anti-climax and fiasco, our consciences and our common sense would have obliged us to abandon. At the same time Major Pingle was a little nervous of producing this evidence because, being ignorant of its full value as evidence, he doubted its efficacy as bait.

This is what the information was:

It came from Murika, the chief of a Kalapalos village on the Kuluene. Murika began by describing Fawcett's itinerary from Cuyabá to the Kuluene; this itinerary tallied, point for point, with the trail which Dyott followed in 1928. Murika related how Fawcett and his two companions had arrived, unaccompanied, at the southernmost port[1] of the Kalapalos, which is

[1] Judging by our own experience with the Tapirapé Indians, and Commander Dyott's with the Anauquas, this port was probably no more than an uninhabited

situated on the Kuluene just south of the little tributary called the Tanguro.

Fawcett announced his intention of continuing his journey into the unknown country lying east of the Kuluene. The two young men, who were suffering terribly from sores on their legs and greatly weakened by privation, were reluctant to go any further. The Kalapalos joined with them in attempting to dissuade their leader from so desperate an enterprise, warning him that he would come up against dense jungle which it would be all but impossible to pass. But Fawcett was adamant; he would not turn back until he met defeat.

But before he left he asked Murika to get together a party of Indians and to follow up his trail with a supply of *mandioca*. (*Mandioca* is an unappetizing but sustaining root, the staple food, in one form or another, of all those tribes.) Murika promised to do this. His tribesmen ferried the three white men across the river in canoes and watched them disappear into country of which it is reasonable to suppose that the Kalapalos themselves knew little or nothing.

Murika, looking east, saw smoke for eleven days. On the twelfth there was no smoke, and he set out, as he had said he would, with a ration-party. At Fawcett's last camp they found (to quote the type-written statement) 'traces of a massacre': the work (according to Murika, who claimed to be in touch with the tribe) of the Arumá Indians, a fierce and wandering people whose warriors scar their faces with slits from the eye to the ear and from the ear to the mouth.

That was all. But it was enough for me. I had left England in the belief that Dyott's theory was the best we had to work on and that his evidence, as far as it went, was sound. Here was a story which independently confirmed all his first-hand findings; which gave, in other words, substantially the same account as

clearing on the river bank. In that part of the country the Indians make their villages some way inland, preferring to keep a belt of jungle between their homes and the river, from which, since it is the only highway, there is most danger of attack.

his of Fawcett's journey as far as the Kuluene; and which was at variance with his theory only in so far as it amended and amplified his largely conjectural conclusions as to what happened to Fawcett east of the Kuluene. I was, though I tried not to show it, very pleased.

A few minutes later I was even more pleased. Major Pingle had produced a map — another copy of that huge, brightly coloured and obsolete map with which our Organizer had made such play in London. On this map, very neatly marked, were shown Dyott's route; Rattin's alleged route; and Fawcett's route according to Murika's statement. But it was not the map that pleased me.

'That's a good job of work,' I said.

'Yes,' agreed Major Pingle modestly. About a week later, when I knew him better, I was to realize that he could never have marked those routes himself. Those neatly gummed little discs of paper, that tiny but legible lettering, were not within his powers. If I had realized this at the time, I should not have been so puzzled: though I should have been no less pleased.

What puzzled me was how anyone who had marked Dyott's route on that map could fail to see the real importance of Murika's story. Major Pingle thought the information important because it was new; its true value lay in the fact that most of it was old. Dyott's theory, after all, was based on information obtained — and obtained in sign language — from Indians with whom he was not on the best of terms, and referred to events which were then three years old. Here was independent confirmation, from an Indian source, that the place to look for traces of Fawcett was east of the Kuluene. At first I could not understand why Major Pingle valued Murika's evidence for itself alone, and not as badly needed support for Dyott's. Then it began to dawn on me that Major Pingle knew a good deal less than I did about the back history of *le cas* Fawcett — that, more specifically, he was not in detail familiar with the Dyott theory.

That was what so greatly pleased me at the time, and through the coming weeks so often reassured me. For there had been present in my mind ever since we landed the suspicion that this new and secret information would prove to be a fake of Major Pingle's. I knew now that this was not so; for if Murika's story was a fake, it was faked by someone with a thorough knowledge of the Dyott theory. This knowledge Major Pingle did not possess.

It was lucky for my own peace of mind that I realized this, and that I did not have to depend for my faith in the value of Murika's story on the assurances of Major Pingle. For it did not need the textual flair of a Shakespearian commentator to see that the style of that type-written statement was not Major Pingle's, being far beyond his severely limited literary powers. Yet Major Pingle claimed to be its author, as he claimed to have marked that map. . . .

Questioned, moreover, about Murika, he returned perfunctory and evasive answers. How long had he known about Murika's story? Oh, about nine or ten months. What was Murika like? Oh, just one of these Indians. Very reliable man. Major Pingle had known him for a number of years. What were the 'traces of a massacre' — had all, or any, of the bodies been found? Murika hadn't said anything about that . . . Had I been less pleased with the new evidence, less convinced of its intrinsic value, I should perhaps have been quicker to suspect that Major Pingle had never seen a Kalapalos Indian in his life.

We passed, however — passed rather hastily, if I remember rightly — to a discussion of our change of route. Major Pingle was all against going up the Rio das Mortes. He said that the country between that river and the Kuluene was very bad indeed. Without Indian guides and porters we should get nowhere, and the Chavantes, who infested all that territory, could be relied upon to be the reverse of helpful. No; the thing to do (said Major Pingle) was to carry on down the Araguaya and go up the Tapirapé. The Tapirapé had never been properly explored, but the Indians who lived on its headwaters were friendly. We would make a base camp on the river in their territory; and then, by judiciously distributing presents, we could persuade a large armed party to guide us across country towards the Kuluene.

I said I supposed the cross-country part would be pretty difficult. Major Pingle said, yes, it would. He wouldn't be able to accompany us himself, because a recent operation on his throat had affected his wind and prevented him from walking long distances: though there was nothing he would rather do. It would be a hard journey, but it would be all right if we took proper precautions and treated the Indians well. Some of the tribes in there were very bad.

This all sounded hopeful to me. The plan seemed a good one, and Major Pingle's attitude to it neither impractical nor irresolute. Our objective I knew now to be worth reaching; and as far as I could judge, this cautious and experienced man fully appreciated the difficulties involved and was as fully determined to overcome them. It almost looked as if we had a chance of something better than honourable failure. I sat down and drafted a cable to *The Times*.

In this cable I explained that in the light of fresh information about Fawcett we had changed our plans. Major Pingle had taken over the leadership of the expedition, and we were aiming now for a point slightly north of our original objective. We should therefore go, not up the Rio das Mortes, but up the Tapirapé, 'from the headwaters of which a party will carry out a 150 mile cross-country journey through entirely unknown country to the district near the Rio Kuluene where we have reason to believe that Fawcett's expedition was massacred in 1925'.

It had been arranged — in fact Major Pingle had insisted — that all dispatches should be vetted by him. (Miss Rosita Forbes had recently published an article in the *Daily Telegraph* which gave great offence to the Brazilians. Major Pingle was afraid that I would commit a similar indiscretion.) When I had finished it, I showed my cable to him. He passed it without criticism.

'That's right,' he said. 'That's just what we want to say.'

I called his attention to the sentence I have quoted. I was myself rather doubtful whether the whole of that cross-country journey would prove possible; I wanted to find out what he really thought himself.

'That doesn't commit us to more than we shall be able to do, does it?' I asked him. 'We don't want to announce a lot of intentions and then fail to carry them out.'

Major Pingle was emphatic. 'No, no,' he said. 'That's quite all right. We're going to do just what you've put in that cable.'

For reasons which will shortly appear, this cable never reached *The Times*. But it is very important to remember that I thought it had.

CHAPTER IX

# SNAKES AND A REVOLUTION

SÃO PAULO is like Reading, only much farther away. Brazil is a young country, and there industry still sprawls, has not yet acquired the spurious glamour with which Russian films and the more acquiescent modern poets have partly succeeded in investing the trappings of a mechanical age. São Paulo's skyscrapers, though more plentiful, seem scarcely less ill at ease than Rio's. Her innumerable trams have not that air of bland inevitability which is the true source of a tram's dignity. You almost expect them to shy at the traffic lights.

But you must not suppose that São Paulo is in any way quaint. Far from it. The air is brisk; the streets clang; electric signs challenge the stars with hyperbole. I find many people in England who think of São Paulo as a raw, new place, full of the rough romance of the extempore: the sort of town where tanned and wary men, riding in from great distances, scatter the poultry in the rutted streets and leave their ponies outside the saloon. The truth is very different. As you watch the straw hats bustling in and out of Woolworth's you feel — with satisfaction or regret, according to your nature — that here is the South America that matters, the South America of the future. One day the whole sub-continent will be like this, and then purists need have no misgivings about exploiting the accepted implications of the epithet 'transatlantic'. 'Order and Progress'. . . . But, as you shall hear, our visit was perhaps hardly the occasion for underlining the application of that motto.

\*　　\*　　\*

'To Throw Stones at the Serpents' (said the notice) 'is an Indication of Bad Character.'

We were in the snake farm at Butantan, outside the suburbs

71

of São Paulo: a most amusing place. There are two main en-
closures, one for venomous, the other for non-venomous
varieties. A low wall surrounds two squares of sunny turf, and
the turf is dotted with little round huts like foreshortened bee-
hives. Here the snakes live, a representative and contented community. If they want seclusion, they can retire into the little
huts. If they want exercise, they can go whipping round the
outside of their enclosure, a questing head held high, their eyes
for ever gauging the height of that incarcerating wall. If they
want a change of scene, they can climb the little trees and hang
in looped contemplation of São Paulo's remoter villas. If they
want a thrill, they can then relax their muscles and fall heavily
to the ground: a thing they do with surprising frequency, reck-
less abandon, and a kind of brittle plopping sound which is
indescribably sinister. And if they want to study human
nature, there is always a foolish fresco of faces on their
horizon.

Some of these snakes were extremely handsome: notably the
coral snake, in a devil's livery of black and red, and a snake
whose name I do not know, long, whippy, and apple-green,
with large deer-like eyes. But what I admired most was their
solution of the problems of social life in a confined space.

Watching those aimlessly circumambient reptiles, I was reminded of the promenade deck of our liner. In their lithe and
prowling passage round the edges of their prison I saw reflected
our own dyspeptic pacings of the deck. But with what a
difference! We human beings had cut particularly silly figures
on those solemn, self-consciously redundant circuits. To march,
for the good of our livers or our souls, round and round the
deck was in itself a sane, and should have been a satisfying,
practice. The trouble was that there was always someone else
doing it at the same time. One met them (if they were going in
the opposite direction) twice in every furlong. One could not
ignore them, even if they were strangers; there was not
room.

# SNAKES AND A REVOLUTION

At the first meeting one grinned at them with that protective self-mockery proper to a situation which both sides admit to be ridiculous and unnatural. At the second meeting also one grinned, for the awkward comedy of encounter lost nothing by so swift, so predestined a repetition. It was not until after the third meeting that one suddenly foresaw the impossibility of conjuring up the same broad, spontaneous, and slightly deprecating smile sixteen times in every mile: not until after the fourth that one discovered how difficult it was to replace it. One could not, now, disown that recurring and perambulatory figure. One could not, after that initial smile, stride past him with a set face, as if intent solely on exercise, on breathing deeply through the nose. That line of defence was already undermined by shared laughter. So both parties were driven to take refuge in a series of the most paltry evasions. By staring fixedly at an imaginary object on the vacant horizon: by feigning a rapt and frowning meditation: by blowing the nose: by examining the wrist-watch — by these, and a hundred other base superfluous shifts, one contrived to ward off the impact of too frequent recognition. It was a fine example of man's degradation by self-consciousness.

The snakes were gloriously free from anything of the sort. In the narrow ditch on the inside of their prison wall conditions were exactly analogous to conditions on the promenade deck. Snake was constantly meeting snake on a tour which both must have recognized as futile and rather ridiculous; and between snake and snake existed the same delicate barriers of class (or, as they would put it, species), the same awkward ties of fortuitous acquaintanceship, as complicated the encounters of passenger with passenger. But the snakes were perfectly equipped to deal with these petty emergencies. For their outlook — for their attitude to the social conventions — I cannot speak. Nor need I, since their anatomies were alone equal to the occasion.

However confined the space, however abrupt their meeting,

the snakes never found it necessary to recognize each other's existence. They did not have to swerve, to stand aside, to deflect or interrupt their progress. They simply went straight on. Splendidly indifferent, they crawled over each other. Their speed, their poise, their air of purpose, were unaffected. With bodies touching at half a dozen points, they could still ignore each other. Their capacity for aloofness had no physiological limitations. Enviable reptiles.

There was another enclosure, this time surrounded by a little moat, where the rattlesnakes lived. Their keeper was a bright-eyed little man with a detached, professional air: a little man, it seemed to me, of the very highest courage. His gaiters reached no higher than the knee; his hands were innocent of gloves. We had already watched, torn by anxiety for the welfare of all three parties concerned, while he drew a gigantic frog from the recesses of an anaconda's throat. Now we saw him leap the moat and, with an instrument something like a hoe, rudely evict the rattlers from their huts. He hoicked them out, bundles of fat and thrashing worms, which quickly coiled into malignant brown pustules on the bright turf. Their rattles whirred: a thin dry note of anger. Smiling indulgently, as though he were playing with puppies, the little man kicked them gently with the toe of his boot. Soon he had three or four striking with horrible speed and fury at his legs. The darted heads hit his gaiters with sharp bitter little thuds. The rattles made a scurrying, impatient noise, like dead leaves blown along a frosty road. I have never seen hate so well dramatized.

Presently he pinned a snake down, picked it up in those ungloved hands by the back of the neck, and brought it over the moat into our midst. (The Brazilians, I noticed, showed hardly any of that instinctive revulsion which would have flickered through a European crowd.) Then the little man produced a shallow glass saucer and, thrusting it into that pale soft mouth, showed us the vicious action of the fangs. As they closed on the glass, poison flowed out in yellow mucous jets. There was a surprising amount of it. I wondered what would happen if the little man got cramp, or had a stroke ... But neither of these things occurred; I suppose they never do. When he had finished with the snake he threw it carelessly back over the moat; its body bounced on the hard ground like a driven partridge's. We went back to our taxis, considerably impressed.

The whole time I was up in the interior I never saw a snake of any sort.

It was on our first day in São Paulo that we went to the snake farm. We expected (how slow we were to learn the lessons of Brazil), we confidently expected to leave by train for the interior in two days' time. We set about buying ammunition and films, and selling sterling cheques for prices twenty per cent above the official rate of exchange for milreis, and repacking our luggage, the bulk of which was to be sent round the coast to Pará to await our arrival at the mouth of the Amazon. Meanwhile, two things of some importance happened to the expedition.

One was the appearance of Neville. The nice thing about Neville was that he really did look like an explorer. That massive, fair, and cheerful presence might have stepped — or, more probably, hacked its way — out of the pages of the *Wide World Magazine*. Moreover, since leaving Eton (where he had been a contemporary of Roger's and mine) Neville had lived and worked in many distant places. He knew the Somerset Maugham country. He was no novice to the tropics. Perhaps the most significant thing about him was that no less than two of his friends had sent him (independently) that advertisement from the Agony Column on the day it appeared. He was clearly a notorious exception to the rule that modern young men are not adventurous. He had gone straight out from England to wait for us in Brazil.

The other important thing was Major Pingle's insistence that we should abandon our declared intention of increasing the world's geographical knowledge. He said that the difficulties of doing any useful survey-work would be almost insuperable, and that we had much better leave our theodolite in São Paulo to be sent back to the Royal Geographical Society and sell the small wireless set which we had brought out for picking up time signals. In this, as things turned out, he was wise. We were to find ourselves on our journey always pressed for time, and Roger practically single-handed, could hardly have coaxed any valuable results out of the theodolite by the hand-to-mouth methods which we should have had to employ. At the same time the decision stripped our enterprise of its never very convincing façade of scientific purpose; it would no longer be possible to offset a failure in the Fawcett hunt by brandishing a nice, new, accurate map. Our eggs were all in one basket now: a flimsy basket, though sensationally coloured.

Our second day in São Paulo was spent by Roger and Neville and me and the bull mastiff at a place called Santo Amaro. Though it produced nothing of the least interest or importance, I can remember every detail of this day with curious distinctness. In Santo Amaro I saw my first and last armadillo: it was cantering down the street with a *dégagé* air in the middle of a crowd of children. (But this alone would not suffice to make the day as unforgettable as it has proved.) There was also an ocelot in a cage by the side of the road; and a golf course; and an enormous artificial lake; and on the shores of the artificial lake an artificial sailing club. This last was a magnificently unreal place. As if it had been a scene in a musical comedy, the words Sailing Club on its gate did not purport to describe its functions; at the best, they offered a perfunctory and colourful excuse for its existence. In spite of the fleet of little boats at anchor, I had the feeling that — as in musical comedy — this sunlit lawn had chosen to pass itself off as a sailing club for some reason which no one could quite remember and which in any case had never been very cogent. This feeling was heightened by the behaviour of the habitués. These (with the exception of one inexplicable and overwrought monkey) were young, vigorous, and American. They all wore bathing dresses with that air of passionate inconsequence proper to the members of a sailing club in musical comedy; but they did not bathe, and viewed with disapproval and amazement our own attempts to do so, which were finally successful.

But I see now that I can never transfer to paper the impression which that day at Santo Amaro produced on me. Nor indeed would there be any point in doing so were it not that I suppose everyone, at one time or another, finds themselves in places which seem to belong nowhere, which they visited only by chance and where nothing happened to them; and which nevertheless they remember with a kind of dream-like vividness and of which the picture in their memory, disproportionately clear-cut, outlives the pictures of more memorable scenes and becomes at last encrusted with an eerie and importunate significance. I know that the only thing I am capable of forgetting about that day at Santo Amaro is its meaninglessness, its complete unimportance. And this, perhaps unwarrantably, I have now recorded.

When we got back to our hotel, they told us there had been a revolution. It had broken out the night before, and was now in full swing. This meant that there was not a hope of our starting up-country the next day, for the banks were shut and the train service dislocated. We were very much annoyed. We were also a little piqued. None of us had had any previous experience of revolutions; but from all we had heard of them, to be in the middle of one and not to know anything about it until eighteen hours after it had started seemed to argue a certain want of perspicacity. Your trained observer, we could not help feeling, would have been on to this business a little earlier in the day.

Still, there it was, going on (so they said) all round us: a full-dress South American revolution. We had better make the most of it; there might not be another that season. We had, as things turned out, five days in which to study the phenomenon at close quarters.

They were dull days. I suppose one's first revolution — like one's first experience of anything to which one brings preconceptions coloured by literature and the drama — is always rather disappointing. From the point of view of local colour, the first of the five was easily the best. On that day there were at least to be observed lorry loads of citizens, clearly in a state of considerable excitement, who careered through the streets at eight or ten miles an hour, shouting. There were also students, with sashes slung round their shoulders, who stood at strategic points holding inferior guns at angles perilously acute, and carrying on long, theoretical arguments with the more obviously non-combatant elements in the population. There was also, best of all, a real machine-gun. It stood on the steps of the post office, wrapped up in newspaper. But these were the only outward and visible signs of an event from which one had a right to expect something much more sensational. No shots were fired in anger and very few, I believe, by accident. Boat Race Night was Armageddon to this.

The second day did nothing to restore our faith in the dramatic value of revolutions. They even took away the machine-gun. But by this time it was clear that we had been expecting too much from the revolution. We began to realize why it was that the atmosphere in which we were living more nearly resembled that created by a vote of confidence than by a *coup d'état*. Everyone in the city of São Paulo was strongly in favour of the revolution. Where all are united by a common cause, your fiery patriot is scarcely more interesting to the onlooker than your keen anti-vivisectionist. All either of them can do is to carry banners about, distribute pamphlets, and get up subscriptions. In the streets of São Paulo these practices were rife. If exciting things happened at all, they happened down the line at Cruzeiro, where the railway crosses the Rio frontier. And they were a long time happening.

Meanwhile the unfortunate newspapers of São Paulo, cut off from communication with the outside world, had nothing to report save the symptoms of internal unanimity. These, amplified and elaborated in almost hourly extra editions, acquired with the passage of time a certain air of the ludicrous. The tremendous abstractions, the abundant exclamation marks, and the throbbing adjectives of the leading article were badly let down by the news items. In one column we were told that the heart of a people had never more gloriously vibrated to the call of Liberty; in the next we read that the Associated Pigeon Fanciers of São Paulo had placed 500 of their best birds at the disposal of the Commander-in-Chief.

The advantages of being On The Spot are often over-estimated. In the autumn of 1931 I was in Mukden a week after the Japanese had seized Manchuria; and though afterwards one behaved as though one's memories of sand-bags and impassive little sentries had given one an abnormal insight into the Far Eastern crisis, one knew that in reality this was not so, and that one had been hardly any nearer coming at the truth behind the situation than if one had stayed at home and read *The Times*. Everything nowadays takes place at such long range that the man on the spot had often less chance of seeing both sides of the medal than the man at a distance; one can no longer get a just impression of Crécy from the nearest windmill. Though it is, of course, pleasant to pick up one's misapprehensions at first-hand, and to have them coloured by one's own, and not by other people's imaginations.

About the Civil War (for it was something more than a revolution) of which the duration almost exactly coincided with my stay in the country I was hardly any the wiser for having been to Brazil. A fortnight after its outbreak we went out of touch with civilization and thereafter heard no more of the revolution or anything else than the Orkneys hear of Opera;

and during that first fortnight there were only rumours and propaganda. So, although from a sense of duty I will now append an estimate of what I understand to have been the significance of the revolution, you must not suppose that I understood it at the time.

The revolution took all Brazil, and even most of the inhabitants of São Paulo, by surprise. Its immediate causes were three. First: survivors of the old political regime, which had been swept out of the saddle by the revolution of 1930, were numerous in São Paulo, and had influence. These were anxious to get back into power before the elections, promised for 1933, confirmed the status and strengthened the hands of Dr. Getulio Vargas's Provisional Government (the victors of the 1930 revolution). Secondly: the industrial magnates of São Paulo were no less anxious to see their own friends controlling the country from Rio, for they urgently required that the tariff walls which now barely sheltered them (and which the Provisional Government threatened to lower) should be raised, or at any rate maintained at their present height. Thirdly and lastly: the local banks had made over-generous advances to the industrialists and therefore of necessity saw eye to eye with them.

Besides, there was an economic crisis, in Brazil as elsewhere; it looked as if there must be something wrong, and the government — who in truth had no very dazzling record — were the obvious people to blame. In Brazil, where four-fifths of the population are illiterate and they all have untidy minds, it is virtually impossible to get any accurate information about anything, ever. So it is hard to tell which of São Paulo's grievances were genuine, and which the result of artful misrepresentation.

# CHAPTER X

# FALSE START

On the fifth day of the revolution we left São Paulo by the night train. The invaluable Captain Holman had obtained safe-conducts for the party from the Chief of Police. But the troops of Matto Grosso — the only state to make good her promises of support to São Paulo — were on their way south and likely to be monopolizing transport facilities. So it seemed doubtful whether we should get very far by rail.

But everyone was delighted to be off. There was a general feeling that at last we were getting near the Real Thing; and this feeling was betrayed, rather prematurely, in the costume of several of our number. If from now on civilized clothes were an encumbrance, khaki was definitely an indiscretion; and some of us failed to achieve the picturesque without suggesting the military. I retain a vivid memory of jodhpurs, sustained by a portentous cartridge belt, plunging steeply into mosquito boots which would have aroused comment in Sherwood Forest. I have never seen the *Two Gentlemen of Verona* acted in modern dress; and I am afraid that not until I do will my fancy be recaptured by figures so romantically accoutred.

But, after all, there had been nothing so far to suggest to us that Brazil was glutted with romance. I like to think that that small but noisy group of aliens, half of them dressed for Death or Glory, and the other half for a good long walk in the country, brought into the lives of the station officials that element of colour and surprise which they must have sought in vain among the straw hats of São Paulo. That may have been the case, or it may not. What is certain is that we brought into their lives considerably more ammunition than they thought was decent. There was a scene. They were voluble, and we aghast. Betrayed by its weight, the squat suit-case full of .45 ammunition sat on the platform in a patch of lamplight, acquiring with each precious minute a more unmistakably political significance. Protests, disclaimers, threats, and mollifications eddied round it. Passes were flourished, regulations invoked, bribes hinted. The train whistled. It seemed as if we were going to be cruelly snatched back from the very brink of departure. But at the last moment, by one of those happy accidents which are so rare in the untemperamental atmosphere of Nordic officialdom, someone turned up who — either because he had a reputation for broadmindedness to keep up, or because he liked the English, or because he was out of sympathy with those of his colleagues already on the spot — was prepared to stretch a point. In a moment opposition had evaporated in a cloud of courtesies. Eager hands seized the suit-case, which now contrived to look infinitely commonplace and smug, and rushed it along the platform to our carriage. The stares of the onlookers mellowed. The train whistled for the last time. We had got away by the skin of our teeth. We rattled northwards through the night.

Dawn found us facing further delay. The railway service, having landed us at Ribeirão Preto, made its excuses and turned to business of national importance. Troop movements were being prophesied with confidence and — when they occurred — acclaimed with enthusiasm. Someone important was said to be coming down the line with his staff. If any trains did leave for the frontier, nothing so irrelevant as our expedition had a hope of getting seats on them. We drove through chill and sparkling air to the hotel and ordered a great many fried eggs.

The morning was full — as many of our mornings were destined to be — of rumours and false alarms. We were starting in an hour's time by car. We had got a special train. We should be here for a week. The bridge over the frontier had been dynamited. We were starting in half an hour. We were

going back to São Paulo. We were going to be arrested. ...
Everything, as usual, was rather uncertain. Eventually we
started the next morning, by road.

Ribeirão Preto was a pleasant little town. Its streets tailed
off with an air of relief into grass-grown tracks which led
through the coffee to distant fazendas. Its suburbs were the
merest huts, full of a casual squalor. Its chief civic ornament
was a large trim garden which filled the centre of its only
square: a cheerful green place, laced symmetrically with little
paths and shaded by impressive trees. (Almost all the little
towns we passed through reproduced this garden, with its raffish
but derelict bandstand and its bestiary of shrubs clipped to the
shapes of animals and birds.) Several cinemas looked on to
the square, their posters crying the wares of Hollywood. In the
streets battered cabs, drawn by small horses of a pinkish colour,
were elbowed, amicably rattling, out of the way by shiny self-
important cars with long American bonnets. In the blue sky
vultures hung meditatively; as they always do in Brazil.

The political situation lent the sleepy place a more than
ordinary air of animation. It frothed agreeably with excitement: an excitement without consequences, such as you see
expressed by the chorus in an opera. Spurs jangled in the bare
and sanitary-looking lobby of the hotel. Warriors came and
went with an air of preoccupation which did not conceal from
me the fact that their chief, if not their only, purpose in coming
and going was to maintain an atmosphere of *va et vient*. Girls
with bold eyes and secret ambitions to become *vivandières* sold
flags for the Red Cross, though it was as yet by no means certain
whether anyone had been wounded. Posters exhorted them to
'give our young men courage': an injunction which I suppose
they thought it would be easier to obey if they first broke down
the young men's sales-resistance.

Every now and then a small detachment of troops, straggling
and *désorienté*, would appear from nowhere in particular and
march aimlessly about the streets, while the populace expressed

their enthusiasm by clapping. The clapping, where one would have expected cheers, sounded odd. According to our standards of applause, it should have signalized the accomplishment of some difficult or curious feat; and one found oneself instinctively searching the devoted ranks for some soldier who was balancing his rifle on his chin, or swallowing his bayonet, or doing card tricks on the march. But after a time one got used to the custom, and when a troop of cavalry appeared it seemed quite natural to join in and clap too. For the cavalry were a very different kettle of fish from the infantry. The men sat their wiry little horses well, without affectation. There was an air of fancy dress about the infantry; you felt that carrying a pack and a rifle was not their job, though they enjoyed doing it before a crowd. But the troopers were at home in their saddles — were men born to manœuvre on horseback, if only against steers.

In Ribeirão Preto there happened one of those tiny, casual incidents from which one gets — or imagines that one gets — an insight into one aspect of a people's character. I was sitting on a high chair outside the hotel, having my shoes shined. A hundred yards away, at the corner of the square, a loud-speaker was blaring propaganda from São Paulo to the assembled citizens. One after another, all the oldest tricks of rhetoric came blundering through the evening air over the heads of the crowd, creaking in their flight like swans. At last the speech came to an applauded end. There was a pause filled only by those terrifying asthmatic crackles which rend the ether for some reason which I can never remember. Then the National Anthem began, flooding the cool square with its deafening and pretentious strains. Instantly the crowd removed their hats and stood as if magically pollarded by that blast of sound. From their chairs in cafés and outside shops, from the seats in the public garden, men and women rose to their feet and stood respectfully erect. My bootblack excused himself and faced the music. A very small negro boy with a bundle of newspapers under his arm whipped off his cap, clapped it between his knees, and stood saluting with the hand thus freed. His eyes were very solemn, his body very stiff; only his jaws moved, completing with an air of ritual the consumption of a sweet. The policeman on point duty was saluting too, dapper and motionless, while the four streets controlled by that now patriotically rigid arm were slowly choked by traffic. The moment was an impressive one.

But it outlived its psychological effect. The National Anthem, played once, was played again; and this time (what we had supposed impossible) slightly louder. Our feeling of consecration wore off. We began to catch each others' eyes: to smile in spite of ourselves, and then to look quickly away. There was undeniably something a little ludicrous in that crashing and redundant music, which had frozen us all into postures of formality and now seemed gleefully reluctant to break the spell. Our artificial solemnity trembled painfully on the edge of farce.

Then, suddenly, the music choked and died. Everyone relaxed and began to talk. We acknowledged with smiles our narrow escape from bathos. With a grinding of gears the glaciers of traffic at the cross roads dissolved into motion. We had that pleasant feeling of being all sharers in a subtle joke. For a full minute the loud-speaker was silent.

Then, with a roar, the music was on us again; and it was still the National Anthem. The situation was a delicate one, but the Brazilians met it in exactly the right way. Again they stood up and bared their heads. But they did it now with an air of humorous resignation. The policeman smiled as his salute once more paralysed the traffic. Even the little nigger boy looked less dutifully rapt. On all sides anti-climax was frankly admitted; the crowd discharged its patriotic obligations with a deprecating air.

This, I thought, was greatly to their credit. People are never more apt to be silly, and to behave in an unreal way, than when their dignity is at stake. The citizens of Ribeirão Preto, finding themselves made publicly ridiculous by their loyalty to a convention, neither disowned the convention nor pretended they had not been guyed. They admitted the loss of their dignity and wrote it off with a good grace. They made the best of an unnatural situation by doing the natural thing. This does not happen often among civilized peoples.

# CHAPTER XI

# FRONTIER INTERLUDE

UNTIL the last moment it was uncertain when, if ever, we should leave Ribeirão Preto. But the last moment came, quite suddenly, at ten o'clock on our second morning there, and we found ourselves packing our persons and possessions into two cars and a lorry before an amused crowd, who had formed the habit of crying, in an explanatory but illogical manner: 'Ah, os scientistas!' whenever they saw a pair of jodhpurs. For a few minutes before our departure the expedition held the centre of the stage. The military bustled and swaggered in vain. It was our drivers who were the heroes of the hour; for who knew what terrible things were happening up at the Minas frontier? The devoted fellows, I observed, hardly did themselves justice in the roles which popular imagination had assigned them. They had already successfully demanded double pay in view of the risk involved in making such a journey at such a time; they were now haunted by the fear that the dangers which they had so feelingly sketched would not turn up to justify their exorbitance.

We dashed off, hooting, in a cloud of dust. I enjoyed that first day's drive immensely. Release was in the air. From now on we should be seeing our fences. If we met delay, we should at least meet it at first hand. We should no longer have to take its causes on trust, or endure it in circumstances remote from all emergency. The expedition had taken a step towards reality.

All day we drove furiously along roads heavy with a reddish dust, the *terra roxa* of the coffee country. The country was rolling and empty, but not at all exotic. The rare villages looked poor, stagnant, and impervious to hope or despair. One had a Russian name, another a German; they had originally been foreign settlements. We met few other cars, but it was a point of honour with our drivers that at each meeting we should rub shoulders with disaster. The Brazilian chauffeur appears to believe that it is his business, like the matador's, to reduce to its narrowest the margin between life and death.

We reached a place called Igarapava with an hour of daylight in hand. The frontier between São Paulo and Minas Geraes, represented at this point by the Rio Grande, was only two miles away. Being anxious to get across that night, we pushed on to the military post at the bridgehead. Here there took place a mildly fantastic scene.

The western sky, already yellowing into sunset, jaundiced the wide unhurrying waters of the river and provided a lurid, theatrical background. The long steel bridge — the only bridge — which carried both road and railway across to Minas looked gaunt and enigmatic and more than capable of being dynamited. It was, in any case, closed to traffic. It was obvious that we should never get our cars across. At our end it was blocked by a sprawling, amateurish redoubt which formed the spearhead of some shallow entrenchments. There was a similar redoubt at the Minas end, and 100 yards of lackadaisical barbed wire entanglement in the middle of the bridge. The opposing forces were still on speaking terms; but they would remain so only until such time as the Minas authorities made up their minds to withhold from the revolution that support to which the Paulistas regarded them as pledged.

The expedition, stretching its cramped limbs and trying to remove from its features a thick layer of russet dust, stood beside the cars beneath a little siding on the railway. The garrison was engaged in the occupation, by no means uncommon in Brazil, of waiting for a meal to be cooked. In their extreme youth, their untidiness, and the antiquity of their equipment, they resembled a detachment of the Chinese army. What they thought we resembled it was — fortunately, perhaps — impossible to guess; but they examined us closely, with that faintly incredulous curiosity which our appearance undeniably invited. Meanwhile Major Pingle questioned the officer in charge about our chances of getting across the river that night. The officer in charge thought them slender. A discussion ensued in which representatives of all ranks took part, for Brazil is socially, if not politically, a democratic country, and when it comes to talking, an officer, though he may reasonably hope for precedence over his men, will not claim a monopoly of the conversation. So everyone had their say, and what they said was not encouraging. It was impossible to guarantee our safety on that bridge in the twilight. We might perhaps get across to-morrow, *si Dios quizer*. . . .

The soldiers, naturally anxious to impress us with the importance of their position and thereby with their own military qualities, enlarged on the fieriness, the irresponsibility of the troops on the opposite bank. They might fire on us, or they might not. Who could tell? We were to understand that they were a wild and incalculable type, the Mineiros. . . . The only constructive suggestion came from a civilian, a swashbuckling and intolerant nigger with a raking black hat and an incisive manner. He it was who pointed out that if we tried to go across dressed as we were we should indeed run some risk of being shot up; unless we could find some more obviously civilian clothes we had better wait and try in full daylight on the morrow.

At this the expedition started a feverish search for the subfusc; Roger, with notable presence of mind, put on a dark blue fisherman's jersey. But in the flow of talk minutes had been wasted and indecision was abroad. In the end it seemed best to Major Pingle to postpone our attempt till to-morrow. We turned back to Igarapava and slept among squealing children in a filthy hotel.

In the bland and reassuring sunlight of morning the military were less inclined to be alarmist. By ten o'clock we were in the Paulista emplacement at the bridgehead, waiting to be ferried across the river and saying good-bye to our drivers. These were all excellent men, and the negro in charge of the lorry had a bent for the lowest forms of comedy which made his loss doubly bitter. Major Pingle had done good work that morning. Advancing to the barbed wire under a white flag, he had persuaded the Minas commandant to endorse our safe conducts and to telegraph up the road for cars to meet us on the other side. He had also arranged for a boat to take us across.

The boat was a small one, with an outboard motor which bore every appearance of having been home-made. It would only hold four of us at a time. As we chugged across the broad and shining river the embattled bridgeheads, seen from below, were altogether less contemptible and comic; we hoped that our non-combatant status had been very thoroughly explained to the soldiers who manned them, for they could hardly have been offered a more tempting target.

We landed on a little beach and scrambled up a steep bluff to the bridge. Behind fortifications which were so perfunctory as to appear almost fortuitous the defenders of Minas were taking things easy. They sat under the lee of their sandbags, smoking cigarettes with their backs to the enemy. Memories of O.T.C. field days in Windsor Great Park rose unbidden in my mind. Had it not been for three or four public-spirited civilians of the mendicant class, who were taking the keenest interest in all that was, or might be, going on, the bridge would have been virtually unguarded. One of these addressed me in execrable French. He was the true type of the malcontent, a grubby little man with a dissatisfied mouth and several days' growth of beard. But he wore his tatters of Gallic culture with an air. He considered himself greatly superior to the soldiers; and in this, I dare say, he was right. They were men, he said, of the very lowest type: mere brutes. Indeed, all the people in these parts were on a level with the animals. I would find, as he had, that for a man of intelligence and distinction their society was intolerable. As for these revolutions. . . . He spat, rather

90

ineffectually. In the last revolution, the revolution of 1930, he had lost all his money and the soldiers had destroyed his home. Politics were a kind of madness in Brazil. What a country. . . .

I expressed a guarded sympathy, praying that none of the soldiers understood French. But it must be confessed that the soldiers did not, just then, present a very formidable aspect. Without a murmur they had yielded up their rifles and were placidly watching a demonstration of arms drill which conveyed the spirit, if not the letter, of the British War Office's Infantry Training Regulations (Part I). By the expedition's gramophone, which had arrived in the first boatload of luggage, they were metaphorically disarmed as well. The voices of Herr Richard Tauber and Mr. Douglas Byng, trailing incongruously out through the heat-haze towards the barbed wire, entranced them. They listened, puzzled but content. A faraway look came into their eyes. They unbuttoned their tunics. Even the disgruntled linguist mellowed, and became wistful instead of bitter. He had once owned a machine like that, he said: like that, only larger. They had stolen it from him in the last revolution, the revolution of 1930. . . .

Meanwhile, for some reason which was never made clear, the ferry had refused its office. About a quarter of our luggage was still on the other side. I was told to go back across the bridge and see what had happened to it. A soldier with a broad, unhelpful face was detailed as my escort. He picked up his rifle with a sigh, and together we scrambled over the parapet, on which previous consignments of luggage had already produced signs of wear and tear. With a pleasant (but unwarranted) feeling of self-importance we marched down the long bridge, ducking and straddling our way through the barbed wire entanglement, which had been erected on Heath Robinson principles. In the Paulista emplacement I found the invaluable Humphreys, who had come out from England as man-of-all-work to the expedition. He was mopping his brow and regarding with a pained but indomitable eye an immensely heavy trunk and a still heavier wooden case. Owing to a misunderstanding — or more probably, to misappropriation of their pay — the men whom we had hired as porters had gone on strike. We would have to get the things across ourselves.

I remember the next half hour very vividly. Most of it the two of us spent on all fours, coaxing those gigantic burdens under the barbed wire entanglement. We cursed. We sweated. We tripped up. We tore our shirts. We cut our hands. We lost our tempers. The heat leapt up into our bodies from the concrete and the sun beat down on them from above. The bridge, with the elasticity of mirage, grew longer every moment, and the luggage, with the smug malice of the inanimate, heavier. And all the time our antic exertions were watched, from either end of the bridge, by two large groups of able-bodied men who were not allowed to help us. How right the malcontent had been, I thought. Politics were a kind of madness in Brazil. I cursed the revolution more bitterly than ever.

But for all that it was rather fun. Two hours later, lying on a pile of unripe bananas in the first railway station in Minas Geraes, I realized that I had enjoyed that morning at the bridge more than anything since we left England. The incident had been fantastic, strenuous, and crowned with success: which is, for me, perhaps the most attractive combination of qualities that any incident can offer. Besides, we were outside the state of São Paulo; from now on difficulties ought, by rights, to be fewer and further between.

But we made almost no more progress that day. Most of it we spent in that small and barren railway station, with nothing to eat but oranges scrounged from a deserted orchard. At last, towards evening, the cars turned up, and we drove on northwards to the town of Uberaba, trailing our swollen plumes of dust across the fiery face of sunset.

# CHAPTER XII

# THE ROAD UP COUNTRY

In my memory the next five days are of a piece.

You got up while it was still dark and left without regret the grimy cupboard of a room which you had shared with two others. You drank black coffee with *pinga* in it and helped to load the lorry. Outside it was quite cold. Everything was grey and expectant. The street lamps burnt with a sickly, lessening glow which could not touch the walls behind them. Footfalls in the town were very distinct; there was a vague uncertain stirring behind closed shutters. Stars still pricked a pale, enormous shell of sky. The thin sound of a bugle came from the barracks. Then the driver of the leading car raced his engine, and you lost that prized accompaniment of dawn — the birth of small familiar sounds into a world of silence.

It was yours again for a moment on the outskirts of the town. The convoy was halted at a fiscal post; while formalities were discharged and road tax paid your ears caught once more the voice of the day's youth. Now there was more to hear. A dog barking in the middle distance: cock-crows: the crack of a whip: the thudding of an axe on wood. All these sounds came singly to you across the still clear morning, each one delicate, finished, and perfectly subdued to its setting. They had a special quality of remoteness without withdrawal. They were at once mysterious and immediate: altogether different from the sounds of evening or of noon. If you had shut your eyes and banished your sense of time, your ears would still have told you that it was early morning.

The sun had just risen. Its light no more than grazed the world, gilding the crests of ridges, from the blue hollows between them picking out little save the tallest trees and the wisps of vapour which hung wherever there was water. But it plunged at hazard through the window of the poor house outside which your car was standing and there discovered, among its furthest shadows, the head and shoulders of a mulatto girl. A moment ago the window had offered only gloom and dim shapes and the sound of crockery. Now there was this sudden image of the girl pinned by a lance of light. She was chewing a bit of sugar-cane. Her face was grave and intent. With each bite she twisted her head slightly and drew it back, like a puppy with a bone. You could see the play of muscles in her neck, and the way her face grew peaked and her cheekbones were defined as she sucked the juice. Like a mechanical toy in a glass-case she went through her deliberate repertoire of little actions over and over again. Then gears ground and your car moved forward. The girl chewing sugar-cane in a back room was left behind.

After that you went on, hour after hour, along a white, swooping, empty road. The dust was many inches deep. Sometimes the surface underneath it was smooth, and you flew like the wind. Sometimes it was pitted and scarred and tortuous, like the bed of a stream, and you lurched painfully along at a walking pace, clinging to the fiercely tilted coachwork. Your horizons closed and opened, now swerving sharply in on you, now veering carelessly away; but always keeping that watchful and competitive air which a road beside a railway has when you look at it from the train. Sometimes you could see for miles across a tufted plain to remote blue hills. Sometimes you scurried down an aisle barred by the shadows of tall trees. Sometimes the road narrowed and the scrub closed in, so that for a long time you were blinking fretfully behind an arm raised to ward the whipping branches from your eyes. Your impressions of the country and the day were always undergoing change.

There was most to see in the early morning. Flocks of green parrakeets dipped and darted over the road. From one steep wall of forest to another toucans, direct and unhurrying, flew high across the valleys like blackcock. They were always in pairs, yet never together. It was as if they were bound to respect some queer convention of aloofness, some formal and obligatory habit of pursuit and evasion. They never flew side by side, like the parrots. Tall secretary birds pranced anxiously down the road before our cars with the stupidity of poultry and the gait of *haute école*. Sometimes an emu watched us, grey, unobtrusive and puzzled, from among the little twisted trees of the campo, drawing an ineffectual broadside from revolvers in the leading car.

But most of the birds were a discreet compromise between the exotic and the familiar. Plover loitered gracefully against the deep blue sky in something very like the magpie livery of peewits. Little doves, smaller and quicker than a thrush, pecked in the dust of the road and whirred away like quail at your passage. There were heavier pigeons, of a dark slate-colour, and rotund, pompous partridges, and woodpeckers with splendid orange throats, and many kinds of hawk. But as the sun climbed higher the birds grew scarce. By noon there was little stirring on those parched and ragged uplands. The only live things you saw were the big lizards and the humped zebu cattle, incongruously Asiatic, who stood carved in shadow-dappled groups under the trees.

There was hardly any traffic on the road. Sometimes you passed a horseman, and carried with you for a moment the fleeting impression of white teeth grinning in a dark face, an excited pony stamping backwards into the scrub, a saddle-cloth of gaily dyed sheepskin. More rarely there was an ox-cart: a high primitive affair travelling with infinite leisure on two solid wheels behind eight or ten couple of phlegmatic beasts. The axles of these carts are never greased; the harsh yet curiously peaceful rhythm of their screaming is held to encourage the teams. They move at a foot pace. The sound of them is peculiar and memorable. If I heard anything like it now, I know that the Brazilian highway would be conjured up entire and that I should remember many small things which I have forgotten.

Though at that season in that country there is hardly any water, the road crossed many water-courses of all sizes. The bridges over these were responsible for whatever of delay or anxiety we encountered. They consist of an openwork structure of wooden beams designed on the principle of a railroad track. That is to say, there are two large beams which run longitudinally beneath a number of smaller ones placed latitudinally. The name for these bridges is *Mataburros*, or Mule-killers, and their special virtue is that no livestock can cross them without running grave risk of being disabled by missing its footing on the beams. Motor traffic is exposed, though in a less degree, to a similar risk. This is especially so when (as is very common) the smaller latitudinal beams are not, through age or any other cause, equal to bearing the weight of your car. It is then necessary that your wheels shall run only on the more substantial lengthwise beams — not as a rule a difficult thing to manage, if you approach the bridge cautiously and take your time. But this our drivers were excessively reluctant to do. All our entreaties, and the fact that the car I was in had some two feet of play in the steering wheel, did not deter the driver, a man of spirit, from taking his bridges at full speed. He would dash sharply down an incline, bent, as it seemed, on the total destruction of bridge and car alike. At the last minute, with a tremendous but nonchalant wrench at the steering wheel, he would contrive to hit off the longitudinal beams. The gleam of rocks and water below us; an angry ripple of sound as the cross-beams leapt in their places at our passage; two more wild wrenches to correct the aberrations of our steering gear; and we had somehow scrambled across. It must have been good management; good luck would never have held out for 600 miles. But it never felt like good management.

About noon we would stop in a village and order a meal. The meals were always the same, and they always took an hour to cook, and we always ate too much of them. The groundwork was *feijão* — a mixture of rice and black beans. Undeterred by the discovery that you had taken much more of this stuff than you had meant to, you piled on to the same plate several kinds of roast, fried, and boiled meat: eggs: sometimes fish: and a rather enigmatic selection of vegetables. You washed this down with warm inferior beer or a coarse red wine which was often rather good. Then, sleepy and surfeited, you got into the cars again and drove on till dusk.

In the villages where we stayed the night we were treated with kindness and a certain incredulity. The *pensão* was invariably, at first sight, far too small to accommodate the whole expedition; and, no less invariably, the whole expedition slept there. A huge meal, the exact counterpart of luncheon, was consumed, while the inhabitants glared or giggled according to their sex. Major Pingle disappeared with our papers to obtain the blessing of the local *delegado*. With a zest which clearly could not last, the expedition wrote up its diaries by candlelight.

In all these places we were careful to show no interest whatsoever in the revolution. If we had, it would in any case have been ill-repaid. Nobody knew what was happening; but nobody admitted his ignorance. So the air was full — as it often is in the interior of Brazil — of huge, colourful misapprehensions. In some places a large part of the population, with memories of 1930 fresh in their minds, had taken to the jungle to avoid all danger of being pressed into military service. There were no mails, either incoming or outgoing, and all wireless sets had been confiscated; nobody yet knew for certain which side they were on, so the radio propaganda from Rio and the radio propaganda from São Paulo were impartially proscribed. This is one of the best ways of what is called Preserving an Open Mind.

There was a dangerous tendency — due, I think, to our heavy armament — to invest the expedition with some sort of politico-military significance. In Minas, and even further north in Goyaz, a half-formulated fear of a Paulista invasion was abroad; an officious man with a squint, who held us up at the point of the carbine outside Uberlandia, clearly imagined that he beheld in us the advance guard of the revolutionary forces. Fortunately, our Portuguese was not yet sufficiently fluent to commit indiscretions in, and we presented such a ridiculous appearance that the fears aroused by our arrival died down as soon as people had time to get a good look at us. There were several half-hearted attempts to obstruct our progress; but in the end they always let us through. To hold us up would indeed have been as foolish and un-Christian an act as to impound a menagerie; the officials were very properly loath to deny their fellow-countrymen further north such innocent pleasure and amusement as our passage through their homes was certain to provide.

We found no community so small or so ill-informed that a mention of the name of Fawcett failed to create a stir among its members. As a topic for controversy and conjecture the Colonel's fate enjoys in Brazil a popularity accorded elsewhere only to the sea-serpent. Nothing so stimulates the Brazilian's powers of invention, nothing so enlarges his credulity, as a conversation about Colonel Fawcett. Enough legend has grown up round the subject to form a new and separate branch of folk-lore. Everyone has his own theory; and since the best sort of theory is clearly one based on personal experience or private information, personal experience and private information are coined for the occasion. It became harder than ever to believe that Fawcett had really existed; under this battery of apocryphal side-lights our *ignis fatuus* threatened to vanish altogether.

Still, we gave it out that we had all been at school with one of Fawcett's sons, which was a likely appeal to sentiment and slightly reassured our more sophisticated critics who — taking their line, I imagine, from General Rondon and the Rio newspapers — were apt to regard us as imperialistic claim-jumpers, anxious to plant metaphorical Union Jacks on the untapped mineral resources of the interior.

It was during this stage of our journey that I first detected an ominously genuine scepticism in Major Pingle's references to our search for Fawcett.

# CHAPTER XIII

## ASSORTED ENCOUNTERS

I HAVE said that all those five days on the road are of a piece in my memory. But at the time each had a pattern and texture of its own; each was coloured by moods and events of which I have forgotten the order and significance. When you have tidied up a room, there are certain objects for which you cannot find a place, though you know they once belonged there. In the end you take them out and store them, in indiscriminate irrelevance, somewhere else. In the same way there were incidents in those five days which I do not like to jettison, yet which will not fit into their setting.

There was the wrangle with our drivers in Minas. They evolved a theory that their cars would be commandeered when we crossed the frontier into Goyaz, and on the strength of it stood out for still more money. Successfully, as far as I can remember.

There was the time when Major Pingle, the only man in his car who knew the road, went to sleep and did not wake up till they were ten leagues out of their way and had run out of petrol.

There was the large black and silver iguana which stood in the middle of the road, looking (as well it might) suspicious, until I hit it in the off fore with a revolver, third shot. This was the first blood drawn by the expedition.

There was the place where the road-tax was levied by an official suffering from small-pox. We did not wait for our change.

There was the birth of a conversational gambit which (though this we could not have foreseen) was to dominate our intercourse with the natives for the next three months. It consisted of asking them how far it was from the place where we were to the next place. The answers given were always inaccurate.

But above all there were two encounters which were so oddly opposite in the impressions they produced that I will record them for the sake of the contrast. Both were enjoyable. Talking to Dr. Carlos was like reading the *Arabian Nights* — but then this was Brazil, where one expected colour in the conversation; perhaps Baghdad is not the best place to appreciate the *Arabian Nights*. On the other hand, in Baghdad the *Morning Post* has the charm of all transplanted things, the tang of incongruity. That evening with the missionaries was like the *Morning Post* in Baghdad.

We were summoned to it, as we walked back to our inn at dusk, by a piping, matter-of-fact little voice. 'Mother-says-would-you-like-to-come-in-for-a-cup-of-tea,' cried the voice, panting slightly. Coming from the shadows of that wretched village a pistol-shot would have surprised us less — considerably less — than that English invitation. We halted: peered: discerned a child: and followed her, rather incredulously, to her parents' house. Here there were more children, and the two excellent missionaries, and large nostalgic cups of tea. The little room was full of dogmatic, reassuring texts and photographs of the missionaries' relations, looking confident. The children brought the photographs to me, one after another, and asked me if I loved the people therein represented. I said Yes, I did, and it must have been the right answer, for they did not seem at all surprised.

When I had been shown all the photographs twice I began, in self-defence, to ask the children those foolish and perfunctory questions with which the adult at bay tries to justify himself. Such as: how old were they, and could they read yet, and what were they going to be when they grew up. But all these questions were parried, with uncanny skill, by references to the fact that one of their number (Timmy) had had a fit the year before. This alarming occurrence had made a profound impression on their minds, but I think they perhaps overestimated its news value. In one's conversation with children it is often rather difficult to pretend that one is making much progress; with every avenue of approach blocked by Timmy's fit I felt that my task was hopeless indeed. All the same, I enjoyed that evening. The tea and the texts: the tight little domestic world landmarked by a series of bed-times: the ill-informed discussion of last night's supremely uninteresting wireless news from London — all these things supplied an entertaining note of contrast in that hot, careering journey: like a bowler hat in a battle.

Dr. Carlos had a very different value. He was a vivid little man, with deep-set eyes and a lined face. In his hunched and forceful shoulders, in the way he turned his head very quickly and decisively to give you a keen bright stare, he suggested a small hawk, perhaps a merlin. He was courteous, intelligent, and full of a curious learning. He spoke good English and bore a name long honoured in Brazil. It was he who reminded us what cause our imaginations had to be fired by the prospect before us. He spoke at length, in a level deprecating voice, of journeys he had made into the unknown forest area called São Patricio. He told us of fungi which at night gave forth a blue light, strong enough to read by, and of the Indians' skill in witchcraft, by which he seemed to mean a kind of voodooism, backed by great subtlety in poisons. In those forests there are blacks living (as elsewhere they do not) wild with the Indians: a strange, doomed, and beastly people. They are a degenerate type. He showed us a photograph of a little stunted man with a tail eighteen inches long, standing in a humble fawning attitude between huge tree trunks. He showed us giant beetles, and the skins of snakes. He told us legends of the first explorers, the bandeirantes, and made it easy to believe them. He talked well, rehearsing romance with the manner of a scholar.

But he gave more than lip-service to Romance. He had hunted buried treasure on the coast of Uruguay and very nearly died in the process. With this story he took, I think, especial pains; for these English, traditionally insane and quite possibly wealthy, might be persuaded to return to South America next year with an objective more profitable than the bones of an explorer. It was a good story, irreproachably grand in manner. Against a background of death-beds on which faded charts repaid the debts of gratitude, the original protagonists played their parts with a nice respect for the conventions. They were an English crew, buccaneers of the eighteenth century. Hard pressed by British men-of-war, they ran their ship aground on the coast of Uruguay and buried their booty under a cliff on which they carved, with something of Hook's hankering after respectability, the Royal Arms of England. They themselves were later surprised and cut to pieces by a landing party from the men-of-war. Only a few escaped to attempt a desperate journey across country, they could not tell whither. One man came through this alive. He found himself in the enviable (but often surprisingly unremunerative) position of possessing the sole clue to the whereabouts of untold wealth. Now Dr. Carlos had arrived, by the approved death-bed route, in that position. It was one which he was peculiarly fitted to hold. He had gone to Uruguay, had searched its coast line for the coat of arms, and had at last, when far gone with illness and privation, found it. But alas, the sea had advanced, gnawing into the base of the cliff and permanently covering those rocks over which the lion and the unicorn stood wardens in the alien stone. To get at the treasure would need many men and much tackle. Dr. Carlos had been forced to abandon his quest; but it was not (he said, looking at us) abandoned for ever. He meant to go back there one day; he only needed the right companions, and a little money.

A nice man. He was ready for anything, and I think would have done some things well. Unlike the missionaries' children, whose existence, ever since Timmy's fit, seemed doomed to anti-climax, Dr. Carlos would always be finding new things under the Brazilian sun.

CHAPTER XIV

# DELAYS AND DOUBTS

GOYAZ ought to be a charming place. I seem to remember that when we first got there we found it so. But in Goyaz, as in so many other places in Brazil, we had to stay much longer than we meant to. Enforced familiarity bred something more bitter than contempt.

We had to stay there much longer than we meant to because most of our supplies had disappeared. Major Pingle had forwarded them in advance to railhead, which is a place called Leopold Bulhões, about 100 miles south of Goyaz. But the revolution had caught them in mid-journey, and only a fraction of the consignment had reached its destination. It took time to find this out, and more time to replace the stuff which had been commandeered by purchases in Goyaz. In all we lost five days.

They were all spent in Goyaz. As I say, it ought to be a charming place. Its crooked streets are blinding white in the sunshine. A little river runs through it with a cheerful noise. The town crouches close under wooded hills, and the sun sets behind a grinning jagged row of peaks. It is not a big place, though it is theoretically destined to become, in the incalculably distant future, the capital city of all Brazil: the idea being, I suppose, that the nation's heart will beat more evenly if situated at some point more nearly in the centre of the body politic. To-day, however, Goyaz is small and sleepy. A quarter of an hour's walk will bring you out of the sight and remembrance of man's work. There are no trams, no sky-scrapers, and the cinema functions once a week. The gables are gargoyled with vultures, and small wild boys on small wild ponies clatter inconsequently over the cobbles, with huge spurs strapped on to their bare feet.

There is nothing at all to do in Goyaz. All day long the women sit at their windows and stare, in an ardent and provocative manner, at the empty street. All day long the men, with the air of philosophers in training, sit on little chairs outside their front doors, wearing straw hats and heavily frogged pyjama jackets. (This combination, which struck us at first as curious, was the nearest approach to a national costume that we found in Brazil.) Occasionally one of them gets up and goes indoors, to lie down. Nothing else happens.

We stayed in an inn kept by a bent but active old woman with a heavy moustache. She had had some previous experience of the English, though what form this experience had taken I could not make out. Her acquaintance with our fellow-countrymen I took at first to be confined — wide though it was — to unmarried females. It was not until she referred to Roger as 'Miss' that I realized that this prefix, which played a dominating part in her reminiscences, had for her no sex connotation.

We used to go for long, purposeful rides on scraggy ponies or, when these were lacking, on swart, embittered mules.

'There be some sports are painful, but delight in them
    Labour sets off',

says someone in *The Tempest*; and we used to pretend that these rides came under that category. There was certainly no concealing the fact that they were painful. The Mexican saddle has a great deal to be said for it; not so the Brazilian. Instead of high vertical pommels fore and aft you have an ordinary open saddle with a long raised guard in front — a heavy and ornate affair, bent sharply back towards the rider, who derives no sort of benefit from it. I never saw the *boiadeiros* roping steers, but I doubt very much whether a rope hitched round that awkward bulwark would take the strain of the beast; it seemed to me to serve no conceivable purpose. For us the stirrups were not — as they say of windows in stage-directions — practicable. Those stout leather buckets looked pleasantly medieval, and in thick country they gave valuable protection to the feet. But we, who wore boots of the sort charitably described as 'sensible', could scarcely get our toes into them at all, and could not hope to keep them there. When we returned, dusty and excoriated, through the glaring streets, the townspeople of Goyaz used to go through the process known as Permitting Themselves a Smile. And small wonder.

Otherwise I cannot remember that we did very much. A circus had pitched its tent on a piece of waste land near the river, and on the first night most of us went to see it. After we had occupied our seats for three-quarters of an hour, with only the municipal orchestra to keep us amused, I went home to bed. Later, they tell me, a female tightrope-walker appeared and fell heavily, breaking her parasol. Even so, it was a poor kind of a circus.

Then there was the time when I was to have gone out after deer with the dentist, who nightly slung his hammock under some fruit trees and shot the unsuspecting creatures by the light of a torch. But the dentist failed at our rendezvous, and the project came to nothing. I remember also the afternoon when Roger and I set out to bathe in the river, and in the end somehow found ourselves talking to a bald Dutchman in the malt-room of a German brewery. The Dutchman drank a great deal of beer and perspired with a freedom amounting to licence. He had a violent admiration for the English. His two favourite authors were Zane Grey and Sir Walter Scott; which did I think the greater of the two? I said that each was exceedingly good in his own way, but for my part I slightly preferred Scott. But Zane Grey also was great, was he not? asked the Dutchman anxiously. I said Yes; those most familiar with his work often referred to him as great. We also had talk of three Germans who had set out, a couple of months ago, for the Rio das Mortes: 'on horsey-back', according to the Dutchman. Two of them lived in Goyaz. The Dutchman did not expect to see them again.

# DELAYS AND DOUBTS

The expedition had the honour of being received by the Interventor of Goyaz. The post of Interventor was created (I think) by Getulio Vargas's Provisional Government, which came into power after the revolution of 1930. The Interventor corresponds in effect to the Governor of a State under the old regime; he is an unconstitutional agent of the Provisional Government, wielding — subject to inspiration from Rio — something like dictatorial powers. He is, in fine, a man of real importance. Major Pingle, who is a snob, was delighted when we got our invitation to the palace.

The palace looked out on to the principal square, with its neat turf and its inevitable bandstand. We filed oafishly into an ante-chamber, past informal sentries and a derelict typewriter. In the ante-chamber stiff little plush chairs stood symmetrically, and with an air of expectation, round a burnished spittoon. A secretary waved us to them. We sat down, making those little wordless whimpers of gratitude which one always does make on such occasions. We were acutely conscious of our disreputable appearance. In Brazil rigid conventions govern all matters of *tenue*, and you may not (for instance) travel in a train unless you are wearing a coat and a collar. Tucking our hobnailed boots underneath us, we hoped devoutly that the Interventor would know an Old Etonian tie when he saw one.

The ante-chamber had what I can only describe as a non-existent air. This was chiefly due to the fact that its mural decorations were executed according to a formula perfected by the scene-painters of the nineteenth century, and which to-day survives only on the remoter provincial stages. On the plaster walls of that room not only had a rich oak panelling been boldly painted, but a series of huge and ambitious oil paintings were represented, in the same medium, as hanging in elaborate gilt frames on top of the panelling. A wainscot had been painted round the floor, and a frieze round the ceiling. Even the prospect from the tall windows, obscured as it was by yellowing curtains of imitation lace, gave the impression of having been painted on a backcloth and hung a few inches from the un-glazed sashes.

It must be confessed that as a *trompe-l'oeil* the thing was a hopeless failure. What will pass muster as 'Act III. The Library at Fritters. Midnight' was never meant to stand close scrutiny and sunbeams. Those massive frames too obviously lacked a dimension; not even by moonlight could you have been deceived into thinking that the room was really hung with pictures. As for the false panelling, it was so blatantly false that it made even the solid walls seem spurious. When the door opened, you half expected to see the plaster sag in before the draught, like old scenery. In the midst of this elaborate and unsuccessful sham the authenticity of the spittoon was almost painful.

The Interventor was a slim young man with a discerning eye, a sense of humour, and a gracious manner. He must have found us funny, but he did not show it. He began pumping Major Pingle about the state of affairs in São Paulo, discovered that Major Pingle knew nothing worth knowing, and turned to listen politely to our views about Fawcett, jaguars, and the scenery of Brazil. These were made clear partly in Public School French and partly in dumb-show, and occasionally obscured by my stilted and unfruitful excursions into Spanish. To all that we said he listened with every appearance of interest, and most of what we tried to say he guessed. There was nothing perfunctory in his reception of us. Brazil is one of the countries (which I suppose nowadays are very few) where courtesy is *successfully* practised for courtesy's sake. At last we got up and shook hands and clumped out of that weird room like a deputation of eighteenth-century peasantry leaving a great house in England.

Outwardly, nothing happened to the expedition while it was becalmed in Goyaz. I have sketched in the small events of those uneventful days because they were a background to internal developments of some importance. Our ponies, our landlady, the comic Dutchman and the unreal palace — all these things were distractions of which we were at pains to make the most. For we were in poor form, and we thought — at least Roger and I thought — that we were in a bad way.

You must remember how we were situated. Against all good advice, we had come to Brazil on a probably hopeless and (when you came to think of it) a rather ridiculous quest. We had invested in the enterprise a certain amount of time and money which we could ill afford. *The Times* had given prominence to an announcement of our intentions in which optimism, resolve, and a discreet bravado supplied the domainting notes. In my cable from São Paulo (I could not know that the revolution had prevented its dispatch) our final plan had been specified in detail, and our determination to carry it out emphasized. Quite apart from our personal wishes in the matter (which may be imagined) we were every way committed to following, to the limit of our powers, a certain course of action. More specifically, in order to justify our existence as an expedition we had to travel down the Araguaya, up the Tapirapé, and from the Tapirapé as far as we could go across country towards the Kuluene, during this last stage making all possible search for the seven-year-old traces of Fawcett's expedition.

It was clear to everyone that Major Pingle fully intended to make the journey down the Araguaya. I was prepared to bet (and, indeed, bet) that he intended to make the journey up the Tapirapé. But I had an uneasy feeling that, when it came to the point, Major Pingle's enthusiasm for that cross-country journey which he himself had planned would be found to have cooled. It was obvious that unless we attempted that journey we could not pretend to have begun to look for Fawcett; but by this time I was by no means certain that Major Pingle particularly wanted to look for Fawcett.

I had picked up rather more Portuguese than he suspected;

and, though it was very little, it was enough to suggest to me that when Major Pingle talked to Brazilians about the expedition, something more than diplomatic understatement underlay his humorous disclaimers of all serious intentions to search for Fawcett. He was in some ways rather a conceited man; he liked impressing people, and he liked us to see that they were impressed. It was a little unnatural, the way he always insisted that the expedition was no more than a shooting trip, when even the most guarded hint that it was anything more would have gained him so much prestige. We were now out of reach of the Press, and I could see no point in throwing off our scent all these people who had neither the motive nor the means to follow it up. It looked to me very much as if it was we, and not the Brazilians, who were being misinformed.

Before leaving Rio, we had all signed a contract, of the informal type known — too often ironically — as a Gentleman's Agreement. The first clause in this contract read: 'The object of the expedition is to ascertain the fate of Colonel Fawcett as far as is humanly possible.' Our chances of achieving this object had been slightly lessened by the outbreak of the revolution, which had involved us — though to no very great extent — in unforeseen expense and delay. But I did not entertain the possibility that Major Pingle, without consulting us, had virtually abandoned this object. I still believed that he would enable us to put up some sort of a Fawcett-hunt, though it looked as though a shooting trip would have suited his book much better. The situation was further complicated by the fact that two members of the expedition had come out mainly for the shooting. They had shown little interest in, and less knowledge of, the issues involved in a search for Fawcett, and they were moreover unsuited to take part in a cross-country journey. They could certainly not be relied on to maintain our objective if Major Pingle showed any signs of abandoning it.

So in Goyaz the clouds of uncertainty, which were to have been progressively dispelled the further we got into the interior, were darker, though less numerous, than they had been in London. I tried to reassure myself by remembering with what alacrity Major Pingle had approved that cable which definitely committed the expedition to carrying out its full programme as outlined by him. For the sake of his own reputation (he had, after all, been named as our leader) he must surely be concerned to see that the expedition acquitted itself honourably?...

I decided to test his intentions further. I had already prepared a despatch for *The Times*, describing our journey to Goyaz and rehearsing our plans in detail. The tone of this despatch was not optimistic; it was designed to break our fall in case of fiasco. In it I pointed out that the rains were expected in September, a month before they were normally due, and that this circumstance, together with the delays and losses which we had suffered in the revolution, might well oblige us to curtail our activities. Major Pingle had not yet seen this despatch.

I now prepared another: a fake despatch, in which all references to our plans were couched in terms of unshaken confidence and heroic resolve. In this document the name of Major Pingle appeared very frequently. Major Pingle had decided.... Major Pingle thought it best.... In the light of Major Pingle's information.... And, finally, 'Major Pingle was determined not to leave the Tapirapé until a part, at any rate, of the cross-country journey had been carried out, and every effort had been made to obtain confirmation for his theory in, or near, the district where Fawcett disappeared.'

If he passes this despatch for publication (as he believes) in England, I thought, it means one of two things. Either he is going to give the expedition a square deal; or else he is a great knave and a great fool. I was sure he was not a fool.

I took the fake despatch to Major Pingle and asked him if it would do for *The Times*. I said I was afraid that perhaps it sounded a bit too optimistic; ought I to tone it down? Major Pingle put on his spectacles and read it through laboriously. Then he grunted, and said it was all right; people would like my description of our troubles on the road, it was very amusing. And the bit about our plans wasn't biting off more than we could chew, I asked him. No, said Major Pingle; it was all in order.

I set about underlining the incident in his memory, so that in the future he would not be able to pretend he had forgotten it. With a sickening assumption of frankness I told him how delighted I was to find that his idea of what the expedition was going to do still coincided with mine; for — to be quite honest — Roger and I had lately been wondering whether he hadn't allowed himself to be jockeyed into a Fawcett-hunt against his inclinations. We ourselves were desperately keen on carrying out the official objects of the expedition, and of late we had feared — no doubt unjustifiably — that Major Pingle was perhaps not quite as keen as he had appeared in São Paulo.

Major Pingle rose to the occasion in a most reassuring manner, protesting that he was as determined as anyone to do all that could be done in the way of a search for Fawcett. The difficulties would be very great, of course; we might perhaps find them insuperable. But if the expedition failed, it wouldn't be through any fault of his. I then tried to corner him into discussing our plans for the cross-country journey, which still remained disturbingly vague; but I did not get very far, for Major Pingle's tendency to digress was impossible to curb. However urgent the matter in hand, you could not pin him down to it. If you asked him about transport arrangements for the next day, he would break off in the middle of his answer to recall the occasion when he cured three Scotsmen of ring-worm in Peru. His passion for reminiscence infected his speech like a stammer. In conversation you could get nowhere without tripping over his past experiences. However wild and woolly, they almost all bore the stamp of truth, and were often amusing. We came to know some of them pretty well.

I felt much better after this interview with Major Pingle. I had watched him closely, and detected no trace of uneasiness in his reception of the fake despatch. By approving it, he had once more committed himself in our eyes (though not, as he imagined, in the eyes of the British public) to doing what he had said in São Paulo he would do. The illusion that I had done something to increase our chances of success was comforting and made all the difference to the immediate present. It is not true to say that illusion is better at doing this sort of thing than reality; but it certainly does it much more often.

# CHAPTER XV

# THE REAL THING

THE last gun-case was wedged into the lorry's mountainous load. The drivers of the two decrepit cars raced their engines and hooted. The crowd raised a faint derisive cheer. The expedition was under weigh again.

The cadets of the Military Academy, who were present in force, withdrew to the pavement. Self-important little girls picked up infants from the middle of the road and deposited them in the gutter. On the steps of the hotel our landlady smiled inscrutably into her moustache. The dentist, with streaming eyes — the result not so much of emotion as of a cold caught in his ambush under the fruit trees — wished us good hunting. Once more the Dutchman implored us to accept the gift of a fantastically inaccurate map of the Araguaya which he himself had made. A middle-aged lieutenant, who lived in the hotel, appeared with five of his beastly little children to bid us farewell; for the last time I remarked the contrast between his placid and dignified bearing and his costume, which, combining as it did spurs with a pyjama jacket, powerfully suggested the exigencies of a night alarm. Craning with precarious nonchalance out of windows all down the street, the beauties of Goyaz risked their necks and their dignity to see us go. We began to move forward, bumping slowly over the cobbles. The crowd cheered again, with kindly scorn. We left Goyaz.

It is about 130 miles from Goyaz to Leopoldina, which was to be our point of embarkation for the journey down the Araguaya and our last contact with civilization for some time to come. There had been stretches of road on the way up to Goyaz which had seemed pretty bad at the time. Not often,

we had supposed, are cars, even in Brazil, called upon to
negotiate going as rough as this; and if worse roads do indeed exist, they can hardly be accounted passable. But the
road to Leopoldina proved this supposition to be gravely at
fault. It was not like other bad roads, which incommode you
with continuous and petty malice. 'Look how far we can go,'
they seem to say, as you crawl painfully along them, 'and yet
still be called a road.' You hate them the more bitterly for the
knowledge that they will keep within certain bounds. They will
madden you with minor obstacles, but in the end they will let
you through. They dare do all that will become a road; who
dares do more is none. However gross the indignities that they
heap upon you, they will yet deny you the hollow revenge of
calling them impassable. You know that they will observe the
letter, though not the spirit, of their contract with your wheels.

But with the road to Leopoldina it was not like this. It had
no quarrel with us. It took no count of us at all. It did not
fight a sly delaying action, raising our hopes only to dash them,
but always keeping them alive. It did not set out to tantalize
or gall us. It seemed, rather, preoccupied with its own troubles.
It had never wished to be a road, and now it cursed itself for
not refusing its function before it was too late. It lashed itself
into a fury of self-reproach. It writhed in anguish. It was
clearly a tormented thing. At any moment, we felt, it might
decide to End It All.

But it didn't. It stuck it out. It saw it through. It mastered
its distress and got us to Leopoldina.

That was a stormy passage. Of the scenery, though I believe
it to have been savage and beautiful, I can remember little.
For in its agony the road plunged so frequently into the jungle
(going there, I suppose, like the people in novels, To Forget)
that we spent most of the journey gazing steadfastly into the
lining of our hats, held up in front of us to protect our faces.
On their crowns the little branches drummed a spiteful tattoo.
The driver was reluctant to slow down, however formidable

the obstacles in his path, so that our sweating bodies were hurled either sideways against each other or upwards at the roof with a tiresome regularity. The driver, as always in Brazil, was an impetuous fellow.

It was a very hot day. We had a breakdown: it was one of those breakdowns (I know so little about cars that I cannot classify even this commonest type of mishap) which everyone believes will be remedied if only the car is pushed along the road for a certain distance. We tried this remedy, several times; but no one — certainly not the car — was any the better for it. We resorted to hanky-panky with a spanner and to grovelling, in the *Punch* tradition, underneath the vehicle: and in the end this was successful. The car started with a triumphant roar. A quarter of a mile further on we had a puncture.

But all this was much better than delay. We were getting on. The prologue, the rather dreary prologue to our enterprise was almost played out. The curtain would rise on the first act when we reached the Araguaya. Towards evening we dropped down off the hills into lusher, more exciting country. This was the river valley. The road was level now, with a surface of thick white sand. The red dust of the uplands we had left behind. Everything was green, and there was water about. A big fish, a surprisingly big, outlandish fish, flashed away up stream as we crossed a little bridge. Palms now stood in delicate independent ranks; hitherto they had been isolated phenomena, or else had preserved their grace with difficulty among a press of trees. The open country between the strips of jungle was dotted with little clumps of vegetation and single trees. It had the persuasive, and so often illusory, look of being a likely place for game. You had the feeling that there was a great deal of life about. That rich cover had a frequented air. When the car stopped you heard the calls of birds which you did not know. For the first time since we had landed at Rio I had the feeling that we had got somewhere.

This feeling was strengthened, and indeed the whole colour

and tempo of life were changed for the better, when we got to Leopoldina. The road swung sharply round a clump of palms and there was suddenly to be seen in front of us a casual galaxy of little white hovels. The setting sun burnished the fluted wands of smoke which stood and slightly wavered above their roofs. I was vaguely aware of non-committal women with folded arms leaning against their doorposts, and listless children tumbling with dogs and poultry in the dust. All these things were familiar, though they had once been remarkable. Like the filling stations on an English road, one had long ceased to take note of them. What was new and sudden and splendid was the river.

The Araguaya was there, in front of us, and beyond it was a reddening sky. The trampled open ground on which the twenty houses of the village stood ended abruptly at the lip of a perpendicular bluff. Beyond that, and forty feet below it, was the river: a river half a mile wide and more: a river so big, so long expected, and so phenomenal in every way that it seemed hardly possible to have come on it so suddenly, to have had no more warning that it was waiting for us round the corner of those palms than we should have had of a dog's dead body in the road: a river fired and bloody in the sunset: a river that we loved instantly, and learnt at last to hate. We gaped at this river. There was exaltation in the air.

It ran slowly but strongly, making no sound at all. The trees on the farther bank stood up, a dark plumed horde. Our own bank — as your own bank always does — seemed terribly commonplace by contrast. We beheld for the first time, and in the most appropriate of circumstances, the frontiers of Matto Grosso.

In the middle of the river, off the village, was a sandbank, a pale, immaculate sliver of land. At its tail end a thin canoe was moored; a small tent of matting showed dark against the sand, and a fire flickered before it. The tent and the fire, like all solitary dwellings and all solitary lights, had an appearance at once confident and forlorn; night would be on them shortly, but they were ready to meet it, as they had met it often before.

The leading car had arrived an hour ahead of us. 'Carajas,' said someone who had been in it, indicating with a knowledgeable and proprietary air the inhabitants of the tent, who had come over to the mainland and were sitting in a row on a log overlooking the river. There were five of them: two men, two women, and a child. They all, except the child, wore clothes of a sort. On the whole the Carajas, who are river Indians inhabiting something like 400 miles of the banks of the Araguaya, have held out pretty well against the forces of enlightenment. But in almost every village there is a minority — drawn, it seemed to me, from those with most intelligence and fewest scruples — who have allowed themselves to be transformed into those regrettable hybrids which spring up, fully trousered, wherever the dragon's teeth of civilization are sown on aboriginal soil. These five were of that sort. They had dark brown, healthy skins and black tangled hair. The women's hair reached below their shoulders, the men wore a shaggy bob. On the men's cheekbones two little circles were cut; they were the size of the rim of a twelve-bore cartridge and showed up black against the skin, as though they had been branded. This used to be a universal mark throughout the tribe, but to-day it is disappearing. I remembered a theory of Dr. Carlos's that Caraja meant 'Four Eyes'; the etymological derivation was plausible, and now those scars, sketching the eyes in duplicate, made the name seem a likely one.

The faces of the Carajas never conformed strictly to a racial type, and the two Indians before us had features very differently cast. Lorian (who was rumoured to have been formerly a chief of great importance) had a wizened, dependable face; he looked capable of wisdom and authority, and had about him a certain innate dignity which I never knew him to parade. He was a mildly impressive man. The other one was called Burity, which

means Palm Tree. The name did not suit him. He was much
younger than Lorian, to whom he stood in some sort of blood
relationship which he himself always had difficulty in defining.
He had a round, smooth, bucolic face, with a suggestion of the
Mongol in it. I have seen vaguely similar, though less cheerful,
faces on both sides of the frontier between Russia and Manchuria. Perhaps the thing that struck you most about him was
his capacity for silliness. It was not an irritating, or a dangerous,
or an obstructive silliness. He was a little moonstruck; that
was all. It came out in his shrill and ready laughter; it came
out in his fatuous smile. But he was a nice oaf, for all that,
though not nearly such a good worker as Lorian.

That was a good moment, our arrival at Leopoldina. We
scrambled down the bluff and bathed in the sunset river.
We were ravenously hungry, having had nothing to eat all day
except some bread: our last bread for many weeks. We had
meant to camp that night on the sandbank (from now on all
sandbanks will be referred to as *praias*), but the lorry with our
equipment did not arrive till close on midnight; so they found
hammocks for us in the village, and we slept in the house of
José Santa Anna.

José Santa Anna was a considerable man in that place. He
was a gigantic negro with a crafty face and the reputation
(a common and often, I suspect, a baseless one in Brazil) of
being many times a murderer. He wore on his head a curious
thing, a kind of cross between a scrum cap and a Balaclava
helmet, with green and black checks on it. For many years he
has been a well-known figure on the river, where he wields
something like a monopoly in the shipping world. The traveller
going downstream must buy his boats and supplies from this
tall and sinister man, for Leopoldina is the only place in the
state of Goyaz where anything resembling civilization impinges
on the Araguaya, and José Santa Anna owns the whole of
Leopoldina. To-day, admittedly, there is not much to own.
But there was a time in the last century when Leopoldina

boasted 500 houses (or so they say) in place of the beggarly twenty that we saw. There was a boom.

This state of affairs was brought about by Couto de Magalhaes, for many years Governor of Goyaz, and a man of energy and imagination. He made superhuman and temporarily successful efforts to open up the Araguaya to navigation; and there are still lying on the foreshore at Leopoldina the rusty skeletons of two steam launches, monuments to a rather splendid failure. One of these de Magalhaes brought up stream from Pará himself; a mutinous crew faced and conquered the rapids at the point of his revolver. The other was carried overland, piecemeal, to be assembled and launched at some point further upstream (Registro, I think). At any rate, both boats were manhandled into the middle of a sub-continent, and there for a time they plied, carrying the rich and various exports of Goyaz down to the mouth of the Amazon when the river was high with the rains. As a boy, José Santa Anna worked on these boats; it was part of his job to wake the crews in the morning with a cornet, and Cornet became his nickname.

In those days Leopoldina was an important place, a place with a future. I do not know what killed the enterprise. Probably it had too many difficulties for ballast, and too little of that buoyancy which in Brazil is supplied only by stark necessity, to ride for long the unplumbed seas of national inertia. At any rate it came to an end. Leopoldina lost her future and was left with several tons of scrap iron and something of a past; which is more than most places of her size have got in that country.

Roger and I, grown wary by this time, had allowed for several days' delay at Leopoldina. Miraculously, we started downstream on our second morning there.

On the first day there was a good deal to do. We unloaded the lorry and took everything across to the praia in canoes. We checked the stores, and sighted our rifles at targets in the sand, discovering in the process that the .44 which Roger and I had bought in São Paulo had a barrel the inside of which was comparable only to those papier mâché grottoes which you whizz through on scenic railways. We watched Santa Anna's men caulking the new boat which was to be the flagship of our convoy, and learnt from Major Pingle the useful lesson that a judicious bet will sometimes reduce delay in Brazil. By launching the boat twenty-four hours after our arrival, the shipwrights won five dozen bottles of Santa Anna's disgusting beer.

We slept that night on the praia, under a million stars. The men slung our seven hammocks between eight poles driven into the sand: an ingenious feat, it seemed to me, though I suppose it was really a simple one. But then I have an untidy mind, and am easily dumbfounded by match tricks. One of the men took a small party upstream to shoot alligators by the light of an electric torch. The rest of us listened enviously to the resultant barrage. I remember—with something of that tolerant incredulity with which one recalls the emotions aroused by one's first bicycle—the excitement with which we greeted their return, towing a small alligator five feet long. This, we told ourselves, was the Real Thing. From the jungle unknown birds sent out stealthy, isolated calls across the moonlit water. A dog barked in the village, and someone said it was a wolf. From time to time a huge fish broke the water with a surreptitious splash. The camp fire glowed in accordance with the best traditions. We went contentedly to sleep, hooped like bows in our ill-slung hammonks. The Real Thing. . . .

Here I must digress, to explain a habit, a convention, an attitude of mind — I don't really know how to define it — which became very strong in Roger and me through the next few weeks. It permeated, though it did not affect, our relations to life within the expedition. And though it was an entirely superficial thing, colouring our conversation rather than our thoughts, it was so constant and so often a helpful feature of that life that I should do wrong not to mention it.

It was our sense of Parody. It had been alive from the first. The whole technique of exploring is overlaid with conventions so unmistakable and so often mocked — has a jargon so flashily impressive and so easily guyed — that the man who at his first essay adopts the conventions and employs the jargon must lack both shame and humour. Even in London we had found it impossible to talk of our plans without apologetically draping the pretensions of such words as Standing Camp in inverted commas. We had been careful to refer to the rains as beginning, not as breaking. We spoke always of going, rather than of striking, up a river.

Now that we had reached our scene of action this habit persisted. Much of what we saw and did was clearly too good to be true. Life was always perilously close to the pages of those books which publishers catalogue under the heading of 'Travel and Adventure'. In self-defence — in instinctive pursuance of that policy of *nil admirari* which is the joint product of repression, sophistication, and all the hot air one hears — we turned to Parody. If Indians approached us, we referred to them as the Oncoming Savages. We never said, 'Was that a shot?' but always, 'Was that the well-known bark of a Mauser?' All insects of harmless nature and ridiculous appearance we pointed out to each other as creatures 'whose slightest glance spelt Death'. Any bird larger than a thrush we credited with the ability to 'break a man's arm with a single blow of its powerful wing'. We spoke of water always as the 'Precious Fluid'. We referred to ourselves, not as eating meals, but as doing 'Ample Justice to a Frugal Repast'. To anyone who did not think it as funny as we did it must have been an intolerably tiresome kind of joke. But it made us laugh, and thus served its purpose. It became an important feature in that private code of nonsense which was our chief defence against hostile circumstance.

# CHAPTER XVI

## ARAGUAYA

AT noon the next day (the last but one of July) we started downstream from Leopoldina. We had four boats, some description of which is, I suppose, necessary. First of all, there was the new *batalõa*, which leaked like a sieve for many days and which carried Major Pingle and the bulk of the stores. A batalõa is a heavy, capacious clinker-built boat about thirty foot long. I should imagine that its design has not changed appreciably since the days of the earliest settlers. The two rowers, who may be increased to four, sit on thwarts in the bows, the spaces between the thwarts being filled with luggage. There is a sort of well amidships where bailing can, and must, be done. The passengers and the rest of the luggage fill the stern. The pilot stands to his helm on a tiny platform, being thus enabled to look down into the water in front of him and pick his way through the channel. The oars are primitive and unpractical, being long heavy poles with a round paddle, like an enlarged ping-pong racket, spliced on to the end. The rowlocks are simply forks, cut out of the jungle as you go along and lashed into their sockets. The oar itself is fastened to them with cord. The whole arrangement is elaborate and unreliable, imposing on the oarsmen a short but at the same time a slow stroke and requiring constant readjustment of one sort and another.

Our second batalõa was a very old one, and leaked even more than the first. A few days after we started we gave it in part exchange for a better one, which had a *tõldo*, a hooped awning of palm leaves, over the stern, and hence became known variously as Honeysuckle Cottage or the Covered Wagon. This was the best boat to travel in for comfort, the worst for shooting.

The other two boats belonged to smaller and faster types. One was a *montaría*, also clinker-built and actually I think a more finished and substantial bit of work than the true montaría of the Amazon. This was paddled by two men, one in the stern and one in the bows, and carried two passengers and all the cooking things. The other boat was an *ubá*, a long, narrow, black dug-out canoe, very unstable until you got used to it, but fast and a good boat to shoot from. The two passengers sat in the bottom of it on their blankets, and it was always paddled by Lorian from the stern.

We were three weeks on the Araguaya between Leopoldina and the mouth of the Tapirapé. For me it was inevitably a period of falling values; the climax came at the wrong end. One began with discovery, passed on to acceptance, and ended in criticism. But it was a pleasant, easy life; if one could have been sure that it was the prologue to something less pleasant and less easy one would have enjoyed it unreservedly. Uncertainty was again our trouble. It became increasingly difficult to foresee what would happen when we reached the Tapirapé — by how wide or how narrow a margin we should steer clear of fiasco, if we steered clear of it at all. There was still too much speculation in the air — too much guessing at questions which only Major Pingle could answer and which we could not ask him yet. Perhaps, after all, those three weeks were not so easy or so pleasant.

Not much in them stands out distinctly in the memory. I can best give you an idea of what our life was like by describing an average day.

The routine of travel was invariable. It was odd how grateful one was for that element of routine. It gave form and substance to those dateless days. It rounded up the bright desolate hours and placed on all of them a brand, however faint, which somehow guaranteed their worth. Little habits, little conventions, little regulations were erected like a palisade against the wilderness. Routine is the most portable form of domesticity, and unconsciously but gladly we took refuge in it. We were nomads by numbers.

You woke a little before six. Dawn was near, and the stars went while you wàtched them. Against a lambent eastern sky the jungle looked black and leaping and alive. To the west it was still huddled and indeterminate. The air was cold, and dew was heavy on your blanket. When you sat up, the litter of camp on the pale sandbank showed up like charcoal scrawls on a white paper. The rack of guns and rifles, close beside you, had a very theatrical air. Two men were squatting beside the fire. A third stood over them, stretching himself and rubbing his knuckles in his eyes. Beyond them were the moored boats, riding lighter than they rode by day, and — partly because of that, and partly because of a little mist that writhed along the smooth dark water — looking larger than you had expected. Everything seemed a little improbable: as indeed it was. It was a moment for disbelief, a moment in which you felt lost. In the process of waking you had to transfer yourself, not from a dream to reality, but from a dream to a dream.

You got up, and put on a sweater, and went down to the river to wash. Other cocoons in the sand were breaking up. There were laughs, and curses, and prodigious yawns. 'Bons dias', said the men at the fire as you passed them. 'Senhor Pedro dormiu bem?' 'Muito bem,' you answered, feeling idiomatic and rather feudal. When you came back from washing they had coffee ready — better coffee than you ever get in England. You drank half a pint of it. Then you rolled up your bedding and put it in a bag and carried it down to the canoes.

After that, with half an hour to spare before breakfast, you took a gun into the jungle. For a quarter of a mile you plodded through the deep white sand, your feet making a silly squeaking noise as distinctive and invariable as the sound of skis through snow. It was always nightmare going on the praias. The most eager stride lost its elasticity in a hundred yards and became a dour, clumsy shuffle. Figures walking in that sand had the air of men spent with exhaustion; their heads were bowed, their arms hung down before them, their feet slugged into the soft stuff glumly.

On the edge of the jungle the sand was thickly dappled with tracks, some of them fresh since the night before. The tracks always fascinated me. You looked first for the jaguars' —suave round cups in the sand, each very nearly straight behind the other, like a cat's tracks in the snow. Then there were the broad, three-toed indentations made by tapirs; their dung, exactly like a horse's, assorted oddly with so outlandish a spoor. The big deer, the *cerva*, had a bold, heavy slot like a red deer, and the little *veado* made delicate tracks like a roe. In the mud on the edge of a lagoon you saw where the small stabbing hooves of peccary had been, and the queer splayed feet of *capivara*, which is a rodent as big as a sheep, a kind of water guinea pig. It was the less important creatures who made the most curious tracks. A big frog marked its route with a design like an undecipherable coat of arms, stamped every six inches in the sand. The tracks of an iguana ran with unswerving symmetry on either side of a deep clean groove cut by its tail. Tortoises and turtles left a broad, purposeful wash in the sand; the marks of their feet were kept always equidistant by the structure of their shells, and this gave to the whole track the air of having been made by a machine.

You hung about the edge of the jungle for a few minutes, and shot one or two of the little pigeons which were coming out over the clubbed tree-tops to drink on the edge of the praia. You had meant to go further and get something more substantial for the pot. But somehow—what with your stomach being empty, and the morning so misty and meditative— you found that you had lost too much time gaping at those tracks and watching a fly-catcher liveried like Harlequin; and now you heard the note of a long home-made trumpet of tin, at once eerie and facetious, which meant that breakfast was ready. So you padded back to camp.

Rice and black beans (which we had now learnt to call feijao) were still our staple food. But there was usually one other pot on the fire, with fish in it, or some sort of game. You seized a spoon and ladled a mountain of food on to your plate, afterwards sprinkling it with a fistful of *farinha*. I had better explain about farinha, which is important stuff in Central Brazil. Farinha is made from the mandioca or cassava, a root of which the chief peculiarity is that, while its juice is a rapidly destructive poison, the flour is a nutritious though insipid food. After the juice has been extracted the mandioca is dried, ground, and baked. The result looks like a pale and rather knobbly form of sawdust, a substance to which it is not noticeably superior in flavour.

After breakfast everything was bundled into the canoes. Major Pingle issued ammunition rations from the store in the new batalõa. The rest of the expedition was split up into pairs, each pair travelling in rotation in the other three boats. It was your turn for the ubá, which meant that you would lead the convoy and get most of the shooting. You got in, with Roger, and settled down as comfortably as you could. By eight o'clock all the boats were under way. As the last one pushed off from the praia, the vultures (which will henceforth be referred to as *urubús*) swooped down in quest of your leavings. The urubús are licensed scavengers, never molested and hence quite fearless. They are black and noisome birds with scrawny necks, which fight silently with a hollow buffeting of wings over the scraps you leave. Looking back at the camp you had left, you saw that the sand, round the still smoking embers of your fire, was alive with this dark and rustling concourse; it was like a sabbath of witches shorn of its mystery.

The first hour of travel was the best in the day. The sun on your right hand was not yet high enough to strip the vast and empty river of the glamour, the almost overpowering glamour, which night had lent it. To the shadows under the eastern bank a thin mist still clung. The wind, the little wind which blew in your faces from the north all through the middle of the day, had not yet risen, and the tall trees stood gravely inverted in the silken surface of the water. Over all the river there was an attentive silence. The sounds were few, clear, and quickly gone. The companionable chattering of a flight of parrots, the mew of a hawk, the noise of some animal evading swiftly through the brittle and betraying undergrowth—these defined themselves sharply and then died. Even the more continuous and orderly noises—the chuckle of the stream against a snag, the methodical tapping of a wood-pecker—dwindled and vanished very rapidly when you had passed their source. Everything seemed in a conspiracy to give the silence its full effect.

But the magic drained gradually out of the day, and you awoke from your thoughts to find that the river had become a hard and customary place. Under a blazing noon you noticed, not the intricacy, but the disorder of the jungle. It no longer challenged and intrigued; it merely enclosed. The wilderness had grown humdrum. Hour after hour you glided forward, running the gauntlet of those ranks of trees. But you no longer thought of them as vigilant, or secretive, or hostile. You no longer felt an intruder or an initiate. They were there, and you were there. That was all. And this was a day like another, without very much enchantment.

You always got a certain amount of shooting during the day. Lorian kept the canoe well in to the bank, and you had the little rifle — the .22 — and a shotgun ready. Sometimes a pair of *marecas* would sit, peering and undecided, at the water's edge until it was too late. They are a wild duck rather bigger than a mallard; the name is onomatopoeic. In plumage they are not unlike the canvas-back of North America; the first one I shot conjured up memories of a bitter January dawn and a little village in Maryland, a place whose retirement and simplicity contrasted strongly with the Epicurian exports (oysters and strawberries) which were its economic life-blood.

Then there were a lot of the birds called *jacú*, a kind of stringy, dowdy pheasant with subfusc plumage, which sat and vacillated in the trees and gave good sport with the rifle. Sometimes we got a *mutum*, a big black and white turkey with a speckled crest; and we often pursued, though never with success, the *inhuma*, a gigantic and mysterious fowl, biggeı than a cock capercailzie but built on more or less the same lines. These would take refuge in the tops of distant trees and thence utter a strange, murmurous and rather asthmatic crooning. Whether they are good to eat I cannot say.

We shot, occasionally and from curiosity, the lovely spoonbills, which are pink and like flamingoes, and — still more occasionally — the *jaburús*. These, more successfully than any of the birds we saw, created something of that *Lost World* atmosphere for which we secretly yearned. They are white storks, with slim black legs, black heads and beaks, and dull scarlet throats; they stand nearly five feet high. They pace the praias gravely, with long, meditative strides: their heads are bowed, their shoulders hunched, their mien preoccupied. Theirs is the gait of the quadrangle or the terrace. They are the incarnation of a thoughtful dignity. In almost all their visual attributes they excel the scholars and legislators whom they suggest. Watching them, I used to wonder whether the experiment of having a stork for ruler need be condemned for a single failure in a fable. Would England fare any worse under a cabinet of jaburús? We should at least be represented at International Conferences by creatures to the manner born, and that philosophic elegance, that imponderable reserve, would not disgrace the lawns of Chequers. The idea merits consideration.

There were many other birds. The *araras*, the big long-tailed macaws, flew always in discordant parties of three. The blue and gold sort were the commonest, but there were also the so-called black araras, which are really a very dark blue, and which I thought the handsomest of the three varieties. (The third is scarlet, a beautifully garish bird. I never saw one wild, though there were plenty in the huts of the Indians, who prize them greatly. There were several sorts of kingfisher, the biggest as big as a wood-pigeon, the smallest smaller than a sparrow: all were gay, brilliant, and effective-looking birds. There were hawks, and herons, and divers, and waders, and raffish crested woodpeckers, and gulls. The gulls included a tiny variety of tern, and a graceful, noisy black and white gull with a red bill. One day I saw one of these do a thing I had never seen before; it drank as it flew. It was skimming low, and not very fast, over the still water; its beak was open, and the lower tip just touched the water, scoring a thin unbroken furrow on its surface while the water ran up into the gull's throat.

Then there were the little birds; but of these I never knew the names, and in only a few cases can I remember their beauties in detail. The most curious were the humming birds, which seem rather mechanical than natural wonders as they hover furiously in front of your face, filling your ears with a tiny but pervasive roaring. Once, in midstream between banks three quarters of a mile apart, we met one of these frantic atomies crossing the river with that air of distracted and unfathomable purpose which takes a bumble bee across your bows in the middle of a Scottish loch.

Last of all there were the *ciganas*, the gypsies, which we called hiss-birds. These curious, unnecessary, and evil-smelling fowl grew steadily more plentiful the further north we got. Of the size of a pheasant, they belong to the same order as domestic poultry, but their toes have gradually become adapted to arboreal life; their plumage is reddish brown, and they carry enormous crests. We found them all along the river bank, perching clumsily in close-packed flocks of twenty or thirty on the low trees along the water's edge. Their flight is ungainly; but having — on account of their stench and consequent inedibility — nothing to fear from man or beast, they were not easily disturbed, and at our approach contented themselves with setting up (like the Fallen Angels in *Paradise Lost*) 'a dismal universal hiss'. There was something extraordinarily sinister and oppressive about this sound, and about the birds themselves a kind of stale horror, the atmosphere as well as the odour of decay. We hated them.

I could write interminably of the birds, but you would not benefit by a catalogue to which the illustrations are in words, mostly ill-chosen. You have had already more than you can stand, and I know that there must be among you those who are disgusted by my slipshod ornithology. 'This fellow is no good to us', they mutter. 'He goes drooling on, page after page, telling us how this bird looks like something or other, and that bird reminds him of something else. In no single case does he tell us, in so many good honest Latin polysyllables, what the birds were. They might be unknown to science for all the reference he makes to their genus and their species. What is the use of worthy and learned men going out of their way to give a bird a name like *Macrocercus hyacinthinus, Lath.* if writers are going to refer to it as "the so-called black arara"? Really, this young man seems strangely ignorant (or damnably contemptuous) of scientific terminology.'

Their suspicions are, alas, all too well founded: their protest only too easily justified. I am indeed ignorant (whether strangely or not I will not presume to say) of scientific terminology. When I saw an arara in the distance, '*Macrocercus Macao* or *Macrocercus hyacinthinus*' was not the question which arose automatically to my lips; nor used I to warn Roger of the approach of a spoonbill by hissing '*Platalea Ajaja*', which would, in point of fact, have been a fairly difficult thing to do. No: there are hardly any birds of which I know the Latin names; and, to be quite honest, this lacuna in my education causes me not only very little inconvenience but also hardly any shame. I am as a rule easily and deeply impressed by the mumbo jumbo of learning. But about ten years ago I discovered, quite by chance, that the scientific name for the

Harlequin Duck is *Histrionicus histrionicus histrionicus*; and ever since that day I have found it impossible, I don't know why, to treat ornithologists' Latin with the respect it deserves. If you want exactitude and scientific terminology, go to Bates, who gives you both in *A Naturalist on the River Amazon* and all the other things I am trying to supply as well. Go to Bates in any case. His is a really good book.

Before I leave the subject of etymology, I had better make a declaration of policy with regard to the use of foreign words: words like *urubú*, and *praia*, and *jacaré*.

From my youth up I have lost no opportunity of mocking what may be called the Nullah (or Ravine) School of Literature. Whenever an author thrusts his way through the *zareba*, or flings himself down behind the *boma*, or breasts the slope of a *kopje*, or scans the undulating surface of the *chapada*, he loses my confidence. When he says that he sat down to an appetizing dish of *tumbo*, or that what should he see at that moment but a magnificent *conka*, I feel that he is (*a*) taking advantage of me and (*b*) making a fool of himself. I resent being peppered with these outlandish italics. They make me feel uninitiated, and they make him seem pretentious. Sometimes he has the grace to explain what he is talking about: as in the sentence 'The *bajja* (or hut) was full of *ghoils* — young unmarried women — who, while cooking the *dô*, a kind of native cake, uttered low crooning cries of "*O Kwait*", which can be freely translated as "Welcome, Red-faced One. Life is very frequently disappointing, is it not?" ' But this does not improve matters much, for the best prose is not so cumbered with asides, and the poor man's muse moves stiffly in the uniform of an interpreter.

I have always regarded the larding of one's pages with foreign words as an affectation not less deplorable than the plastering of one's luggage with foreign labels. I swore that if ever I was misguided enough to write a book of travel my italics would be all my own; my saga would be void of *nullahs*. But I find now that this self-denial is not altogether possible. It appears, after all, that the *zareba*-mongers had some excuse. Let me try, at any rate, to make out one for myself.

When I consider how to dispense with the foreign words which I have already used, and which I intend to go on using, I see that the difficulties of doing so are threefold. Each word, that is to say, is necessary on one of three grounds.

First of all, there are the words like *bataloa* and *rapadura* and *mutum*, which denote things unknown outside Brazil, and which it is therefore impossible to translate. I am so far relying on your memory as not to repeat the explanation of their meaning which accompanies their first appearance: also there is a short glossary at the end of the book. Secondly, there are the words of which a literal translation is for one reason or another inadequate. The word sandbank, for instance, gives you a very niggardly idea of what a *praia* is, and the word *plage*, which conveys an image nearer the truth, has unsuitable associations. Similarly, an *urubú* is a far more scurvy and less spectacular creature than the popular conception of a vulture. Thirdly, there are a few words which can be translated perfectly well, but which we, in conversation, never did translate: words like *jacaré* and *arara*. We never said 'There's an alligator', or 'There's a macaw', but — I suppose because of the presence of our men — always used the native words. So it is easier and more natural, when writing of these things, to give them the names under which they live in my memory.

That is my apology for having seceded to the Nullah (or Ravine) School of Literature and broken the rule that italics should be heard and not seen. I hope it is a sufficient one.

# CHAPTER XVII

# TICKS AND TOFFEE

I SET out, in the last chapter, to describe a typical day in those first three weeks on the Araguaya. Types are the product of a process of selection, and I, with too much to select from, have failed so far to present a very clear-cut specimen. But the typical day was half over before these late digressions intervened to spoil its literary format; and now I shall take up the tale again at noon.

By noon it was pretty hot. But we were on a plateau which was over 1000 feet above sea-level, and it was a dry heat, not the enervating and prostrating heat which goes with humidity in the atmosphere. The Brazilian sun has a further quality of mercy in that its rays are powerless (or at any rate are supposed to be powerless) to give you sunstroke. Why this is I do not know. We used to tell each other — in the imprecise but confident tones in which one asserts, at Maskelyne's, that it is All Done by Mirrors — that it was due to Something in the Air. Whatever the cause, I know that I never wore a hat, even on the equator itself, and felt no ill effects: though I should not recommend this course to anyone who is easily subject to sunstroke.

There was usually a breeze blowing upstream, sometimes hard enough to delay the progress of the boats. When this dropped, the flies attacked us. But, although they were sometimes annoying, they were never the menace we had expected them to be. If you were camped on a damp praia, or close to the jungle, the mosquitoes were liable to be bad — but not very bad — at sunset. By day the worst pest was the *pium* fly, a little black creature the size of a midge, which covered your hands and anything else it could get at with small hard red pimples.

These itched furiously when the sun got at them, or at night when you were hot. But after a time we seemed to become more or less immune to their bites, which for some reason — probably because I am dark — troubled me much less than the others. There were also *motuca* flies, which looked like a lethal and slightly futuristic form of blue-bottle, and whose bites drew blood and oaths but had no worse effects.

In the jungle, and especially in long grass, we used to collect large numbers of ticks called *carapatos*. We had heard a great deal about these creatures, none of it in their favour; and at first the revulsion they aroused in their victims was tempered by a certain pride, a feeling that their attentions, though unwelcome, constituted a part of the Real Thing. 'By God, these carapatos are hell', we used to say, feeling tropical and intrepid. Frightful stories went round about what happened when you pulled them out and they left their jaws and head in your flesh; and in deference to legend we used at first to singe them to death with lighted matches. This method was open to criticism on several grounds. It was excessively painful, for you could not singe the tick without also singeing yourself. It had the effect of permanently affixing the creature to your flesh, for in its death agonies its jaws tightened and it was almost impossible to pull away. And it was quite unnecessary, for the carapatos could always be detached by the usual methods; and if, as sometimes happened, the head and jaws were left behind, nobody was any the worse.

For the carapatos are one of the many perils of the Brazilian interior which will not (in their capacity as perils) bear close inspection. It is true that if you did not find and evict these creatures at once they battened on you, growing to an enormous size and acquiring a very sinister appearance. But the bigger they got the less chance they had of escaping detection, and in the process of battening they did not inconvenience you at all. It is, of course, damaging to one's self-respect to find oneself dotted with insects against whom popular prejudice is so strong that I begin to wonder whether I should ever have mentioned them at all. But one's self-respect was the only thing that suffered, for they caused no pain or irritation. It must however be placed on record that a family of these devoted creatures, travelling incognito, accompanied one of us back to England and there proved beyond all possible doubt the insect's ability — nay, determination — to breed in captivity.

So much for the insect menace.

About noon we stopped for lunch. It was not really lunch, but a meal called *jacuba*, consisting of a saccharine mixture of farinha, *rapadura*, and water. *Rapadura* requires some explanation. It is a product of sugar-cane, and is manufactured in rectangular blocks six inches long. It looks exactly like a huge slab of home-made toffee, than which, though not at all sticky, it is much harder and (I suspect) much more nourishing. You can eat it in hunks; but for purposes of *jacuba* you whittle it off with a knife from the main block, making a kind of coarse powder which you mix into a sodden mass with water and the so-called flour. The result is a quickly prepared and sustaining substitute for a meal. To the palate, however, we found that it could not be calculated to appeal indefinitely.

After jacuba you re-embarked and went on. The hours marched slowly with you down the river. The sun worked round on to your left hand. Incidents were few. Perhaps you passed one of the other boats, or they passed you, and sleepy greetings would be exchanged as you rested on your paddles. Perhaps you landed for a few minutes at a Caraja village, and what you saw there I will tell in a later chapter. Perhaps you encouraged Lorian to sing his strange inconsequent songs, which rose and fell in stumbling cadences remote from any recognized plan of melody and ended abruptly in a long-drawn-out moan, the very accent of anti-climax.

Perhaps you passed close under the lea of a forest fire. Its bitter smoke rolled out across the river, and the air was full of the charred ghosts of leaves. Flames leapt and roared and ravaged among the desperate blackened silhouettes of trees. The sunlight thickened to a dun and dingy glare. A frightful, greedy crackling ate up the silence. A few birds called in panic and flew erratically through the smoke. Only the opportunist hawks kept their heads and warily patrolled the spreading frontiers of the fire, vigilant for fugitives.

There was always a fire burning somewhere. I suppose the Indians burn the jungle as keepers in Scotland burn the heather. I know it seemed to me that about a tenth of the interior of Brazil was perpetually in flames.

By four o'clock the leading boat was on the look-out for a praia to camp on. There were two hours of daylight left, but Major Pingle insisted on camping early. He said that it was no good expecting the men to go on working after four o'clock, and that it was essential to get dinner cooked before night fell. This, as experience taught us later, was a fallacy. But we could not know it then, and the expedition, though sorely pressed for time, accepted a custom which — taken in conjunction with similar unnecessary delays — lost it something like a week between Leopoldina and the mouth of the Tapirapé.

The phrase 'making camp' has a professional ring, but for us the process could hardly have been simpler. You disembarked, tied up the canoe, took out your bedding, scraped a shallow trench in the sand to sleep in, and cleaned your gun, while the men made a fire and started cooking dinner. There were no tents, no tin-openers — none of the appurtenances of that Simple Life which in England is so complicated and so insanitary a business. Exploring in Matto Grosso is a soft option compared with caravanning in the Cotswolds.

The last two hours of daylight Roger and I usually spent in search of food and exercise in the jungle. The latter was a good deal easier to come by than the former; we were, in point of fact, very unlucky with the shooting. But there were always those skeins of tracks in the sand to arouse our hopes; and when these flagged we had only to stand still and listen for a moment. The cover was dry and dense and brittle, and when you stopped crashing through it the silence came down on you with an impact almost as startling as a clap of thunder. But while you listened it was broken — broken by stealthy continuous movements which receded or approached. Leaves rustled, twigs snapped; something was afoot. It might be — it almost certainly was — only a lizard or a rat; but in these desiccated forests the smallest creature could make almost as much noise as the largest. So anticipation was continually nourished on surmise; there was always enough suspicion in the air to keep you alert and amused.

You got back to camp at nightfall, hot, and full of thorns and ticks. You stripped and bathed and had dinner — the usual mountainous, unregarded meal. After dinner there was nothing to do but sit and talk and listen to the maddeningly familiar repertoire of the gramophone. It was the chief disadvantage of that life, that night came too early, outstripping — after a comparatively inactive day and half a pint of black coffee — the desire to sleep. We had no light to read or write by, and in the darkness the boundaries of our little world contracted, the uncertainties which were its only permanent furniture domineered over idle imaginations, and the gramophone, which on the voyage from England had provided an accompaniment for doubts and misgivings, was, after all these weeks, providing it still.

What would happen when we reached the Tapirapé? Major Pingle, bland, irrelevant, and enigmatic, presided inscrutably over our destinies. 'Talk to you about that later,' he would mutter, when approached, with a friendly wink for you and a hostile conspirator's glance at whichever member of the expedition happened to be in his bad books at the time. The future remained uncertain.

Eventually you lay down in the sand to await sleep. Everything was lovely, clear, and dramatic in the brilliant moonlight. The great river slid past silently. The frogs made a steady mechanical *tok-tok-tok*, very like the hammering of a Lewis gun. Birds called, sadly or in fear. In the jungle behind you a wolf barked. Between your head and the teeming stars night-jars cut the air with a whickering of wings. The world seemed very empty. You went to sleep.

# CHAPTER XVIII

# INDIANS AND OTTERS

So far I have tried to describe the Araguaya subjectively: I have tried to show what living on it was like from our point of view, from the point of view of interlopers. But this is no place (I am afraid you will be grumbling) for the subjective method: you don't go to a practically unknown part of the world to say what it was like from your point of view. Give us a few facts, a little accurate observation.

I wish I could. This book is all truth and no facts. It is probably the most veracious travel book ever written; and it is certainly the least instructive. For this there are a number of reasons, which will appear most clearly when we pass from the interlopers to the indigenes.

I am appalled when I think how little I know about the Carajas. I cannot write of them objectively, for my data are inadequate and unreliable; and I cannot write of them subjectively, for I cannot say for certain that I understand them.

For these two admissions there are two main excuses. The first is that we spent only a comparatively short time with this tribe, and where there was close contact it was on our terms and not on theirs: that is to say, they were living with us, in our fashion, and not we with them in theirs. The second excuse is that all the information I received about them (like all the information I received about anything in Brazil) was unreliable and open to contradiction. They themselves took an obscure delight in being — wantonly and without motive — inaccurate. One instance will suffice. On a certain stretch of the river we noticed that the villages had been deserted by the men; there were only women and children left. At the first village where we enquired the reason for this we were told that all the men had gone to a place some days down stream, where the whole tribe was rallying for a great war against the white men. At the second village, that they had gone down to the Tapirapé, to trade and hold wrestling matches with the Tapirapé Indians. At the third, that there was so much sickness in all the villages that the men had gone off on a fishing expedition. So far as I know none of these three explanations was the true one.

So you must take what I have to say about the Carajas as the result of superficial observations which it was impossible to check.

Physically the Carajas are a fine race. They are taller than most of the tribes in Brazil, the men often standing as much as five foot eight in their bare feet. Their skin is dark brown, and of a fine texture. Paddling has made them deep-chested, but their wiry legs are muscular and well-formed. Their features — though the type varies widely — suggest a Mongoloid variation on the conventional Red Indian of illustrations to Fenimore Cooper. Their hair is black and snaky; the women mostly wear it hanging below their shoulders, but some of the more civilized of the men have it cut short, or in a bob. They have no hair anywhere on their bodies, and they pluck out their eyelashes and eyebrows.

In their natural state the men go naked, and the women wear only a kind of fibre apron. But contact with the forces of enlightenment, and increased opportunities for acquiring what they regard as finery, have in a few cases resulted in the appearance of skirts and trousers. The condition of these garments is usually an offence against hygiene, and their wearing an entirely unnecessary prop to the natural modesty of the Indians. The use of the tribal mark — the circle cut with a stone on either cheek bone -- is said to be dying out. But most of the children still have a hole cut in their lower lip, through which a variety of ornaments are stuck: a sliver of mussel shell, or a spindle of bone (usually the howler monkey's bone), or a six-inch slip of dried palm frond, which hangs down below their chin, an unnatural but a curiously graceful appendage. They often pierce the lobes of their ears with similar ornaments, the most prized being a capivara tooth.

Their bodies are sometimes pigmented, though not, as far as I was able to gather, for any particular reason or in accordance with any particular design. Occasionally their trunks, more often only their legs, would be ringed and striped with an inconsequent pattern of black and red. (Once I saw a man who had painted his hands, and nothing else, jet black. It made him sinister in a subtle way.) Their red paint they make from the *urukú* berry, the black largely from soot, and the blue-black from the *genipapo* fruit.

I remember in Guatemala it struck me that the Indians there, the Maya Indians, had a wonderful natural eye for colour. Every village wore a kind of livery of its own, though the style of dress varied little — loose short trousers, a kilt, and a sort of blouse. But the Indians were skilful weavers, and made many different dyes from strange recipes (the juice of snails figured in one). In their clothes they mixed the gayest, the most vivid colours, with assurance and success; their taste never faltered, their motley and kaleidoscopic rags never clashed. I fancied that there was among the Carajas something of that unerring instinct for the right colour, though they had far less chance to exercise it, possessed by the gaudy little tribes of Guatemala. When they carried a blanket or a cloak, or when they stained a mat or an earthenware pot, they seemed always to hit on something in the narrow range of shades at their command which harmonized well with their surroundings.

The Carajas inhabit the banks of the Araguaya along a stretch extending roughly from lat. 15 south to lat. 7 south. There is some sort of variation between the northern and the southern halves of the tribe, the northerners being lighter in colour, more industrious, and richer, the southerners bigger in build and more warlike. They are purely river Indians, and they never go far inland. Apart from farinha and mandioca, their staple diet is fish. These they catch in a number of ways, but chiefly by shooting them with arrows. The arrows are four or five feet long, gaily feathered, and tipped with bone; the bows are short but very strong. The shooter stands in the bows of the canoe, and the helmsman guides it softly through the shallows, where the fish can be seen clearly against the sandy bottom in three or four feet of water. The Indians are very good shots, knowing by instinct how much to allow for the refraction. They will score perhaps three hits out of five. The arrow transfixing the fish sticks up in the water, wavering and jerking to and fro uncertainly; the canoe ranges alongside, and the fish, impaled, is easily retrieved. They lose very few arrows, which are precious.

The Indians have no nets. The very big fish – the *piraracú* and the *pirará* – they harpoon, following them up the lagoons into the shallows and there joining a battle in which it seems certain that the precarious canoe will be overturned. For catching ordinary-sized fish they have one other very curious method. They cut great faggots of a certain bush, the name of which I have forgotten, and then a number of them stand round the shores of a small lagoon and thrash the water into a froth with these branches. The leaves of the bush contain a poison, and this, spreading through the water, stupefies the fish, which rise to the surface unconscious and are at once collected. I have heard that there is a tribe somewhere in Africa which does much the same thing.

In the rainy season the Carajas live in villages on the high bluffs along the river bank, out of reach of the floods. The huts in these are permanent erections; big, solidly built, and well thatched. But in the dry season they move down to the praias which the falling water has left bare, and on these they build themselves flimsier huts, to last until the next rains come. As a rule there are six or eight huts to each dry season village, and the villages are mostly a day's journey apart, or rather more.

It was always fun calling on the Carajas. The women and the pot-bellied children would come crowding round as the nose of the leading canoe grated on the sand. The women are said to speak a different language from the men, the principal variation being the omission — or slurring — by the men of the K sound. How much etymological truth there is in this I do not know, but certainly there is a great and striking difference in tone, inflection, and cadence between the speech of the sexes. Difficult as those who are accustomed to polite female society in civilized countries may find it to believe, there is no more maddening sound in the world than the conversation of a Caraja woman. She speaks hurriedly, in a plaintive, petulant sing-song, and until you get used to it you think that she is going to break at any moment into rather angry tears. The voices of the men are by contrast dignified and deliberate.

We would land in the middle of a friendly gabbling crowd, and for a few minutes barter would go forward briskly. If we were lucky, they would offer eggs, bananas, yams, mandioca, and perhaps a turtle, and these we could buy for handfuls of salt and cuts of twist tobacco. (The Carajas, men and women, are enthusiastic smokers. They stuff the tobacco into stubby little pipes like enlarged cigar-holders, at which they suck very noisily indeed.)

The not very weather-proof leaf huts are about thirty feet long, and each is inhabited by one large and loosely defined family. The Carajas are monogamous, and for a primitive people their moral standards are very high; only the chief may have more than one woman, though custom permits the superannuation of wives. The huts are furnished only with mats, on which the occupants (who do not, like the Tapirapés, use hammocks) sleep. The best hut in the village is set aside as a store in which are kept the ceremonial costumes and the feather head-dresses for the *Dança dos Bichos*, or Dance of the Beasts. I never saw this simple though lively masquerade performed, nor was I able to discover what, if any, was its religious significance. Some of the feather head-dresses are extremely handsome.

As far as I could make out, the Carajas have no religion worthy of the name. They do not seem to feel the need for anything more than an elastic and often contradictory code of superstitions, and they betray no signs of being profoundly influenced by these. They are a people not easily susceptible to awe, and though they are for the most part timid, the graver doubts to which mankind is subject find no lurking place in their sunny and superficial natures.

The Carajas are devoted to their children and their pets. The children's podgy necks were loaded with bright cheap necklaces, the poor fruits of a slender trade. They looked well fed, and it was clear that their mothers adored them. Considering how few were the possessions of their parents, the children were very well provided with toys, which consisted entirely of miniature reproductions of those possessions; tiny canoes, tiny paddles, tiny bows and arrows, tiny clubs and tiny pots. You could always (the method holds good in other parts of the world) ingratiate yourself with a family by patting the more sanitary-looking infants on the head; they were often very attractive — plump and black and bright-eyed, like fallen cherubs.

The villages swarmed with livestock. At nightfall parrots warred with scrawny poultry for roosts along the roof-pole. Pigs, and dismal dogs, and fantastically prolific cats, and tame wild ducks wandered in and out of the huts through holes in the wall. In almost all the northerly villages cormorants paddled among the litter round the cooking fires; sometimes their sombre plumage had been decorated by the children with tufts of red arara's feathers fastened to their wings. The sight of them brought back memories of swaying snake-like heads along the gunwales of a sampan in a yellow Chinese river, and I told the Indians that they could train their cormorants to bring them fish if they fastened rings round their necks. In conception, rather than in execution, this project amused them very much; it was clear that they thought of the birds always as guests, never as servants.

Sometimes there were more unexpected pets. A stiff, aloof heron; a night-jar being cherished by a child; a scarlet-throated woodpecker chattering on an old woman's shoulder; a hawk; *a coati*, a reddish ring-tailed animal like a raccoon, which we sometimes shot in the jungle, only to find that their skins had been spoilt by fighting. The Indians were very fond of all these creatures, and treated them well; they asked prohibitive prices for their parrots, and the big red ones they would not sell at all.

We ourselves were animal fanciers for a time. The Araguaya — and for all I know the other great rivers of Central Brazil — are inhabited by a kind of otter not found elsewhere. It is a huge beast, and is said to measure as much as ten or twelve feet in length: though the biggest adult that I saw out of the water was not more than seven feet long. Almost every day we passed a family of anything up to a dozen of these otters, which the Indians call *arirânhas*. They would hang about in the offing, fifty yards away from the canoe, a little knot of intelligent-looking heads, like the heads of seals, only flatter. All the time they kept up a sort of chattering mew, interspersed with snorts of resentment and alarm. When they craned their necks to get a better view of us, you saw on their cream-coloured throats a dark-brown horse-shoe, exactly like the marking on a partridge's breast. They carried magnificent pelts, but we learnt that it was impossible to retrieve them unless you shot them in shallow water, which they rarely frequented. We only brought one skin back.

The Royal Zoological Society had asked us to catch a pair of these otters, if we got the chance; and one day Roger and Burity cut off a couple of young ones from the main body of their family and somehow got them into the canoe without much loss of blood. They were comical creatures, with heads too big for their sleek little bodies. Their small but protuberant eyes and their luxuriant whiskers gave them an elderly, an almost Anglo-Indian look; and they uttered continuously a fretful whiffling sound, exactly reproducing the tone in which very old men in clubs reprimand the waiter for bringing them the wrong liqueur. We never became very deeply attached to them. They were what nurses call a handful, and they seemed to regard us in the light of so many mouthfuls.

But they were an amusing feature of camp-life. At first we tethered them both to a paddle stuck in the sand; then we discovered that, owing to their unfailing lack of unanimity on the question of which direction to go in next, it sufficed simply to tie them to opposite ends of the same piece of string and let them roam; and in the end they learnt to love us for the huge quantities of fish which we gave them, and it was not necessary to tie them at all. They fought almost incessantly, but they were really very fond of one another. They shared our life for about two months, until at last one died, and the other, turning savage, had to be released when we came to the bad rapids on our way down-stream.

But to return to the Carajas. There was a village called Santa Isabel, where the Brazilian government had established a post from which their officials were to disseminate culture and enlightenment among the aborigines. Good work, I believe, was done while the funds lasted; but when we arrived there, there were only the labels left to show how zeal had been expended. The School of Sewing was tenanted by two parakeets, who sat, solemnly regarding each other, on top of the blackboard; from time to time they defaced it with an air of abstraction.

That was a place which you might call symbolic. Three layers of civilization had been laid across that hut-dotted clearing at the top of the steep high bluff. The first things you saw when you scrambled up from the landing-place were two old, old cannon, aimlessly covering the wide but empty river.

An ornate scroll, just forward of their touchholes, bore the following inscription:

1751

MANOEL GOMES DE GARVALHOES SYLVA
THENENTE GENERAL D'ART<sup>RA</sup> DO REYNO

If you were feeling romantic, you tried to imagine the feelings of the man who put a match to those long-empty breeches to answer the farewell salute from the guns of Lisbon, as the sails filled and the expedition plunged out westward across the Bay. You wondered whether he had survived to bring his guns as far as this: and, more particularly, whether he had got back to Portugal again. . . .

Then your eye was caught by a large notice in green and yellow (the national colours of Brazil) prohibiting the import into Santa Isabel of alcoholic liquors, and you saw over the doors of half a dozen white-walled huts similar notices, announcing the purposes of enlightenment to which these buildings were variously devoted. But they were all, like the School of Sewing, empty. The outposts of culture had been evacuated. Only the brave green and yellow notices remained.

The wheel had come full circle. The naked Indians who had endured the cannon of the eighteenth century and the kindergarten of the twentieth were still there. They were not so naked now, and not nearly so numerous; they had picked up a few of the white man's bad habits and some of his diseases, and the clothes which he insisted on their wearing had made them more susceptible to the cold at night, and so to fever. They were dying out, but they were still there. They came to meet us, with feather head-dresses and ceremonial spears for sale, asking exorbitant prices. They had learnt one of the first lessons that contact with civilization teaches a primitive people: that sacred things are the easiest to sell. . . .

What more is there to say of the Carajas? That they can swim like fish under water. That the women mourn for a death with a low, continuous wailing. That they speak to each other across huge stretches of the river without raising their voice, so that often when you think your helmsman is talking to himself he is still in conversation with a canoe which you passed five minutes ago. That when they tried to steal from us they were handicapped by their nakedness and consequent lack of pockets: so we could see them, as they squatted in our camp, apparently entranced by the gramophone, furtively burying the coveted objects underneath them in the sand, in hopes that they could return and unearth them after we had gone away. That they are mortally afraid of the Chavantes, who inhabit the Matto Grosso bank of the river, and who occasionally massacre small parties of the Carajas. (I know nothing about the Chavantes, except their evil reputation. Contact with them seems to have been established only at the wrong end of a spear. They are undoubtedly bad Indians, and perhaps cannibals. The smoke from their fires was a regular feature of the western landscape as far as the mouth of the Rio das Mortes. Major Pingle once saw a pair of Chavante legs hanging from poles in a Caraja village; the children were shooting at them with bows and arrows.)

Those, then, are my woefully unscientific impressions of the Carajas. They are a nice, cheerful, rather silly people: children in most things. It was sad to see them being civilized; but their numbers are dwindling fast, and before the process of civilization is complete I think the tribe will be extinct. Even in Paradise, you cannot afford to be as improvident as they are.

# CHAPTER XIX

# THE LAST OF THE DRAGONS

A PROMINENT, but on the whole a disappointing, feature of life on the Araguaya was the alligators.

There is little awe left current in the world, and little of that little is well bestowed. Formerly men went in awe of real things, like Tyrants, and Thunder, and Snakes. These things (which affected their lives) had about them some mystery or force of which men had imperfect comprehension or control. Awe was given on account of some quality not quite natural: a touch of the monstrous.

Many, indeed most, of the products of modern civilization are superficially monstrous; but we rightly do not allow them the status of monsters. The dullest peasant in the furthest lane still takes more count of one piebald horse than of twenty charabancs. And the once fashionable nursery game of Marvelling at the Strides Made by Science has clean gone out, for science has got her seven-league boots on and leapt the layman's horizons. In any case, we are all too blasé to be caught in the attitude of savages gaping at a gramophone. There is very little left remarkable beneath the visiting moon: remarkable, I mean, in this special sense which implies awe.

There is, however, in most of us an unused deposit or residuum of awe which is at the command of certain outlandish things: as, for instance, Volcanoes, Chinese Pirates, Prairie Fires, and the Octopus. We read about these things in our early youth (probably in books of the last century, when awe was cheap). They seemed to us then worthy of awe; and we should to-day, if we were to come in contact with one or other of these things, be prepared to experience a sensation of awe.

Very commonly included among these outlandish things is

the alligator. Most people hold the alligator in awe; nor is it difficult to see why. For here is the last of the dragons, a creature old in evil, of secret ways, living in noisome places: armoured, baleful, and as ugly as Miltonic sin. Hearsay does not detract from his menace; and the mere malignancy of his outward form stays any possible suspicion that this, almost the last of our bogies, is a turnip-ghost lit by travellers' tales. We believe so firmly all that we have heard of his cunning and his ferocity that we do not scruple to call them incredible.

Alas, the alligator is a fraud. His cunning and his ferocity are all my eye and Sir John Mandeville. His formidable reputation — as empty as his skin, which mountebanks formerly hung in their booths — is, like that skin, a hallowed device of quackery, a trick to fire imaginations which have to take the tropics on trust. The alligator is a fraud.

He took us in at first, I admit. Those two discreet little projections, his snout and eyes, furtive yet non-committal conning-towers, the spearhead of a silent ripple on the lagoon's surface — they, surely, were index to a power for which experience would enhance our traditional respect. We gave him credit for timing his dives, and placing his reappearances, in accordance with some deep-laid scheme. And when we first saw him ashore, lying on a sandbank, hunched in his startling carapace, we thought him inscrutable because he did not blink his pale eyes at our approach, and fearless because he (sometimes) delayed his dive until it was too late.

In those early days, when we still took him seriously, we used to go after him at night in fine romantic circumstances. An Indian in the stern of the canoe; a rifle in the bows; and someone with a torch amidships. The beam, reaching out over the black water, picks up two specks of sultry red: his eyes. Our bows swing to them; the paddle bites the water silently. The two specks do not move; we gauge his size by the distance between them. Soon we are very close, and still he waits for us, giving no sign of fear or fury. Number One covers him;

Number Two's torch shines down the sights into those smouldering ineffectual eyeballs, now close below our gunwale. Literary precedent demands that he should charge and upset the canoe, as he very easily could; common sense dictates submersion. Our alligator takes neither course. The rifle roars, and the dull beast dies melodramatically in a flurry of stained waters.

Of the many we killed a very few did not die tamely. There was one hit three times in the head with a .375 and dragged ashore. (It was a very big one. We wanted to measure it.) In the night it revived, and before an incredulous torchlit semi-circle of its butchers took six revolver bullets in its pulped skull, still blindly lunging at us with its jaws. There was another which, with one eye destroyed, for a long time carved foaming circles in a still lagoon, straining through the water with its head reared high: an oddly formidable sight.

But the alligator — at any rate the alligator of Central Brazil — is a fraud. For two months we saw him every day; we slept within reach of him, we swam in his waters. He was content to look malignant and live on his reputation. If he is not a fool and a coward, he might just as well be, so assiduously hidden are his cunning and his courage. I am sorry to expose him, because such frauds colour life and do no harm. But I doubt if he minds very much; it would be hard to find a creature with less self-respect.

Perhaps we expected too much from the alligators. I know that we were disappointed, and acquired so great a contempt for these unenterprising creatures that, after we had killed well over one hundred in a month, we almost gave up shooting them. The biggest we retrieved was fourteen feet long; and the silliest I ever had anything to do with was one which I shot in the belly with a revolver as it lay staring foolishly at me from the bank. I was anxious to get a photograph at close quarters, and landed quickly, cutting off its retreat to the river. The .45 bullet had done it no great harm, and at my approach it scrambled with undignified haste underneath a small bush and there stayed, cheating me of my photograph, while I prodded it vindictively with a paddle, like a beater trying to evict a rabbit from thick brambles. That was a contemptible monster.

There was only one occasion on which the alligators inspired in me the faintest sensation of awe, and then they did it by sheer force of numbers. After supper Neville and I had gone out to wait up at the head of a small lagoon behind our camp, where we had seen many tracks of tapir and peccary and deer. As we came quietly through the scrub that fringed it, we were surprised to hear a deafening and continuous uproar going on in the lagoon: a boiling, squelching, thrashing sound, as if a herd of elephants was wallowing in it. We emerged on to the shore and found ourselves in the presence of all the alligators in the world. When we flashed the torch across the water most of them dived; but even so I counted forty pairs of red eyes in its narrow beam.

For two hours we lay in the sand at the head of the lagoon, and all that time the water, from its margin twenty feet away to the furthest point illuminated by our torch, seethed with alligators. What they were doing heaven only knows. But by degrees the presence, close at hand, of so many slimy armoured bodies moving motivelessly in the sticky dark became oppressive. Almost with surprise I realized that for once the alligators had filled the role which our expectations had assigned to them: that I was thinking of them not altogether with contempt.

As a matter of fact, most of the terrors of the Central Brazilian jungle had a way of paling into rather ludicrous insignificance when you looked at them closely. In the dry season Matto Grosso is more of a health resort than a White Man's Grave. I suspected before I went there, and I know now, that it owes its evil reputation largely to a combination of circumstances which I have seen at work in other parts of the world. If a country contains regions very remote and almost unknown, everyone conspires to paint them in the most lurid colours possible, for two very good reasons: the few men who have been to them naturally want to make a good story out of their experiences, and the many inhabitants of the country who might have been to them like to have a good excuse for not having done so.

The only danger which was perhaps a real one, and against which we did take certain precautions, was the *piranhas*, the little man-eating fish, which are of the size of a roach and attack men and animals in fierce shoals. We restricted our bathing to places which the Indians said were safe from these, and I dare say this was wise and necessary; my conclusions with regard to the extent to which these fish deserve their hair-raising reputation are reserved for a later chapter.

# CHAPTER XX

# ONE THING AND ANOTHER

THE journey from Leopoldina to the Tapirapé was very easy going; we began to feel more like beachcombers than explorers. There were few happenings worthy of record, and the days were so very much alike that it is by sights and smells and sounds, rather than by events, that that stage of our journey is marked in my memory. There was, however, one incident sufficiently comical to deserve a mention.

One night Roger and I, plunging at hazard into the jungle behind our praia, found the going easier than usual, the country more open. There were big clearings, and the low, rather scrubby forest between them opposed us less than usual. We were glad of the chance to walk upright and at a decent pace, instead of twisting and ducking through dense cover which protested all too loudly at our passage.

At the end of one long clearing we saw a little deer, a veado. She was feeding in the gentle evening light, a distant delicate toy, russet against a dun background. We stalked her without success, zig-zagging upwind from one clump of trees to the next, bending double in the long grass when dead ground failed us. It brought back to me very clearly Ardnamurchan, and September evenings after roe, and the thoughts of a boy. In the end she got away, and we were not sorry, for as she disappeared under the trees, we saw that there was a little fawn, not bigger than a hare, at her heels.

We went on, and Roger, with the .22 shot a toucan, whose grotesque and flaming bill, miraculously surviving all mishaps of travel, came with us back to England. We stalked an emu, and another deer, and thereafter found our memories of what had been our course confused. We had certainly come a long way.

But we thought the river near. If we headed back for the sunset we must hit it soon; there was no immediate hurry.

We squatted in the dry mud on the shores of a rank little lagoon. All the time in Brazil we clung pathetically to a belief that, sooner or later, given luck, we should find some place where the animals came at evening to drink — some place where an ambush at sunset would be (as Baedeker says) 'repaying'. This secret trampled pool aroused our expectations. We thought we could afford the time to test its possibilities; so we squatted there and waited.

But nothing came. Nothing stirred. In that part of the jungle thirsts, if slaked at all, were slaked elsewhere. The ciganas, the hiss-birds, clambered heavily and made their uncouth sounds in the branches above us. A gilded kingfisher flashed silently, and with an air of caprice, over the clotted water. Presently an egret dropped down through the tree-tops, gliding through the air softly but giving a little lurch at every stroke of its round owl-like wings. It settled on a tiny island opposite us, a slim pale ghost with a fastidious manner. We coveted the feathers, and Roger raised the rifle quietly. At the shot the egret rose with a struggle into the air and went across the lagoon with a convulsive flight, to fall dead on the further bank.

As it fell, a swirl broke the surface of the shallows twenty yards away. The eyes and snout of a small alligator began to move with purpose through the water towards the white and broken bundle on the mud. Stealthily, as though drifting, the flat skull drew nearer its objective, trailing a silent ripple; and presently there was a paddling sound as the alligator crawled out on to the mud. He had been covered all the way, and now I fired. The poacher twisted and died in the shallows. We got up and worked our way round the lagoon to retrieve the bird.

By the time we had got it it was nearly dark. We started back at a good speed towards the embers of the sunset. We were not on, and we did not seem to be near, the route by which we had come out. The jungle was much thicker. We made slow and exasperated progress. Soon it became very bad — so bad that the exasperation left us and we tasted that fierce and irresponsible delight that comes when you are contending with odds to the limit of your physical energies. We barged through thickets; we crawled under fallen trees; we writhed and danced and threw ourselves into strange contortions to escape from the lianas which lapped themselves round our legs and seemed so pliant, so submissive, that you went forward two or three steps, expecting them to yield or snap, and thus fatally tightened their hold on you. The light was going, and in the thickening dusk it was harder than ever to avoid the slim black thorns, like needles, which go in deep and cause an instant swelling and are difficult to cut out. We bled and sweated and cursed and laughed. Inexhaustible reinforcements of black trunks paraded against the red and genial sunset. With a splendid incompetence we had got ourselves bushed.

But at last the trees thinned suddenly, and we burst through a wall of undergrowth on to the river bank. But it was not the place at which we had been aiming, nor anywhere near it. Camp, and the half-mile-long praia on which it stood, were out of sight. We were perhaps two miles, perhaps more, downstream of our objective. We began to make our way along the steep and overgrown bank. But night had now closed down — a night without a moon — and all hope of progress along the bank was strangled in a labyrinth of fallen trees. We stopped to consider the situation.

Opposite us, a sandbank gleamed dully in midstream. As we stood there, a little fire sprang into life on the sandbank; we thought we could make out two or three figures and a canoe. They must be Indians; we could promise them tobacco or salt, and perhaps they would take us back upstream to camp.

'Caraja acu!' we called. ('Acu' corresponds to 'Hi!'; or, for that matter, to any loud cry.)

There was a moment's silence. Then a voice answered in German.

It was a strange echo to have woken in the heart of Brazil. While Roger carried on across the water a fluent conversation in matter-of-fact tones, I reflected that this was perhaps the most bizzare proof I should ever be given of the value of an expensive education.

Presently a canoe came across from the sandbank, manned by a German, a Brazilian, and an Indian. The German was a missionary of sorts. He was on his way upstream to a point from which he hoped to strike across country to the Rio das Mortes. This was his holiday, he explained; his wife was with him. And there, to lend the incident its crowning touch of improbability, was the wife, a demure and childish figure in pigtails, pacing gravely beside us along the sand as we glided under the lea of the praia.

We spent, alas, only a few minutes with these charming and well-encountered people. From their sandbank we could see our own camp fire, far away upstream; when we fired a shot a Verey light rushed up, with a sound like a very faint sneer, leaving a sheaf of green spangles to wither quickly in the sky. A minute later, a deprecating 'acu' came out of the darkness at our elbow, and there was our tip-tilted ubá, with Lorian's unobtrusive dignity in the stern. We had to say good-bye and go straight back to camp with him, for the others might be getting anxious. Lorian had come out to look for us on his own, without instructions. He was a good man. For this piece of rescue work we gave him a pair of my trousers and the title of Captain, which pleased him greatly. He made a skull cap and an armlet out of an old red stocking, and wore them always, as the insignia of his rank.

All our men, as a matter of fact, were good men, and we got to know them well in those long empty days and garrulous dusks. First there was José Diaz, a keen effective little man, by profession a taxi-driver in Goyaz, by vocation an excellent cook. Everyone was sorry when, half way to the Tapirapé, memories of his deserted taxi ousted the visions of adventure which had brought him with us, and he left us to go back upstream to his lawful business.

José Tiburce succeeded him as cook. He was almost a pure negro; he had great courtesy and humour, and took our palates very seriously.

To Raymundo, who was white, there clung a kind of faded distinction; his battered Trilby had a civilized air, and the little black cord which attached it to his filthy shirt somehow suggested that its owner had once been a man of elegance, a careful and respectable citizen. He was inclined to be glib and unreliable, and he was a coward; but he was sincerely devoted to our interests, and it was impossible not to like him.

It was on the other hand comparatively easy not to like João Morro, who was half-Indian and a well-known figure on the river, where he has fished and traded for many years. He was a cunning and rascally old man, for whose allegedly invaluable services Major Pingle offered a high wage. Once we had engaged him, he strutted about in a very horsey waistcoat of black and white checks, gossiping and giggling and giving out inaccurate information about the places on our route. He was never much use to the expedition.

Then there was the man whom we christened The Aesthete, on account of his habit (it was more of a policy than a habit) of resting at frequent intervals on his oar and pointing out some object of natural beauty in the landscape with an ecstatic cry of 'Que belleza!'. This trick was usually good for a five minutes' 'easy' for himself and his fellow-oarsmen. The Aesthete's digestion was always in a terrible state, but he could in no circumstances be deterred from eating enormous quantities of turtles' eggs. He was a puny and excessively dirty little man, but there was, nevertheless, something likeable about him.

José Francisco was a good man. He always wore a dagger and a terrific slouch hat, and thus looked, with his fierce but sentimental eyes, exactly like a Victorian artist's conception of a Corsican brigand. But the most useful member of that motley, amiable gang was Queiroz.

Queiroz was twenty-two. He was a very small and unattractive man, with hardly any neck at all and a face like a malicious hedgehog. He had only one eye, but his powers of endurance were considerable, and he was the only Brazilian I met who was capable of doing anything in a hurry. In his native state of Maranhão he was a clerk in some sort of government office, and on the trip with us he expended the best part of a six months' holiday. He had a squeaky, irritating voice, great courage, a regard for accuracy, and an almost Teutonic passion for collecting information. He was the only one of our men who was literate, and round the camp-fire at night he used to read out to the others, with obvious relish, passages from an old newspaper which he had with him. He served us well, and plays an important part in the later chapters of this book. Though in the end he let us down over a money matter, I still have a great respect for him. If I thought that there were many more Brazilians like Queiroz, I should be inclined to predict a different future for that country.

During this uneventful stage of our journey the only domestic development worthy of note was the gradual obsolence of jokes about beards. We almost all grew these useful (and, as some maintain, honourable) appendages, and they had now reached a decent degree of luxuriance. The spirit of keen emulation in which their development on rival chins had been anxiously watched through its earlier phases was abandoned; and at last the time came when it was no longer considered necessary, on our all sitting down to a meal together, for some reference to be made to the Last Supper. The practical value of the beards easily counterbalanced their aesthetic drawbacks, for they meant that at least some portion of one's face was protected from the insects, who rather surprisingly overlooked their considerable attractions as nesting sites.

# PART TWO

## HAND TO MOUTH

# CHAPTER I

# AT THE CROSS-ROADS

WE reached the mouth of the Tapirapé in the third week in August and camped opposite it, at the foot of a little conical hill on the shores of the island of Bananal, the largest effluvial island in the world.

I remember that little hill with affection. It was not more than 300 feet high, but it was the first eminence of any sort that we had seen since we dropped down into the river valley at Leopoldina three weeks before. Somehow it made a great difference. The wide impersonal river had become a prison. The wider it got, the more marked, the more oppressive, grew the sense of captivity. The emptiness of our horizons had created in me a need which was not acknowledged until the little hill satisfied it. It added, almost, another dimension to our world. It belonged to the order of eternal, reassuring things from which we were indefinitely parted but of which we did not consciously feel the lack: things like Saturdays, and bacon, and bare branches against a grey sky. I was grateful for the little hill.

Roger and I climbed one of the trees which crowned it. Below us, half a mile away, was the mouth of the Tapirapé; a sufficiently romantic-looking mouth, with a little island set in the middle of it. Beyond the mouth the silver coils of the river writhed mysteriously westwards through dense jungle. We were encouraged by the sight of what looked like big stretches of open country breaking the green opacity of the forest. Far away to the north-west — how far, in that hazy light, we could not even guess — we could see high ground which was not marked on our map and which, indeed, since our course thereafter lay south-west, we never identified.

163

This was all very stimulating, and as we clung to the ant-infested branches of our tree we indulged that tendency to wild surmise traditionally associated with equatorial peaks. But we indulged it with heavy hearts, and in a more or less academic spirit. The country before us was indeed our Promised Land; but it seemed at the moment highly improbable that any of the promises made in regard to it were going to be kept. Between us and the Great Unknown stood the virtually omnipotent figure of Major Pingle, now a foreshortened and brooding manikin among the familiar litter of camp on the praia below us.

The situation, which had come rapidly to a head in the last three days, was as follows:

Major Pingle had come out into the open. He did not want to go up the Tapirapé. He did not want — he never had wanted — to look for Fawcett. The root of the trouble had been the deplorably incomplete liaison between our headquarters in London and his own in Brazil. Not until a few weeks before our arrival had he been given to understand that we purported to be a serious expedition bent on clearing up the Fawcett mystery, and not a casual shooting trip. His first impulse on learning this had been to wash his hands of the whole business; but his good nature, his fatal good nature, had prevailed, and when we all arrived — as keen (to use his own vivid phrase) as mustard — he had not had the heart to disappoint us. A kindly man, he had undertaken to do what he could.

He had done it. He had done his very best. But the run of events had been against him; the revolution had bothered him a lot, and that cooling of our enthusiasm which he had foreseen as an inevitable result of discomfort and privation had not taken place. He now freely admitted that he did not want to go up the Tapirapé; and that if in the end we did go up he would see to it — for our own sakes — that the expedition's search for Fawcett was confined to asking the Tapirapé Indians (whose language nobody knew), if they could tell us anything about events which took place, seven years ago, 150 miles to the south-west of their territory. It was obvious that this could produce no useful results; and for his part he would vastly prefer to take the whole expedition straight on down the Araguaya to Pará. We should, after all, thus complete an instructive journey through the middle of a vast and little-known country. What more could we want?

He was reminded that we had come out from England in order to make a serious attempt to clear up the mystery surrounding Fawcett's disappearance: that, more specifically, he had brought us up country from São Paulo — and had in fact been paid in advance — to carry out a certain plan of action, drawn up by himself, in which the most important item was a cross-country journey from the headwaters of the Tapirapé towards the Kuluene. It was further pointed out that he had authorized for publication in England despatches committing us, on his authority, to a programme which, now that the time had come to put it into practice, he characterized as futile and impracticable. . . .

Poor Major Pingle· His good nature had landed him in an awkward position. He had bitten off more than he could chew; and if, in my account of subsequent developments, his behaviour appears to the reader occasionally odd, the reader must remember that Major Pingle was actuated throughout by (among other things) a strong regard for the personal safety of all members of the expedition, and that the situation in which he found himself was one to the handling of which his character and temperament were singularly ill-adapted.

When we expressed, in temperate terms, our reluctance to abandon the expedition's primary objective without having satisfied ourselves that it was unattainable, Major Pingle agreed to carry out a drastically modified version of his original plan: he would take the expedition up the Tapirapé, interview the Indians there, and return without delay. Any more extended operations — any attempt to carry out the plan in full — he refused to countenance. And he reminded us that, in the Gentleman's Agreement which we had all signed at Rio, we had pledged ourselves to recognize his authority as leader and to obey his orders implicitly.

It was hardly worth-while to point out, in our turn, that the first clause in that contract read: 'The object of the expedition is to ascertain the fate of Colonel Fawcett as far as is humanly possible', for Major Pingle's authority, whether we chose to recognize it or not, was effectively paramount. As leader, he held the expeditionary funds; he controlled the men, whose language we spoke imperfectly or not at all; and to get at the supplies without his consent would entail the use of force. Major Pingle had the whip hand, and knew it.

By failing, for reasons which could obviously not be made public, and by a fantastically wide margin, to carry out the intentions which it had so confidently proclaimed in *The Times*, the whole expedition would appear in a light which could most charitably be described as ridiculous. The right and obvious course was to take the law into our own hands and discharge Major Pingle, relieving him, if necessary by force, of the balance of the expeditionary funds and property. This, however, meant presenting a united front; and there were so many differences of opinion as to the degree of rashness and impossibility which would in fact be found to characterize our plans for a Fawcett hunt — as to whether, in other words, it was worth taking so much trouble to achieve an honourable failure — that a united front was not practical politics. So the right and obvious course was out of the question.

Roger and I were probably keener on the Fawcett hunt than anyone else. Certainly I stood to lose most by its complete failure, for my letters from São Paulo to Printing House Square had guaranteed a good Fawcett 'story', and hinted at the possibility of a very good one. At any rate, Roger and I went to Major Pingle, implied that he had bitten off more than he could chew and that we knew it, and offered to resign from the expedition with a view to attempting to carry out on our own those plans to which my obligations to *The Times* committed me more unequivocally than anyone else. We asked that he would leave us a share of the supplies and the money for our passages from Pará to England, to which (under that famous contract) we were in the circumstances entitled. All we wanted, we said, was to confirm by our own experience his statement that the journey which we had come all this way to make was indeed impossible. We would do nothing rash; as soon as we came up against an impossibility we would turn back, our curiosity and our consciences alike satisfied. And, since he was (rightly, no doubt) so insistent on the dangers involved, we would give him before we parted a signed and witnessed statement absolving him from all responsibility for our fate and making it clear that we were following a course of action directly contrary to his wishes and advice.

Alas, it was no good. Major Pingle drew a hair-raising picture of the perils which awaited us up the Tapirapé. If not for our sakes, then for the sake of his own good name, he said, he was not going to allow us to commit suicide. He became very angry. We left him.

But if he was angry, he was also rattled. He had finally committed himself to taking the whole expedition up the Tapirapé and down again: a flying visit. But he knew that there was trouble in store for him when we reached the Indians on its headwaters. He foresaw (and I encouraged him to foresee) that supposing, when we got there, the first stage of a cross-country journey towards the Kuluene did, contrary to expectation, prove possible, nothing short of force would prevent Roger and me from attempting it. And when it came to force Major Pingle no longer had the whip hand.

These were anxious times for Major Pingle. Looking down from our tree at that lonely and diminished figure on the gleaming praia, I felt a certain pity for it.

The next day (several hours late, as usual) the expedition started up the Tapirapé. At last, after all these months of talk and travel, after all these brief elations and all these long delays, we had reached the scene of operations. We were Taking the Field. Few ventures of a similar kind can have been so firmly rooted in the ludicrous. From the mouth of the river to its head-waters, where we should meet the Indians, was said to be a six days' journey. It would be a difficult, and perhaps even — on account of the lowness of the river — an impossible journey; and it was freely admitted by all to be a useless one, unless we did a great deal more than simply paddle up to the Indian port and paddle back again. Our leader did not want to make the journey at all, and at intervals said so to those members of the expedition with whom he was still on speaking terms. Further-more, it turned out that our supplies had somehow or other been limited to food for sixteen days. I was filled with a kind of forlorn glee when I reflected that all this would one day have to be translated into that impressive, non-committal prose, with its slightly technical flavour, in which the activities of explorers are recorded in *The Times*.

The bataloãs were left behind. They went downstream, with Humphreys in charge and the bulk of the supplies on board, to await our return at a mission station situated on Bananal, a day's journey north of the Tapirapé. We had said good-bye to Lorian and Burity. Their tribe has an ancient feud with the Tapirapés, and no Caraja would come with us up the river. We started in three ubás and the montaría. There were seven explorers, including Major Pingle, and six men — João Morro, Queiroz, Raimundo, José Francisco, a new man, a good worker, whose name I forget, and Chico, also a new man, who had made several journeys up the Tapirapé; he was to be our guide, and he pretended that he was also going to be our interpreter. He knew the river well, but his information about the Tapirapés was limited and imprecise: partly, I think, because he was secretly very much afraid of them.

# AT THE CROSS-ROADS

Besides supplies for sixteen days, we had with us a largely irrelevant assortment of medicines and a box of presents for the Indians — tobacco, cutlery, necklaces, and some rather silly toys. In addition everyone had the irreducible minimum of personal equipment: a blanket, a mosquito net, a revolver, and in some cases a change of clothes. There was not much room in the canoes, and we aimed at drawing as little water as possible. We left camp about eleven o'clock in the morning. Roger and I were in the last (and heaviest) canoe, with Chico. It was a very hot day. As we crossed the wide river we saw a strange canoe, also headed for the mouth of the Tapirapé, coming upstream under the Matto Grosso bank. Chico said it was one of the missionaries from the Bananal station, carrying out his annual visit to the Tapirapé Indians. The strange canoe, heavily laden, but with four paddles going, passed us just inside the mouth. The missionary, in a broad-brimmed hat and a khaki shirt, sat amidships.

Comedy — good comedy, though of an elusive kind — was rife that day. I thoroughly enjoyed our encounter. There came a moment when the two canoes rode motionless, within a hundred yards of each other, on the polished river; water dripped with a gentle deprecating sound from the blades of paddles laid across the thwarts. No other sound broke the silence. No other sound broke the silence, in spite of the fact that three Englishmen were here unexpectedly brought together in a place which, broadly speaking, was as remote from anywhere as it is possible to be. The forces of desolation, the notoriously demoralizing effect of the tropical atmosphere, were alike powerless against the tradition of English reticence. Nobody spoke.

It was I (to my shame) who hailed our fellow-countryman. He answered in a cultured, amiable voice. We exchanged almost equally stale rumours about the revolution, and — as his conscientious paddlers bent once more to their task— promises to meet again shortly. Before long he was out of sight.

I had two reasons for welcoming the appearance of this missionary. In the first place, the fact that we should be accompanied, if not preceded, up this virtually unexplored river by the man of God lessened the chances of the expedition as a whole being lulled into a sense of achievement by the mere completion of the journey up the Tapirapé. In the second place, the presence in the district of a man with medical training might conceivably salve Major Pingle's conscience in the matter of turning Roger and me loose in the wilderness. Little though he knew it, the young man in the broad-brimmed hat had already been enrolled as a pawn.

I was too busy with my own thoughts, and with the unaccustomed business of paddling continuously and against the stream, to give to our surroundings the attention they deserved. But it was clear that we had come into a new world. Between the Tapirapé and the Araguaya there was all the difference that there is between a lane and an arterial road. Progress was no longer either monotonous or smooth. The new river (although on this first day, near the mouth, it was reasonably deep and sluggish) was narrow and tortuous. The jungle no longer kept its distance, but plunged along beside us, dominating the channel, making a great display of its powers. The channel itself wanted watching. The river at this point linked up an intricacy of lagoons, and the channel had a habit of making sharp, furtive, and unlikely turns, so that without Chico's local knowledge we should have been side-tracked time and again into the lagoons, those plausible culs-de-sac.

What with our late start, and various stops to cut poles for the canoes and to readjust their lading, we made comparatively little progress that first day. When evening came there was no praia in sight, so we slung our hammocks in the jungle. Mosquitoes were present in fairly large numbers, and Major Pingle (who had made great play with the terrors of insect life up the Tapirapé) announced with ill-concealed satisfaction that we had with us only a tiny quantity of that well-known insecticide which is regarded by most Englishmen as an indispensable adjunct to foreign travel. (This preparation, as a protection against the insects of Central Brazil, had an almost purely talismanic value. Those who applied it always appeared to feel easier in their minds, just as negroes do who carry a hare's foot to ward off the Evil Eye. But their sense of security was, in my opinion, ill-founded. In all the insects I came across the merest whiff of it aroused the most ungovernable craving, and it was pitiful to see them struggling to get at those parts of your person which you had sprayed with the stuff. I never knew an insect to suffer the smallest ill effect after an orgy, however unrestrained, of that well-known insecticide.)

The minor — the very minor — discomforts of camping in the jungle had the charm of novelty. But there was tension in the air, and it was not until the early hours of the morning that familiar and deafening snores from Major Pingle's hammock announced that our leader's troubled spirit had found a temporary oblivion. I lay awake, wondering how long things could go on like this. The chances of averting fiasco — and fiasco in fairly unpleasant circumstances — appeared indescribably slender. But the situation, I decided, had still certain rather desperate possibilities; and even when hope gave out, there were always the irony rations to fall back on.

At that moment, as if to warn me against undue optimism, my hammock broke. I picked myself up, mended it, and went to sleep.

Early the next morning our fantastic life underwent its sharpest, its most unexpected, and its happiest change. Coffee was boiling, and the canoes were being loaded in a world from which the tentative sunlight was still excluded by the trees. Major Pingle, looking baleful and a little anxious, stood in the centre of the clearing where our hammocks had hung. Suddenly he called my name.

His tone was of the sort described by novelists as pregnant. Every one turned to listen.

'Well, Fleming,' said Major Pingle, looking at me with marked distaste, 'you can go up the Tapirapé if you like: and any of the others who want to can go with you. I'm going back.'

'Thank you,' I said, with all the ambiguity I could muster.

Major Pingle went on. He said that he wouldn't mind betting that we should have had enough of it after a couple of days more: that there was so little water in the river that we probably shouldn't be able to get up it at all; and that in any case we should serve no good purpose if we did, as he had pointed out all along. For his part, he would wait for us at the Mission Station; he infinitely preferred the clean and healthy Araguaya to this futile and uncomfortable venture.

Now one of the chief planks in Major Pingle's platform during all our debates about the Tapirapé had been his own powers of physical endurance. 'Very well', he had almost always ended up by saying, 'we'll go up the Tapirapé. But you won't like it. You won't last as long as I do. I'm tougher than any of you. You see if I'm not.' And at this crucial moment, while I offered bewildered but unconditional thanks to the fates, someone had the disastrous indiscretion to remind him of his boasts.

'But I thought,' said someone, 'that you were going to be the last to turn back?'

It was an agonizing moment. Major Pingle's decision to leave us to our own devices, prudent though it was from his own point of view, could hardly have been taken without certain qualms of conscience. It was not an unalterable decision; and nothing was more calculated to alter it than a challenge to his *amour propre*.

Luckily the challenge was not taken up. Major Pingle, to my infinite relief, found a familiar sanctuary in the irrelevant. A quarter of an hour later we had parted — for sixteen days only,

## AT THE CROSS-ROADS

Major Pingle reminded us; sixteen days at the outside. He disappeared downstream with João Morro and the smallest canoe. We went the other way, suppressing with difficulty a tendency to break into ribald song. From the ashes of our first camp on the Tapirapé a thin plume of smoke rose towards the laced branches, like the most delicate of exclamation marks.

# CHAPTER II

LOST LEADER

FIVE days after Major Pingle left us we reached our objective, the port of the Tapirapé Indians called São Domingo.

They were five good days — the best so far — and none the worse for the fact that they ought to have been six. For the first time in its history the expedition did something in less time than it had expected to take, instead of in more. We had got a move on.

The absence of Major Pingle, whose rule over the whole equipage had been despotic, created a holiday atmosphere. We were on our own — at liberty to make our own mistakes, our own plans, our own small innovations in that casual scrambling life. It was a pleasant feeling.

It was fairly hard going. On the Araguaya we had done a certain amount of paddling, putting in an hour or so at a time whenever we felt the need for exercise. Now I found myself paddling all day, from six in the morning till five in the evening, with a couple of hours off for a meal in the middle of the day. Paddling is the individualist's sport. Your exertions are not rationalized, as they are in rowing. Your stroke can vary with your mood. But the day's run is a comment on your character, and only a good deal of self-discipline can make it a favourable one. I now shared Chico's canoe with Neville, while Roger in the montaría, with a compass and a watch, made a map of the river under exquisitely difficult conditions. The third and largest canoe was heavily laden and burdened with two non-paddlers; so it was up to us to set the pace. Our efforts were unremitting, but until we acquired the knack we used to waste a lot of energy. It was a salutary experience, after a particularly well-sustained spurt, to be told by Chico, languidly plying an expert blade in the stern, that we were 'people clearly unaccustomed to work, though of a good courage'. At this rate, he added philosophically, it would take us eight days to reach the port.

The river became lovelier and lovelier, and more and more nearly impassable. I was terribly afraid that we should be held up altogether. The twisting channel narrowed, and the current grew stronger against us. There were places where the river was all but choked by fallen trees. Sometimes the trunks were submerged, and we pushed and hauled the canoes over them to the accompaniment of ominous raspings. Sometimes they cleared the water by no more than a couple of feet, and these we negotiated by a technique analogous to that used by circus people who jump from the backs of their horses through paper hoops. Occasionally we had to cut a passage with the big knives called *facões*; but this was always an easier matter than it sounds.

It was the shallows, the ever more frequently recurring shallows, that gave me most cause for anxiety. To get out and drag the canoes through two or three hundred yards of knee-deep water was not very hard work. But it lost us time, and — more important — it broke the rhythm of our progress: so that the whole sly and delicate business of building up, by bets and jokes and challenges, a good morning's run had to be begun over again.

But the difficulties we encountered were not very great, and the obstacles, although they threatened to become at any moment insuperable, were really very ordinary ones. I hope I have not made it sound otherwise. I so easily might have: just as you might so easily make a considerable impression on the inhabitants of Matto Grosso if you circulated among them even quite a bald account of a bicycle ride out from Oxford to Boars Hill. They, never having seen a bicycle, would form a high opinion of your daring and your powers of endurance as they read how here you pushed the machine up a hill, and how there you avoided collision with something called a charabanc. Truth is a perishable commodity; considerable care must be exercised in shipping it across the world.

Enchantment has, I suppose, its drawbacks; there are penalties for dealing in magic. On the whole the Tapirapé let us off very lightly. Trespassers in fairyland, we were cautioned and discharged.

When I say fairyland, I mean the antique fairyland. Make no mistake about that. I mean a green, an old-established, an incalculable place. Not the choice glades of Spenser, laid out in an allegorical design which no one who follows them is minded to decipher: not Milton's formal lawns, curiously haunted though they are by the truth so high-mindedly travestied upon them: not (above all) that insipid Tom Tiddler's Ground whereon the artfully inconsequent fancies of the moderns can pick up gold and silver royalties to their publishers' content and the corruption of our nurseries. I mean a haunted, lovely, formidable place in which man is always an intruder, never a patron. I mean a place which is the very opposite of unearthly, seeing that it had all the qualities of the earth before it came to be exploited by us.

Our relations with everything had suddenly become closer and more real. With our enterprise, because it was now wholly in our own inexpert hands. With our men, because they were now directly under our inarticulate control. With the trees, because from these imminent converging banks they claimed our attention as successfully as shop windows in a street. With the birds, because they were tamer, and stood their ground, inviting detailed inspection. With the fish, because we could see them plainly through the clear shallow water. With our food, because there was not so very much of it. With our bodies, because they were for the first time called upon to endure some strain. We began to feel much less spurious. The label of 'fantastic', which our journey had so far flaunted as its sole excuse, became merely a subsidiary recommendation.

If we felt many things that we had not felt before, we saw little that was altogether new. The river alternately writhed in paroxysms which came near to boxing Roger's compass and offered us, for a mile at a time, lagoon-like stretches of nearly stagnant water, too deep for poling. Praias were comparatively few and far between; but when, searching for a place to camp, we found one at last, it had always a singular freshness and beauty. Firewood was scarcer, and mosquitoes much more plentiful, than on the Araguaya. But these small tongues of silver sand, their shores overshadowed by the jungle on the opposite bank, had the charm of the miniature. We did not regret the vaster, more commodious deserts of the big river. We had exchanged a full-dress beach for an unsuspected cove. It made us feel exclusive.

One praia in particular I remember. It was late, and my canoe was leading. On the pale, exiguous promontory before us three jacú stalked with the pompous uncertainty of the farmyard. A big black duck, a pato, outlined against the yellowing sky on a whithered branch, drew ineffectual fire from the .22 and fled away, croaking. Some pigeons were drinking at the water's edge, and a family of little wise-faced monkeys made disproportionate upheavals in the overhanging greenery. An alligator cruised out slowly towards the opposite bank. It was almost too representative, too composite a scene; such packed grouping would have caused comment even in the glass cases of South Kensington. I felt very alien as I landed on a beach strewn with *jatobá* nuts, of which we subsequently made a dish as nauseous as any I have ever tasted.

Alligators were more plentiful and more unsuspecting than ever. Every hour or so there would be a burst of fire and a jubilant shout of 'Matou!' from one or other of the canoes. Then the whole convoy would utter a wailing and ironic cry of 'Viva o Brasil!' in tones of burlesque enthusiasm. This was one of the expeditionary jokes, and never failed to please the men. We would go on our way, leaving a livid upturned belly to swell and desecrate the beautiful, unholy aisle: and, incidentally, to offend the nostrils of the missionary, whom we had passed on the second day.

He was sitting outside a neat little green tent when we passed him. It was a long time since we had seen anything so spick and span as that tent. We wondered what had held him up, for it was the middle of the morning, and we had been going for a good three hours. We exchanged greetings, and he came down to the water's edge and told me how his men had found 'a huge tortoise in the forest': how they had tied it up, but omitted to turn it over on its back: and how in the night the provoking creature had dragged its moorings and returned to the forest. But he gave no hint of what was delaying him, and it was not until afterwards that we learnt that he had stopped because he would not allow his men to paddle on Sunday. Sunday! We had forgotten all about it. To stumble on it suddenly in the middle of that uncalendared wilderness, and to find, moreover, that its existence could discipline this bright unruly life was as surprising as if we had discovered a degree of latitude embodied in a high brick wall. In waste places time is also waste; and a notice bidding us Keep Off the Grass would not have seemed more incongruous than this heroically irrelevant homage to a seventh day. We went on upstream, marvelling. The missionary, tortoise-bereft, sat down once more before his little tent.

It was on the Tapirapé that we first made the acquaintance of the *arrayas*. These are a kind of freshwater sting-ray. There appeared to be two sorts. One was dun-coloured, with a long tail, and this was the more dangerous of the two, being difficult to see and thus easily trodden on as it lay in the sand. The other was of a blackish colour, with large pale spots, and had a short, rather stubby tail. You could see them everywhere, gliding along close to the river bed, and they aroused in the men something of the animus which jays arouse in a keeper. The canoe's stability was imperilled, and its progress arrested, while bow lunged at them vindictively with the pole. About one stab in three was successful, and the creature would be held aloft transfixed, a nasty, flapping trophy.

The arrayas looked excessively malignant, and to some extent they deserved their very evil reputation; for the long jagged sting in their tail (which the Indians sometimes use as barbs for their arrows) can do you serious hurt. But it only required circumspection in getting out of the canoe, and vigilance in wading, to avoid them. When, as sometimes happened, they came for your legs, they did so, in my opinion, by mistake; what if you were romantically minded you took to be a charge was in reality a misdirected flight. And whichever it was it was easily avoided, as long as the water was clear and you could see what you were doing. One day, when Neville and I were towing the canoe over a patch of shallows, a very big arraya, jabbed by our pole, came downstream so fast that Neville had not time to sidestep; but he jumped instead, and it shot harmlessly underneath him. None of us ever got stung.

To these long days beneath the wheeling sun urgency lent an added interest. It is rarely that the mere fact of being in a hurry fails to increase one's self-importance; as we struggled slowly through that wide and faintly contemptuous desolation we as it were buried our heads in our haste and overlooked our own insignificance. Like a bee in a cathedral, the expedition fussed along and kept awe at bay with a buzz. We had seen so much time wasted in Brazil that now we fell in a kind of fury on the flanks of delay, whenever these were exposed. Not that they were exposed very often, or to any great depth. A more than usually flying start might save ten minutes when we broke camp at dawn. The cook might pare off a fraction of our two-hour stop at noon. We might make an extra league or so by camping late. Perhaps despatch gained for us half a day in six.

Of course it was not really worth gaining; it made no difference in the end. But at the time, as I have tried to explain, it gave a tang to life. All round us were hundreds and hundreds of square miles of country on which the march of centuries had left no trace. Since the dawn of time (whenever that was) this patch of the earth's crust had been green and empty; it was green and empty still. Aeons had passed there, unregarded. And now here were we, stealing minutes under the nose of eternity, gleefully counting our petty swag in a place where a century was hardly legal tender. In all this there was a comforting sense of the ridiculous.

On the second day we passed a place called Porto Velho, the Old Port. There was nothing there but an empty clearing on the river bank. Formerly the Tapirapés had had a village a little way inland, and this landing-place had been a kind of market where the Carajas came to barter. But relations between the two tribes had grown strained: there had been war, which I expect meant an irregular series of small-scale massacres by both sides; and now for many years Porto Velho and the village in the jungle behind it had been deserted. The Tapirapés had moved to the headwaters.

On the fourth day we came to another place which had a name and nothing else. This was São João, a sharp bend in the river where a long stretch of open campo came right down to the bank, without the customary intervening belt of jungle. Roger and Neville and I landed and, scrambling up a steep bluff, saw from the top of the bank two isolated hills rising out of the blue and shimmering haze about fifty miles to the northward. It was a good moment. Chico explained that the first village of the Tapirapés lay below the shoulder of the eastern hill; their second village was thirty miles beyond it. He himself had never visited the second village, and he did not know of any white man who had.

Here at last was something which could for the moment be called an objective, and we were duly elated by the sight of it. Our plans were as follows:

At the port (São Domingo), which we were due to reach the next day, the expedition was going to divide forces. We did not expect to find any Indians at the port (which, as I have explained, is simply a landing-place, visited from time to time from some permanent habitation situated in security far inland); so Roger, Neville, Queiroz, Chico, and I, with provisions for four days, were going to make a forced march from the port to the village, a distance of about thirty miles. In the village we would see what could be done about getting food and guides for a journey (based on the port) south-west toward the Kuluene. Meanwhile Bob and the two others, with the biggest canoe and the three remaining men, would push on as far as they could by water up the Tapirapé, continuing the rough map which Roger had made of its course as far as São Domingo. Both parties were to operate independently, though we hoped to establish some sort of contact with the river contingent before we started across country from the port.

# CHAPTER III

# ANOTHER TRIBE

In the middle of a still, hot morning, exactly five days after leaving our camp at the mouth of the Tapirapé, the leading canoe sighted São Domingo. Not that there was much to sight. The river here was at its most sluggish. Its northern bank was unusually steep, unusually muddy, and unusually bare. The trees had been thinned, unevenly, along a front of about three hundred yards. We climbed the bank by a rough man-made track and found ourselves in the first of an inconsequent series of little clearings.

The biggest of them unmistakably bore the mark of the white man. A large thatched shelter, fifty feet long by twenty broad, with a wall at one end, stood in the centre of a bare place studded with the stumps of trees. You could see that steel had been used here against the jungle, and also a certain method. From the shelter a flight of steps cut in the bank led steeply down to the river. Chico told us that the shelter had been put up by the Dominican Friars from Conceição do Araguaya; the Tapirapés liked the Dominicans, who had been very good to them and visited them every year. He said that he himself had had a hand in building the shelter.

It was strange to find so many traces of man and yet to see no one. In the smaller clearings there were the ashes of old fires, and broken calabashes, and the forked stakes from which cooking pots had hung, and the remains of frames for stretching skins. It seemed somehow unfair that the people who had made all this reassuring litter should be so tantalizingly absent. It was as if one had gone into a library and found it empty save for publishers' catalogues and the dust-wrappers of books. I found myself involuntarily standing still and listening for a footstep, a cry, the splash of paddles.

There was a good deal to do. We unloaded the canoes and went rapidly through the supplies, dividing them in two. We had more than half the day before us, and my party, the land-party, aimed at reaching before nightfall a point on the trail leading to the village where there was said to be water. I arranged with Bob to meet him at the port in six days' time. If either party failed at the rendezvous, the other was to go and look for them.

By two o'clock everything was ready and we had had a meal. The land-party supported with precarious nonchalance its very considerable burdens; food for four days, firearms, ammunition, cameras, and presents for the Indians made loads whose drag on our shoulders was heavier and more insistent than we liked. (Within a week, as you shall hear, two of us were to look back on those first loads as the merest bagatelles.)

In the popular imagination explorers are always saying good-bye to each other. It would indeed be pardonable to suppose that the first, if not the only function of a Base Camp is to provide a convenient and conventional setting for farewell scenes. How often (in imagination) have we taken part in them: wringing hands, exchanging gruff facetiae, turning abruptly on our heels, and at last, in spite of the lump in our throats, raising that ragged, that inevitably ragged cheer as the little party files out across the sand, or through the snow, or into the adjectival luxuriance of the jungle. The partings of explorers are sweet sorrow for the reading public.

I am happy to say that in this respect, if in no other, our expedition was meticulously loyal to the best traditions. Within the space of a single week we staged no less than three farewell scenes, in two of which there was at least a strong possibility that neither of the parties concerned would ever see each other again. I am bound to admit that the first two succeeded each other with a rapidity which seems, in retrospect, a trifle inartistic. One lump in the throat would really have done for both of them; had we only known, it was hardly worth allowing it to subside.

But naturally we could not know. So there was only self-consciousness, and the clammy, enervating shadow of literary and dramatic precedent, to temper the fervour with which we wished each other good luck and to stress, in our laconic valedictions, the facetious at the expense of the manly. Grinning in a rather shamefaced way, the land-party strode off at a brisk pace along a narrow winding path which led northward from the clearing.

I cannot say how long the pace would have remained brisk, for it was a very hot day and we were loaded neither lightly nor scientifically. The village was thirty miles away; and thirty miles (we began to reflect before we had covered one of them) was after all quite a long way. But before we had covered the second something happened which made it no longer necessary for us to go to the village.

We had left the jungle which cloaked the banks of the river. The path — a smooth, thin, wavering track worn by bare feet in single file — wound through the campo towards those dim and distant hills which we had first seen from the river on the day before. The country was open; but open with a bad grace. You could not see far. It gave you the feeling that you were crossing an empty illimitable plain, but it would not let your eyes confirm this feeling. The tall sere grass stood up all round you, pricked with ant-hills, rugged blue-grey stalagmites. And although you could see over the top of the grass, the little twisted trees — sometimes singly, sometimes in assertive clumps, bodyguard to a group of palms — cheated and blocked your view. Vistas kept on opening, but they closed always within half a mile. It was specious but deceptive country. It kept your imagination on tiptoe, your curiosities aching.

We had been going for about an hour. Suddenly a thin, curious, and wavering cry came out of the scrub in front of us.

We stopped, everything was jigging in the heat. Again the cry rose and fell, a twisted thread plucked out of the sleeve of silence, a tentative assertion in that negative noon. It died, leaving no echoes, but only, in the dancing waves of heat, a kind of soundless mimicry of its quavers, the empty shadow of a noise.

Queiroz answered with an imitation. We realized, as the unexpectedness wore off, that the Carajas had greeted each other with something very like this cry. Roger yodelled; and at that moment four Indians came into sight, trotting down the path towards us. They were Tapirapés.

We made amicable and expansive gestures with our arms. We grinned. We put on every semblance of delight, 'Ticantó' we cried. We had been told it was the thing to say. 'Ticantó' we cried with desperate geniality; wondering what it meant.

The four naked brown figures came on. We could see that they were smiling. They raised their hands above their heads in a shy salute, quickly repealed, like little boys taking the part of soldiers in a speech day production of *Macbeth*. They had seen a few white men before, but not many. They also said 'Ticantó'. Their pronunciation was better than ours.

They were three men and a woman. They were smaller than the Carajas, and rather lighter in colour. They looked wiry and nimble, and they did not carry those broad, imposing chests which paddling develops in the purely river Indians. None of them wore any clothes, though one or two of the men had tied below their knees those woven fibre garters[1], dyed red, which denote — with them, as with the Carajas — the unmarried state. The woman had a square, rather embarrassed face. The men — though none of them conformed closely to the same type — had features less Mongolian, and rather more easily animated, than the Carajas.

[1] These garters, having been put on when the wearer was very young, are usually too tight. In the little clay dolls or images of the Indians (I could not discover which purpose they served) the swellings which result are reproduced as a normal anatomical feature.

There was no doubt about their friendliness. They were not shy — had not even that silly bashfulness which was always supplanting the dignified reserve of the Carajas. They patted our bodies with caressing little gestures which seemed always to be uncertain and only half finished and yet were clearly a formality as complete in itself and as well-established as shaking hands. 'Ticantó' they murmured happily, beaming up at us. We answered 'Ticantó', and patted them diffidently on the back.

Conversation, of a groping and fragmentary kind, then took place. With the help of Queiroz's few words of Caraja, Chico's still fewer words of Tapirapé, some pidgin Portuguese, and a good deal of dumb-show, we acquired some valuable information. The whole tribe, it appeared, was on its way down to the river, with most of the women and children. Water was short in the village; they were going to spend several days at the port, fishing.

We adjourned to the scanty shade of one of the twisted trees and sat down in the grass, studying each other with interest. These Indians, like the Carajas, wore their hair in a ragged mop; it made a wild frame for wild faces. The three men carried bows and bundles of long thin arrows, gaily feathered and tipped with bone or with the serrated stings of arrayas. They carried also fibre hammocks, slung in brown, greasy rolls over their shoulders, and clubs, and cooking pots, and small (from our point of view ominously small) bundles of mandioca.

They had come a long way and their gourds were empty. We unhitched our two water bottles and passed them round, wresting them by force from anyone whose attitude was too blatantly opposite to Sir Philip Sidney's. We also gave them hunks of rapadura, which they ate wolfishly. We no longer needed the water, for there was now no point in continuing our journey to the village. Presently we all got up and went back to the port along the way we had come, chanting almost continuously 'Ticantó' and grinning foolishly at each other. One of the Indians gave me a bit of mandioca, which I thought was very nice of him. I ate it as we walked along, remembering only afterwards that in its raw state it is supposed (wrongly, I presume) to be poisonous.

By sunset São Domingo had much more to boast of than a name, the marks of axes, and an air of expectancy. In the history of that forlorn place there can have been few days richer in incident than this one was.

We had left it at two o'clock, and the other party had disappeared upstream shortly afterwards. By four we were back, and with us the advance guard of the Tapirapés, who scattered into the fringes of the jungle to sling their hammocks and to light economical little fires. We established ourself firmly in the Dominicans' hut.

The Tapirapés arrived in driblets. Every few minutes an indeterminate little party of men carrying bows and clubs would thread its way through the sparse trees at the edge of the clearing, greeting each plume of smoke with a vague little cry of pleasure. The clearings filled up steadily.

Presently a canoe was hailed. We had forgotten all about the missionary. Every one hurried to the bank. His canoe had just turned into the straight and was coming along nicely, the paddles flashing as they dipped, the men uttering cheerful and humorous shouts. The Tapirapés grinned and gave their quavering cry and chattered to each other with an air of mischief, watching us all the time out of the corners of their eyes, so that we felt like grown-ups at a children's party. Roger yodelled; it was becoming a vice with him.

Suddenly another canoe swung round the bend in the river and came into sight behind the missionary's. That was a bad moment for me. I had visions of Major Pingle's broad, sarcastic smile: saw him puffing complacently up the steps from the water's edge: heard his thick voice announce that he had come to join the picnic after all. If he was in that second canoe, we were in for what they call a Jungle Drama; the *Wide World Magazine* would have to look to its laurels.

I strained my eyes and Roger strained his. We were both fully prepared for the worst. The wide hat, the black torso of the pilot in the second canoe were horribly suggestive of José Tiburce, one of the men from the batalõas. The hunched figures amidships we could not yet identify; but they were not Indians.

The seconds dragged. The distant canoe crawled relentlessly towards us up the dark green ribbon of water. Gradually, cautiously, we put our fears aside. The pilot looked less and less like José; neither of the other figures resembled Major Pingle. At last we could be certain, and our hearts leapt up. Major Pingle was not in that canoe. His image in our minds grew blurred, receded, vanished. We hailed the missionary, as he glided in below us, with extravagant, with disproportionate delight.

We slung our hammocks in the hut and slept that night, for the first time for many weeks, under a roof. The Tapirapés visited us in relays, squatting on their hams in the dusk, gazing at us with humorous, friendly eyes, and smoking their stubby pipes with loud frantic sucking noises. We distributed *palmas* of black twist — a palma is a section measured across the width of your hand — but had to refuse them food, which we could not afford to give away. We let it be understood that the important presents would be distributed in the morning; nothing could be done that night, for their two captains did not arrive till late. I should like to place it on record that one of the Indians, advancing with a shy smile, rubbed noses with me; I suppose he had been reading the *Wide World Magazine*.

The hut was pretty full. Some of the Indians had slung their hammocks under the eaves, and the occupants of the second canoe asked, and were given, our permission to sleep there too. They were a rather unaccountable but charming party of three Brazilians. The leader was a fragile old man with a serene but slightly bemused face and a little straggling beard like a goat's. He had with him a soft-voiced negro boy with a gigantic, a really alarmingly large head, and a tall thin Brazilian of about forty, who wore a huge floppy hat made of leather and was always leaving a fully charged muzzle-loader lying about. This man had a remarkable and attractive face. Light grey eyes, very bright and friendly, were set on either side of a pointed nose in a deeply tanned skin. He had a small, alert head, and his face was strongly and intricately seamed with lines and wrinkles, so that it looked like a knob of some excellent wood on which a carver with a humorous turn of mind had chosen to display his virtuosity. He was as far removed as possible from the traditional Latin American type. The broad shoulders, the swinging stride, the very dexterous hands, above all that odd and eager head, suggested reliability and enterprise. If he had been at all flamboyant, he would have corresponded exactly to my idea of Robin Hood.

They were a hunting party, after skins to trade. They had come up the Tapirapé to shoot the little deer which rumour said (rightly) were plentiful round São Domingo. They were quiet, sound people, and we liked them. They listened gravely and without surprise to my story of three white men who had disappeared seven years ago in the jungle 150 miles to the south-west. They agreed that our chances of getting much nearer to the Kuluene were very slender; but they appeared to find it entirely natural that we should be on this quest.

The missionary too was a nice young man. Professional (or should it be vocational?) etiquette forbade him to make use of the Dominicans' hut, and he camped in one of the little clearings. But he visited us, and spoke with feeling of Tunbridge Wells, where his home was, and fell out of my hammock backwards, to the delight of the Indians. (He was a man peculiarly vulnerable to the force of gravity. A few days later he fell down the steep bank into the river and cut his head badly.) He said he was going into the village on a flying visit. He was as new to the country as we were, and could tell us little about the Indians. But he spoke with some bitterness of evangelistic claim-jumping, and of the base tricks employed by the rival missions in the race for converts. It seemed (as one of us afterwards remarked) that bible-punching was a bit of a racket.

We had already a great liking for the Tapirapés, and they, who were warm-hearted and uncritical, seemed to have no difficulty in tolerating us. They watched all our actions with interest, appearing to find them unaccountable and rather foolish. But they were genuinely impressed and delighted when Neville killed a big jacaré out in midstream with the Mann-licher. It was a very good shot. The beast came drifting quietly down the river, with only his eyes and snout showing. Neville got him at eighty yards, first shot. 'Ticantó' screamed the Indians, hopping up and down with pleasure when they saw the white belly turn slowly uppermost in the bloody water, one broad claw making impotent, aimless gestures in the air. After that we were a better joke than ever.

They had, I think, a keen sense of the ridiculous. Certainly they were a very merry people, and their humour was better than the Carajas'. Both tribes had a certain quality of remoteness in their natures; both had a stake in some world which we could never know. But there was something forlorn and un-happy about the Carajas. Their roots had been partly torn up; they were flustered and dazzled by the proximity of the white man's boundaries, and thus neglected the virtues of their own world. They forgot that they were alien, and felt merely out-cast. Their remoteness was the hesitant, rather miserable re-moteness of the oaf. The Tapirapés were more like elves, capriciously aloof, their native bliss unqualified by envy. They were curious, but not covetous. They came among us as spies operating from a base of self-sufficiency; not as gauche and wist-ful renegades.

Except for their slighter physique, their sharper, less bucolic faces, there was little about them markedly different from the Carajas. As with the latter, their limbs were sometimes pigmented in arbitrary, unambitious designs of black or red. There was one woman whose jowls were dyed blue. And there was a man from the more remote of their two villages (a place, we gathered, now almost entirely deserted) who had a few sparse hairs growing on his chin and upper lip. He wore a permanently sheepish look, for the tribe seemed to regard his beard as a joke, a comic kind of solecism. He moved among them with a guilty and apologetic air, like a man who has come to a dance without his evening dress. This was the only time I saw an Indian wearing hair anywhere but on his scalp. They either pluck it out or shave it off with slivers of bamboo.

Our relations were cordial but rather inarticulate. After an exchange of Ticantós the correct thing to do, we discovered, was to ask them their names. This you did by saying (rapidly and gruffly, to give it the authentic note of dialect) 'Comm' se cha'?': being a corruption of the Portuguese 'Como se chama?' At this their faces would light up, and they would rattle off an intricate and outlandish polysyllable, which (as is so often the case with the names of foreigners) you did not even attempt to remember. However, they seemed to appreciate your curiosity, and were quick to return it. 'Comm' se cha'? Comm' se cha'?' they would gibber, prodding your ribs in an encouraging way. 'Pedro' you replied, and both sides would go on repeating the name until the Indian got it right. The only other point to remember was that you ranked as a captain. 'Capitão?' they would ask, and you nodded, patting your chest and repeating with quiet pride, 'Sim. Capitão.' There were only two captains, or chiefs, in their tribe; so that if — as you claimed — you were one in yours you must be a person of some importance.

The exchange of names and ranks exhausted our vocabulary, but it did not, curiously enough, put a stop to conversation. It is true that our talk was not good talk. The rapier thrusts of repartee were absent from it. No well-turned phrases made it memorable. We could not even, I am sorry to say, command a main verb. Our choice of words was limited to one: Ticantó. Whatever it may have meant (and its meaning I never discovered) this word was a kind of talisman. It created an aura of goodwill. You had only to say Ticantó two or three times, and to smile with vague but overpowering affability, to envelop everything in a haze of bonhomie. It was much more than a civility; it was a vote of confidence in the universe. If every country put such a password to its affections at the disposal of visitors, international relations would be on a much better basis, travel would be more agreeable, and Berlitz would go bankrupt.

# CHAPTER IV

# SIGNS AND PORTENTS

EARLY the next morning Queiroz and I called most of the tribe together and distributed the presents. The Indians sat in a semicircle with the two captains on a log in the middle. The two captains were brothers, and their names were Camarião and Camaira: or as near as makes no difference. Camarião was the senior captain, and wore the tribe's only garment, a very dirty dark-brown shift, of unmistakably missionary origin. He had cropped hair and a smooth shifty face and little uncertain eyes, which were always evading yours, though whether from guile or from shyness you could not tell. The old captain had lately died, and Camarião, cloaked in a new power, was a little self-conscious and defiant, like a child with a toy which it is not certain how to work. His brother was naked like any commoner, and had a rascally look about him. But his face was open and his mind easy to read. He inspired more confidence than Camarião, though he was a less effective person.

We dispensed the riches of Woolworth's with an air of magnificence. Necklaces and mirrors and knives and forks, and some silly toys — little white horses which were supposed to draw a sort of bicycle bell on wheels: only of course the wheels wouldn't go round and the bell wouldn't ring. The Indians regarded these toys, very rightly, with a certain contempt, and we gave them only to the men with wives and families. Everything else they liked, though they seemed to take our generosity very much as a matter of course.

The presents were not quite enough to go round, but we eked them out with further doles of tobacco and oddments like empty tins and old pipe-stems. The beady-eyed, pot-bellied children got brass cartridge cases and lengths of black and red typewriter ribbon. Everyone behaved very nicely, and there were no signs of envy or dissatisfaction. Nor, to our relief, was there any of that importunate stretching out of hands, that petulant and unappeasable beggar's whine, which had always provided a background for our dealings with the Carajas. I never knew the Tapirapés either to beg or steal; they were unlearned in even the most rudimentary arts of civilized life. Belongings which in the purlieus of a Caraja village would have vanished as soon as one's back was turned could safely be left lying about at São Domingo.

When we had given out the presents we got down to business with the captains. Business was not easily transacted on a one-word vocabulary. We had first of all to explain our needs and to outline as much as was necessary of our plans. In other words, we had to tell them that we were going on a long journey towards the Kuluene (of which they had never heard) and that we wanted some of them to come with us as guides. We had also to try and find out what (if anything) they knew of the country we were going into.

Assuming, therefore, an air of confidence and enthusiasm which we had all too little reason to feel, we pointed repeatedly to the south-west and said 'Turi' (meaning ourselves, the white men) and 'Pé pé pé' (meaning that we were going to walk a tremendously long way). This did not go down very well. Their faces went deliberately blank. A certain apprehension flickered in the eyes which followed, obediently but without enthusiasm, our pointing arms towards the south-west. They were afraid of that country. They remained, however, polite and attentive.

The word 'Pé', however often repeated, might suggest no more than a good long walk. We introduced the time-factor by pointing at the sun and sketching its progress across the sky with a sweep of one arm. At the end of every sweep we pillowed our heads on our hands and said 'Dorme'. They understood this all right; we had, as the statesmen say, Found a Formula. By pointing, and by saying in a brisk and reassuring way, 'Turi. Pé pé pé. Dorme. Dorme. Dorme', we successfully conveyed the idea that we were going to march for an indeterminate number of days towards the south-west. The problem now was to make them understand that we expected more of them than a purely academic interest in the scheme.

We began to introduce the name of the tribe into the rigmarole. 'Tapirapé pé pé pé,' we said in wheedling tones. 'Tapirapé dorme.' We patted everyone within reach on the back. 'Ticantó,' we said emphatically, meaning that on this jaunt a good time would be had by all. Finally we produced and dangled before their eyes three large new facões, several fathoms of tobacco, and a blue pyjama jacket belonging to Roger; there was a suggestion that the old and useless .44 rifle might be thrown in too. The captains, whose eyes were glistening, withdrew to consider our proposition.

We had their decision within the hour. They themselves, the two captains, would come with us if we would add a pair of trousers to the wages already offered. This, happily, we were in a position to do. The bargain was concluded.

From the first I doubted both their will and their ability to earn those wages. It was impossible in the circumstances to define the terms of our contract with them very exactly; the semaphored protestations of both sides lent themselves to elastic interpretation. But the understanding was that the captains would accompany, if not lead us, on a journey of many days towards another river, and would receive their presents on our return to São Domingo. When pressed, they showed some signs of having heard of the existence of this river, or at any rate of some river lying in a south-westerly direction. But this appeared to be the sum of their local knowledge; neither they nor any of the tribe, when questioned about the country through which we should have to pass, betrayed anything except ignorance and fear. It looked to me as if the captains were relying entirely on luck to see them through a journey which they had every reason to suppose impossible and which they had undertaken only in the hope of gain. But these suspicions were not important at the time. What mattered was that we were going to be able to start. We were within 150 miles of the place where Fawcett died, and we were not going to be forced to turn back without proving to our own satisfaction that it was impossible to get there in the time, and with the resources at our disposal. Even in my most sanguine moments I had virtually no hope of success; but an honourable failure was within our grasp, and would be staged in country which no white man had ever entered before. The prospect was a stimulating one. We decided to start the next day, at dawn.

There was a lot, there was really too much to do. I left Queiroz to deal with the supplies, which in truth presented no very difficult problem, since it was merely a question of estimating how much farinha and rapadura we could carry in addition to our few, our lamentably few, tins of things like biscuits and Quaker Oats. All through this period of the expedition's history Queiroz worked splendidly; he got on very well with the Tapirapés, who were flattered by his thirst for information.

I sat down in a hammock and wrote a letter to Major Pingle, which Roger and Neville also signed, formally resigning from the expedition. I had warned him at the mouth of the river that, if the first stage of the journey towards the Kuluene did after all prove possible, we meant to have a shot at it. In this letter I told him that the opportunity of getting at any rate a certain distance across country had presented itself: that we were going to take it, since this was what we had come out from England to do; and that, although we fully expected to have to turn back within a few days, it was on the cards that we should be away for some time. It would in the circumstances be unwarrantable to involve the main body of the expedition in the expense and delay which would be incurred by waiting for our return; so we were resigning. The letter contained no hint that Major Pingle had failed to abide by his undertakings to us. In addition to our resignation, I enclosed a further statement absolving Major Pingle from all responsibility for our safety and a letter to the same effect to the British Consul at Pará, of which Major Pingle could make what use he chose. In both these documents it was made clear that we were taking a step, from which Major Pingle had done his best to dissuade us, at a time when we were out of his control. I added that the other members of the expedition were aware of, and approved, our intentions, and were being informed that we were carrying them out. In conclusion I asked that the money for our passages from Pará to London (to which our contract with Major Pingle entitled us) should be left at the Mission Station on Bananal. I should add that our considerate attitude was dictated less by the desire to save Major Pingle's face than by an anxiety to make sure of our passage-money.

Technically, of course, our resignations had to be accepted before they became valid. But then, technically, the leader of an expedition is supposed to accompany it to the scene of its operations; we had not a fortnight's food to waste on waiting for an answer from Major Pingle. My letter (which was polite, though not cordial, in tone and only very faintly flavoured with irony) was designed to cover him in case of the disaster which he had so confidently predicted; if all or some of us got killed my letter would effectually clear him from all blame. We were, it is true, letting him in for a certain amount of anxiety; but he had only himself to thank for that. It was with a clear conscience that I wrote a second letter to Bob, telling him that we were now taking the step of which he had been forewarned and explaining, as I had explained to Major Pingle, that though we should probably be back within a few days it was conceivable that we should be away for some time. I sent Chico upstream after the river party with this letter.

He was back within four hours. Half a mile upstream of São

Domingo the river-party had turned up a tributary (not marked on any map) which forks south-west, leaving the Tapirapé to curl north, and then north-east, in the unexpected semicircle which you can see on the map on p. 253. (It probably rises somewhere to the north of those two hills which we could see from São Domingo.) Chico came up with them not very far from the fork, at a point where fallen trees made the channel quite impassable, and at a moment when they had just decided to return to the port before renewing their attack on the Tapirapé itself. He delivered my letter, and brought back their wishes for our success. He said that it was quite possible that they would be back at São Domingo that night.

They were. That evening there was a short but violent thunderstorm; it was a wet and battered party which disembarked by torchlight an hour after sunset and came scrambling up to the crowded hut for food and shelter. Roger and Neville and I welcomed them, with the missionary — a cordial, unobtrusive presence — at our elbow. I well remember the stentorian and anachronous coughs, the sudden and eccentric interjections, with which we sought (vainly) to divert the torrent of their oaths from his scandalized ears.

We were glad to see the others again. It gave me a chance to get them to confirm their blessing on our separation. In the dim and precious light of a torch, among curved hammocks packed as closely as a set of ribs, I read them my letter to Major Pingle. They agreed that all I said in it was sensible and right; and they agreed further that, if things went well for us and our journey lasted more than the expected two or three days, it would be not only unnecessary but useless for them to wait for us. They could not form a base camp at São Domingo, because there was no food; and there was no point in forming one on the Araguaya, because any useful purpose which it might serve would be served equally well by the Mission Station, a day's journey from the mouth of the Tapirapé. Our separation could hardly have been put on a more satisfactory basis.

There was no room left in the hut, so I lay down on the charred ground outside. It was past midnight. I finished a final despatch for *The Times*, winding up the expedition's official activities and noting in a guarded parenthesis that three members were staying behind for a few days 'to investigate the territory of the Tapirapés and the surrounding country'. I wrote one or two perfunctory letters of farewell, to be mailed from Pará with *The Times* despatch in the unlikely event of our not having caught the others up by the time they reached the Amazon. (This batch of mail had an eventful history, which you will hear in due course.) Eventually it seemed as if everything that could be done had been done, and I went through the process known to novelists of the last century as composing myself for slumber.

But it was not as easy to sleep as it ought to have been. It had been a hectic and — what with one thing and another — rather a melodramatic day. Now that it was over — now that everything had been done, contrary to expectation, against time — now that the heat had abated and the dust died down — I realized for the first time what it was that we were doing; I saw suddenly what the enterprise on which we were embarking would look like from a distance. I was unpleasantly surprised.

For weeks past the immediate future had held little for me beyond the journey on which we were to start in five hours' time. Life had recognized only one ambition — to attempt it: to attempt it and almost inevitably to fail: but in the failure to justify our enterprise and the part I played in it. The aim had become an obsession. The faculty of criticism, the power of detaching myself from my surroundings and seeing the whole comic business in perspective, had deserted me. I was like a monkey in a cage searching diligently for a flea; a plague, a war, an earthquake, an Act of Parliament might render the very existence of the Zoological Gardens precarious and nugatory; but the monkey, intent on his flea, would take no count of that.

When you came to think of it, there was a certain lofty insecurity about the position into which, by my letter of resignation, I had put the three of us. We were in the middle of one of the biggest countries in the world. None of us could speak its language with any approach to fluency. The journey from São Domingo to Pará, the nearest point at which we could hope to find friends and the amenities of civilized life, was estimated to take six weeks, barring accidents; throughout its last stages we should have to negotiate long stretches of more or less continuous rapids, which were said to be tricky and might well, in the present low state of the rivers, prove impassable. Our net capital in cash was the equivalent of two pounds; I put the chances of Major Pingle leaving our passage money at Bananal at evens (in this, as you shall hear, I was unduly optimistic). There was a strong possibility that the revolution had held up in São Paulo both our luggage and our letters to our banks at home instructing them to forward money to Pará. (This afterwards proved to have been the case.) In short, communications along our line of retreat might well have been better secured.

On our line of advance prospects were, if anything, less reassuring. We were on the borders of a vast stretch of entirely unknown country which has (though it only partly deserves) as bad a reputation as any in the world. This we were proposing to enter with a party of six, at least two of whom — the Indians — were obviously unreliable. None of us had any local knowledge or previous experience of cross-country work in this type of jungle. Our food would last us less than a week, unless we were able to supplement it with game; we knew nothing about the chances of getting water. We had only a very rough idea of our position on the surface of the earth, and no means of verifying it; our map (the best available at the time in London) had entirely apocryphal ideas about the Tapirapé, and although Roger's compass traverse enabled us to readjust these to a certain extent, the sum of our relevant geographical knowledge boiled down to the pious hope that if we marched about 150 miles south-west we should hit the Kuluene. What we should hit en route we could only guess.

It was obvious that we could not hope to cover more than a fraction of those 150 miles without guides or food. Neither of these the Tapirapés could supply. So our only hope — indeed the only excuse for setting out at all — lay in our chance of getting in touch with the next tribe of Indians, whoever and wherever they might be. All the Indians in this area were supposed to be hostile; but since no one had ever been there their bad name presumably rested on hearsay and conjecture. I felt pretty sure that it would be possible, if not to establish friendly relations, at any rate to avoid hostilities with any we might meet (excepting, perhaps, the Chavantes, the north-west corner of whose territory I suspected of being unpleasantly close). I reasoned (theorising rather pompously to myself in the darkness) that there were only three sets of circumstances in which we might find ourselves in serious danger from the Indians: (a) at night, (b) if we made fools of ourselves and annoyed them, and (c) if the party got weakened by privation or retarded by someone going lame. If (c) had not happened to Fawcett's expedition I doubt whether the Indians would have attacked him: though that is not to say that he would have come out alive.

But it was sufficiently apparent that we were going to do a foolish thing. We were going to do very much what Fawcett himself had done — enter at hazard, and hopelessly under-equipped, a stretch of country about which nothing at all was known by anyone. We were entering it from the opposite side — were going back, in other words, along what was probably his projected route. He had for his objective lost cities and treasures to the existence of which only legend, and one uncon-firmed report in the eighteenth century, bore testimony. We were looking for traces of three men who were supposed to have disappeared somewhere in this region seven years ago, and of whom it was idle to suppose that many tangible relics still remained. It had now become necessary to take this quest seriously; which I found difficult.

Lying there, waiting for sleep, I decided that from now on we should have to soft-pedal the fantastic and behave, within the limits of our scatter-brained scheme, with extreme circumspection. In the last analysis, of course, practically everything depended on luck; but officially we should have to ignore this factor. I was alive to the possibility of disaster; but I was betting on complete fiasco. Within a few hours of starting, I thought, those Indians will have turned out to be so silly, or the going so bad, that we shall have to come back with our tails between our legs and go downstream to Major Pingle with the others. But if we could only dodge fiasco we were certain to have an amusing time, though we had not the remotest chance of doing any good.

A little puff of wind passed across the clearing, and in the jungle a swift pattering tattoo of drips from the trees lodged a mild protest. I remembered the thunderstorm of that evening. There lay our one really grave danger: the rains. It was now the third week in August. The rains, which normally break in October, were expected in this unusually dry year a month early. If we were caught in them, without so much as a blanket, far less a change of clothes, we were done for. Life in the jungle, thus far absurdly, unexpectedly healthy, would be a very different affair in the rains. Once they began we had not a hope of escaping fever. I was afraid that the thunderstorm heralded their coming. It was the first rain we had had so far. Still, one never knew; and there was nothing to be done about it. It would do no harm, in any case, to start.

I fell asleep, to dream that, in the office of that august weekly journal from which it was now certain that I should outstay my leave, I was commissioning Miss Ethel M. Dell (who wore, I noticed, a beard) to write an obituary of Major Pingle. I said that I was authorized to offer her a pyjama jacket and two metres of tobacco: not more. 'Not more. Not more,' I kept on repeating, until she took offence and changed into the Headmaster of Eton. . . .

CHAPTER V

# FORLORN HOPE

THE days that now followed were the best I have ever known. We got off two hours after sunrise, after a farewell scene rendered pleasantly ludicrous by its redundancy. We left Chico to go straight downstream with Major Pingle's letter; the belongings and supplies which we could not carry with us were to await our return in a cache at São Domingo. Our loads were heavier than they had been for our journey to the village; but the two captains, who showed none of that inclination to stand on their dignity which I had been afraid of, shouldered the bulkiest sacks of food. I lent my topee to Camarião, who looked extremely odd in it. So far it had been used for almost every purpose save that for which it had been intended, and I took it for largely psychological reasons; feeling that there might be moments in the near future when it would be comforting to be reminded that one was, after all, an explorer. Nothing does this so well as a topee.

We started off up the path to the village, clanking rather impressively on account of the knives and firearms and cooking utensils with which we were festooned. About a mile from the port we turned west, and thereafter for two hours marched at a spanking pace over campo on which the grass had recently been burned. Our guides brought up the rear. When we indicated to them that we should be glad if they would lead the way, they excused themselves with amiable smiles and little nods and, when necessary, by the effective process of stopping altogether and waiting until we went on ahead. But they seemed quite happy about the direction in which we were going, so we assumed that there was nothing radically wrong with it.

It was a lovely day. The air was cool after the rain of the

203

night before, and there was a little breeze blowing. We had a tingling sense of anticipation. Roger and I carried on an elaborate and foolish conversation based on the assumption that we were both guests in the same house and now on our way up to the butts for the first drive on the Twelfth. A flight of brown birds with yellow tails flew along beside us, from one clump of trees to the next; their cry was like a fieldfare's. We saw several of the little deer, the veados; their numbers and their tameness boded well.

Often, when I try to remember a day's stalking, or any other day on which there was little to do save exert oneself steadily and in silence, I find the most important clue to its moods and events in some quite irrelevant string of words which ran for no reason through my head and became part of the rhythm of the day. It may be the chorus of a song which someone was playing on the gramophone after breakfast, or a headline in the paper at which one had time only to glance, or a sentence in the book one read the night before; or it may be a verse, or a speech from some once familiar play, which filters up unprompted from the depths of memory, a bubble which declines to burst.

All through this day, and the days that followed, I marched to two ghostly jingles of this kind. One was a bit out of a song:

'Oh, *I'm* quite happy, I'm glad to say.
I've never felt better since Pancake Day.'

The other was two lines from a play, either by Ford or by Webster, I could not be sure which:

'For she is like to something I remember
A great while since, a long, long time ago.'

They had come into my head the night before, and I could not get rid of them. They have nothing to do with the matter in hand, but for me no description of this harebrained journey would be complete without them. They are the ultimate background to those days; against them I can see again the flickering heat-haze, the motionless gesticulating trees, feel the dank pressure of harness on my back, hear the wooden, scratchy shuffle of our feet on the baked earth.

After two hours we struck the Tapirapé again, on its northward curve above the fork. Here there was a lagoon and on it a place, a kind of miniature São Domingo, where the two captains gave us to understand their tribe came sometimes to fish. We made a fire and roasted — partially — a little of the venison we had brought with us and ate it and were off again within the hour. The Indians knew of a ford which we could never have discovered for ourselves, and we got across the river without much difficulty. I began to hope that I had underrated their potential value. A faint track of sorts led us through a half mile wide belt of jungle on the further bank; we emerged on to more campo.

Much more campo. The prospect before us was encouraging. Open country, dead flat and recently burnt, stretched as far as the eye could see. It was bounded by two diverging walls of jungle; the more northerly, the one at our backs, followed and cloaked the course of the Tapirapé; the other slanted away south-west, and presumably marked that new and unnamed tributary from which the others had turned back the day before. 'Agua?' we said, pointing to that solid-looking rampart of green. 'Aa-gua!' answered the captains, nodding vehemently and betraying, I thought, in their bland and ready smiles rather an innocent pleasure in giving the answer for which we clearly hoped than pride in the accuracy of their information. 'Aa-gua', they repeated, beaming.

It was at this point that we finally jettisoned the map. As a guide to the headwaters of the Tapirapé (and surrounding district) it was no more use than the Treaty of Versailles. It was not wildly inaccurate, but its margin of error varied insidiously, and one could never tell quite how far out it was. Every time we looked at it, it suggested new and tempting theories with regard to our whereabouts. It was much better to abandon it altogether and start our own geographical hares.

For the rest of that day the going was very good. Unburnt campo is heavy stuff to walk through, because the grass is long and thick and grows in tufts of which the base makes a fairly solid protuberance on the surface of the ground. But when it has been newly burnt, as this had, walking is almost as easy as on a road. We kept up a terrific pace. 'Bolivia in a fortnight' was the slogan issued for use on the march.

We travelled on a series of compass bearings, taken on the tops of isolated trees. The compass did not have the success it deserved. I made one half-hearted attempt to create an atmosphere of mumbo jumbo round it, for the benefit of the Indians; but they only sniggered politely when I pushed it under their noses and set and released the swinging needle. It was too far beyond their comprehension to impress them. You might as well expect a child who has just learnt to read to reverence the talents of Henry James. Queiroz, too, displayed in his attitude towards this invaluable instrument impatience and a certain scepticism. He claimed to have 'uma bussola na cabeça,' a compass in his head. This may or may not have been metaphorically true; but we had not seen enough of his cross-country technique to rely on his bump of locality.

As the day wore on, we kept on giving our course a bonus of a few points of south, for we dared not get too far from the wall of jungle on our left hand which (we sincerely hoped) concealed the unnamed river and which we should have to penetrate before dark.

It was a strange country to be in, charred and desolate like the crust of some other planet. Smoke from the fires which had ravaged it, or from other fires near by, still thickened the air; you could smell it, but not see it. It made the sunlight dun and baleful. All along the naked black ground ant-hills stood up spikily, ash-grey cones two or three feet high. You broke them as you passed, to blaze a trail. A touch, a glancing blow of your hand as it swung beside you, was enough to behead them. The cone — so dour, so permanent in appearance — toppled in two with an ease which startled you at first. You felt that it had all been arranged in advance; there was trickery in it. It was like a stage property in a pantomime — the brick wall through which the comedian drives his little car, the couch so prompt to disintegrate beneath the dame. In the real world things were not so obsequiously brittle.

The swart little trees had a blasted look, though in reality the fire had hardly harmed them. The breeze had dropped, and the leaves on them were quite still. Those awkward, agonizing branches, those still, still leaves, gave the trees an air of rigidity, the aftermath of horror. The whole empty and unreal expanse was pervaded by a sense of outrage. There were no birds.

Soon after we struck out from the jungle I saw smoke a long way to the northward, too far off our course to be worth investigating. It was smoke from a signal fire, rising in a slim perpendicular column to an extraordinary height: not the diffuse and rolling smoke which marks burning scrub, and from which nothing can be deduced save that the fire was lit within the last three days, and not more than ten miles away. Round the base of that tall stiff smudge Indians were standing while we watched it: from time to time throwing green stuff on the fire with an air of deliberation, searching with abstracted eyes in the hot blue sky for an answering finger of smoke. The thin grey perpendicular on our northward horizon had vivid implications.

Camarião was beside me. 'Tapirapé?' I asked him, pointing to the smoke. He had not seen it before; and now, I think, it was not a welcome sight. He shook his head, smiling only with his lips. He would answer no questions about it. He seemed glad when the southerly tendencies in our course became more pronounced.

There were few incidents in that day's march. The country had a sameness about it which seemed oddly deliberate. It was not the inherent sameness, the obligatory monotony, of the desert. There were plenty of niches for landmarks. Each island of tall, overbearing trees: each sudden wide patch of bare black ground, sparsely flecked with grass-blades only a few days old: each ant-hill which was outsized and grotesque: each shallow pockmarked depression which had held water in last season's rains: — of each of these one said 'At least I shall remember that': and each was duplicated within the hour. That plateau was like the criminal in a case where all the suspects have identical finger-prints: like the Missing Heir in a third act where everyone is leprous with strawberry-marks. I reflected that — compass in the head or no compass in the head — one could get lost there very easily.

About four o'clock (it got dark at six) we sighted a veado feeding a little way ahead; it was the first we had seen for some time. We needed meat; and the later in the day we got it the better, for there is no point in carrying your dinner further than you must. So we sat down under a clump of palms and drank a little of the by now very nearly boiling water in our two water-bottles, while Neville and Camaira went after the deer. They got it, and returned with a ragged, reassuring haunch.

It was by now apparent that we had not much time to lose if we wanted to camp on the unnamed river (and there was no other water available). It was equally apparent that the Indians were out of their depth. Their belief in the existence of a river behind that wall of jungle was on the wane; in its expression there was a lack both of confidence and unanimity. Their attitude to the whole enterprise had begun to display a marked coldness. The ability to help they had never shown; now the will to please had left them. Enthusiasm had given place to tolerance, tolerance to indifference, and indifference was now being superseded by disgust. They were tired; they were to all intents and purposes lost: they were afraid; and they showed signs of going lame. Camarião complained of a pain in his neck, so we gave him three Genasprin tablets, first taking some ourselves to increase his confidence in this somewhat misapplied remedy.

We decided to make straight for the jungle and cut our way in to the river. But would the river be there? 'Agua?' we asked the Indians, looking at them in a stern and disapproving way. 'Aa-gua,' replied Camaira sullenly; but it was an echo, not a confirmation. As for his brother, he set about founding a new school of thought. 'Não tem,' he said with conviction: 'agua não tem.' He turned and pointed back along the way he had come. 'Ahi agua,' he said rather obviously. 'Ahi agua.' His face became animated at the thought of returning.

It was not an authoritive denial, for neither of these men had been as far as this before; we were outside Tapirapé territory. But it was perfectly plausible. All we could see was a wall of trees. We had been assuming that what lay behind it was a comparatively narrow strip of jungle with a river running down the middle of it — a replica of the strip through which we had passed that morning when we crossed the Tapirapé. But this assumption was based on nothing more than a guess and a wish. For all we knew, there was a solid patch of jungle, hundreds of miles square, behind those trees. There was no high ground, and none of the trees which we could climb were tall enough to give us a view over that enigmatic wall of green. We had to trust to luck.

We headed for the jungle. It was getting late. In all our minds there was the comfortless suspicion that we should have to spend the night without water and turn back the next day. As we came in under that towering wall of vegetation the suspicion died and hope sprang up. In this rich green place, we thought, water would easily be found. We were wrong.

We were off the campo, barging through thick and thorny scrub on the fringes of the jungle. Sometimes we had to use our facões to cut a path, though on that first day we met no really dense stuff. The Indians were more miserable than ever: their tendency to lag behind became more and more pronounced.

The long thorns, which look brittle and innocuous, like pine-needles, entered their unprotected legs, and Camaira was going lame. I was afraid they would drop out of the picture altogether and head back to the campo with our sacks of food. I hung on their flank, urging them on with unconvincing cries of 'Ticantó' and broad but inapposite smiles. Their faces remained surly; but they stumbled along as best they could, wincing. Soon the trees closed over us.

Inside the jungle a dimness foreshadowed the all too imminent dusk. But for a little while the going was better. We came on the shallow bed of a dried up lagoon. There was a dark patch in the centre of the pale cracked mud, and round it fresh tracks of peccary. 'Agua' the Indians admitted, when pressed, in tentative, unhopeful voices. We cut a strong sharp stake. Camaira, gripping it with a professional air, began to probe the dark patch of mud with convulsive downward stabs. We watched, licking our lips.

There was something oddly reassuring in the sight of that naked brown figure bowing and straightening, bowing and straightening with an air of ritual, as he drove the stake into the mud. Here was someone who knew his way about, who had a trick or two to beat this bullying wilderness. The Indians were doing their stuff at last. This was their craft, their mystery. We watched with the interest and respect due to an expert. We watched with a growing thirst.

Nothing happened. Between Camaira's feet a jagged hole grew steadily deeper. The head of the stake plunged in with a sodden thud, was withdrawn with a sucking noise, and remained bone dry. The mud was soft but firm, like cheese. There was no water there. Camaira threw the stake away. 'Agua não tem,' said his brother, in a mild, irritating voice. He spoke as one whose judgment had been thoroughly vindicated.

We had a vague feeling that we had been cheated, that they had no right to arouse our hopes by that rather impressive hocus pocus with the stake if they could not guarantee results.

Poor Indians! The prestige with which we had suddenly invested them fell away. Powerful allies a moment ago, they were reduced once more to the status of pathetic encumbrances. We went on, heading vaguely southwards into the jungle.

The going got steadily worse. The next half-hour was anxious, heart-breaking work. Then, suddenly, we found water: or perhaps it would be more accurate to say that we found liquid. The bed of one lagoon was not quite empty. Heavily overgrown, coated with nutritious-looking slime, and affording a popular rendezvous for the insect life of the neighbourhood, it was nevertheless a pool of water on which we had stumbled. That was a tremendous relief.

Uttering glad cries, the Indians, who were covered with blood and sweat, precipitated themselves into the Precious Fluid. As they wallowed blissfully, the surface of the scum was broken and a powerful smell arose. We filled our two cups with a fluid which suggested some rather far-fetched kind of soup and took a few cautious gulps of bacilli. Afterwards we ate some nondescript white tablets which we had with us. It had never been at all clear what medicinal purpose, if any, they were intended to serve; but they seemed to have a good all-round effect, of a largely psychological nature. At one time and another, and never with a complete lack of success, we used them as food: as a cure for intoxication: and as ground bait for fish. They were the one thing we had plenty of.

Of course we ought to have boiled the water; but there was not time for that. I did not mean, if we could possibly avoid it, to camp at that nauseating pool. Apart from the fact that it was a rotten place to camp, I did not want to halt for the night with the river still unlocated, and all our hopes and fears unverified. We should be terribly uncomfortable, both in mind and body, if we camped away from the river that night. Although everyone was pretty tired and would be still more tired if, as seemed likely, we had eventually to come back to the pool in falling darkness, it was doubtful whether we could end the day much worse off than we were already; and if we went on there was an outside chance of ending it in clover, on the river. So we went on.

After half an hour of frenzied hacking there was no evidence to show that we were any nearer that river whose existence in this jungle we were beginning more and more gravely to doubt. Night was almost on us, and the moment had come when we must turn and scramble back to the pool as best we could, before darkness obliterated our tracks.

Suddenly there was a yodel, a delirious yodel, from just ahead. 'Aa-gua!' roared Roger, in fierce and triumphant parody of the Indians. We plunged forward: went heads down through a thicket: and there was the river.

It was smaller than the Tapirapé. It ran briskly and with contentment along a winding channel between high, secretive banks. A little praia, humped, immaculate, and silver in the dying light, offered a perfect camping ground. We went crashing down towards it, uttering elemental cries of joy and tearing off our clothes.

Five minutes later I lay in the shallows, where the current ran chuckling over a spit of sand. I shall always remember that moment. It was full of a soaring, primitive delight. To lie there, and be washed, and let the clean cool water run into one's mouth: to reflect how awful things had seemed a moment ago, and how by rights, but for a slice of luck, they should still be seeming awful now: to shout 'Ticantó' to the foolish but forgiven Indians as they fetched wood for the fire: to taste the luxury of reprisals as one picked the ticks from one's skin: to lie there, and no longer to wade and duck through scrub and lose one's temper with lianas — no longer to feel the hostile, inescapable drag of one's pack — no longer to hoard one's energies and hide one's doubts — to be able to do all this, when all the odds had been against one's being able to do it, was a rich and unforgettable reward. This was true ecstasy.

We ate roast veado and some handfuls of farinha and lay down on the sand to sleep. It was at night that the disadvantages of travelling light (an indiscretion of which, during the day-time, you could not have accused us with impunity) revealed themselves. We had no mosquito-nets, no blankets, and no clothes to change into. It got very cold at night, and the clothes which we had been wearing all day, and which were tough rather than thick, were soaked in sweat. For the first time in Brazil the mosquitoes were really bad: or perhaps not really bad, by tropical standards, for they appeared to me to belong to an ineffectual and degenerate type, and their buzz was worse than their bite. But their buzz was enough to murder sleep. That sustained malicious ping, now advancing, now receding, was impossible to ignore. You could not learn to disregard it, as the older residents in station hotels learn to disregard the noise of trains; for even if in theory you preferred to sleep and be bitten rather than to watch and defend yourself, in practice your instincts would not let you do this. A little inferno of noise raged round your head; and that Healing Silence to which, in works (like this one) about the Great Open Spaces, some reference is almost bound to be made, was denied you as firmly as it would be in a first floor apartment in the Roaring Forties in New York.

Hard though the practised explorer may find it to believe, I was pleased with that first day's progress. We had made, as the crow flies, some fifteen miles towards that objective which we could not hope to reach. We had eluded, for the moment and by inches, complete fiasco. The going had proved easier than I had dared to hope, and the game seemed plentiful. We had got away to a flying start.

I received without surprise and without regret the news that the Indians would accompany us no further. In theory, it was madness to go on without them; but in practice they were a liability rather than an asset. They did not know the country. They were frightened. They showed signs of going lame. As guides, as interpreters, and as water-diviners they were useless to us. Only as trenchermen could they be relied on to pull their weight; they were *bouches inutiles*. On the other hand, their dereliction meant an awkward increase in our loads. Still, they were going home; and nothing could stop them.

The rest which we needed rather badly eluded us. Roger and I huddled over the fire and talked and ate Horlick's Malted Milk Tablets and did our best to decimate the mosquitoes. It got steadily colder, and in the small hours there was a little ominous shower of rain. The Indians suffered worse than we did. They buried their bodies in the sand for warmth and lay staring at the fire with melancholy glinting eyes. Once there was a petulant inconclusive roar in the jungle just over the bank. 'Jarú', they said, which was their word for jaguar. Camaira got up with a grunt and departed into the shadows, whirling a brand over his head; what he hoped, unarmed, to do I could not tell. Soon he came back and shook his head and smiled apologetically. In the end we slept fitfully for two hours.

# CHAPTER VI

# THEN THERE WERE THREE

THE beginning of the next day was straight out of the *Wide World Magazine.*

As soon as it was light I took the .22 and waded across the river, with a view to gauging the depth of the jungle on the opposite bank; it looked, at this point, as if there was campo not far off. In some trees at the water's edge I found a covey, gaggle, or what you will of jacú. (I do not know the right collective term for jacú. It ought, I think, to be a gristle.) Five of these enormous fowl, to our mutual surprise, I killed with the little rifle. We did not want to carry them with us all day; but they would do as a parting gift for the Indians. After a fruitless reconnaissance through an indeterminate mixture of scrub and jungle I returned to camp, where Neville had just killed a large whiskered fish, called a *barbado,* by the unorthodox method of shooting it with the Mannlicher as it cruised in the shallows.

We roasted a bit of this. Our only two packets of chocolate had melted on the march, so we whittled the nasty looking lump into a powder and made cocoa of a sort. The Indians, impenitent and indeed entirely unaware that they might be said to have failed us, chattered happily together; they were very glad to be going back.

We were almost ready to start. Roger was putting the finishing touches to his rough map of our erratic course. Neville was slowly pulling on his boots. I wondered why he was so long doing it. He had been very silent that morning. Suddenly he looked up; his face was unhappy.

'I'm afraid it's no good,' he said. He pointed to his feet.

I had been afraid of this. Three weeks ago, after a long day's shooting round the lagoons at Luiz Alvez, Neville had come in with his feet badly rubbed by a new pair of boots. It was impossible, travelling down the Araguaya, to keep one's feet dry, and a mild form of blood poisoning had set in. He claimed at São Domingo that the sores were safely healed; but yesterday's march had been too much for them, and when I looked I saw that his feet were in a very bad way indeed. He could not possibly come with us any further; and he would have a bad time getting back.

It was terribly hard luck on Neville; he was very keen to go on. But after discussion we agreed that there was nothing for it but that he should return to São Domingo with the Indians and join forces with the river party, who would be passing the port on their way downstream in a day or two. (They had intended to push up the Tapirapé as far as possible; but from what we had seen of the river when we crossed it on the day before, that would not be very far. Neville would almost certainly be in time to catch them; and if he missed them the missionary would give him a lift down to Bananal.)

That was the last and the least blatantly ridiculous of our farewell scenes. We gave the home-bound party all the food we could not hope to carry, and Neville generously left us such possessions of his own as might come in useful. He tried to make me take the Mannlicher, which was the only effective firearm we had with us; but this I would not do, knowing his affection for it, the impossibility of our keeping it in decent condition, and the slender chance he would have of ever seeing it again. We were already so fantastically ill-provided that it seemed hardly worth-while strengthening one branch of our equipment; I was loath to imperil the unity of that atmosphere of caricature which pervaded our enterprise and which I found congenial and comforting.

The Indians, cluttered with the corpses of jacú, scrambled with alacrity up the steep bank, keeping up a running fire of Ticantós. Neville said good-bye, the jaunty arara's feather in his topee belied by his wistful disappointed eyes. We wrote down on odd bits of paper each other's addresses — little echelons of words which seemed, here, to have not only no relevance but no meaning. We ate a last hunk of rapadura together; then he turned and limped after the Indians up the bank. As he halted on the edge of the jungle to wave farewell, he looked — as he always had looked — every inch the explorer. He left us feeling rather amateur.

As well we might. Within twenty-four hours the expedition had lost half its personnel. An inventory of our stores and effects revealed that we possessed, and would have to carry, the following aids to life in the jungle:

WEAPONS:

1 repeating rook rifle [.22]. We were greatly attached to this weapon, which sometimes gave remarkable results. Its position as the most formidable item in our armoury was, however, open to criticism on the following grounds. It was all but useless for purposes of defence, since the wounds it was capable of inflicting were calculated to enrage rather than to incapacitate the Oncoming Savages. For similar reasons it was a doubtful quantity where game was concerned; to kill a veado with it you would have to get a heart or neck shot at close range. It was not in good repair. You could rely on one misfire in every four shots. The stock had come apart in Roger's hands the night before we started, and had been spliced by Neville with sticking-plaster and string. The sling was also tied on with string, and an important section of the mechanism in the breech fell out at intervals, for no good reason. We had 200 rounds of ammunition for it, but no cleaning rod.

1 service revolver and 30 rounds [.45]. This was in many ways an admirable weapon; but its value to us was lessened by our inability to hit anything with it.

1 rifle and 10 rounds [.44]. This rifle not infrequently fired when you pulled the trigger; but it was possible to conjecture only approximately the course which would be taken by the

bullet. The inside of the barrel was a shocking sight; rich mineral deposits entirely obscured the rifling. We had brought it with us solely for its potential value as a present.

2 facões. Nothing could be said against these indispensable implements.

FOOD:
  2 half-pound tins of Quaker Oats.
  ⅞ of a half-pound bottle of Horlick's Malted Milk Powder.
  2 small tins of biscuits.
  1 minute tin of tea.
  2 oz. of chocolate (melted but congealed).
  A little farinha.
  Less rapadura.

An immensely heavy bag of salt, the size of a small football. This was intended as largesse for the Indians. Thinking it over afterwards, we wondered whether we had not perhaps overestimated the attractions for them of this commodity, which they could never have tasted before. Not everyone likes salt, and these tribes had got on very well without it over a number of centuries. The salt was the heaviest item in our packs; we lugged it along with a blind faith in its indispensability.

MISCELLANEOUS:
  2 cameras, and a lot of films.
  2 water-bottles.
  1 saucepan and 2 cups.
  2 compasses, one dated 1900 and a little giddy in its old age.
  3 metres of gift tobacco.
  Some necklaces, mirrors and knives.
  An assortment of medicines, of which we did not know the uses.
  1 spare pair of boots (mine).
  A sort of counterpane belonging to Queiroz. He was very attached to it. Probably an heirloom.

# THEN THERE WERE THREE

1 copy of *Tom Jones* (in case we got bored).

100 milreis, or about £2. A milreis is rather heavier than half a crown; so our burden was materially increased by this useless wealth.

All this, and whatever else I have forgotten, we divided into three equal and enormous loads. Roger had a rucksack; I had an army haversack harnessed to a Sam Browne; Queiroz shouldered a dirty bag, through which the lumps of rapadura bulged stickily. We carried a good deal in our pockets, and a lot more strapped, hooked, tied, and slung on to our persons. We looked like Tweedledum and Tweedledee. When we stood up we felt top heavy; when we sat down we were filled with an overpowering reluctance to stand up.

We set off soon after Neville had disappeared. The sun was still low. Rather than start the day by fighting our way back to the campo through what we hoped was an unusually wide belt of jungle, we decided to stick to the river for a bit, in case the jungle thinned and narrowed further upstream. But sticking to the river was not as easy or as pleasant as it sounded. We kept on being driven inland from the steep banks to avoid dense undergrowth or the overgrown bed of tributary lagoons; and when, on the other side of these, we came back on to our course, there was a tendency for the river to have vanished altogether, writhing away sharply on one of its innumerable bends. Still, we made progress slowly, and got much valuable practice in the use of the facão.

At noon the jungle on the other side of the river looked (as it always does) much easier than on ours; so we waded across and for a time made reasonable speed along the south bank. At the point where we crossed it we fired the scrub, hoping to take a back-bearing on the smoke from our camp that evening.

It was in the middle of this second day that we first found Vestiges. We called them this because Queiroz always referred to them as *vestigios*. There was no trail along the river bank, but every now and then we came on a twig or a branch or the bare stem of a young evergreen shrub which had been broken three or four feet from the ground. Unless you were looking out for them you did not notice them. The break was usually incomplete, and the top of the branch or whatever it was hung down limply. Sometimes it seemed to have been done by a sharp twist of the hand; more often it was a cut, not by steel. Some of the branches on which the break was old carried two or three little gashes just below it, made at various more recent dates. There was no doubt that these were the marks of Indians. Some of them were not more than two days old.

It was great fun looking for them, but they did not tell us much. They were not numerous, and between each set of Vestiges there was clearly an interval of several days. It looked, therefore, as if we were on the edge of some tribe's territory, and a good way from any village (near which the river bank would be more unmistakably frequented). These Vestiges must have been made by small parties of Indians — too small to leave a definite trail, even in thick places. Judging by the height of the breaks from the ground, and by the fact that they sometimes led under low overhanging branches which it would have been easy to circumvent, there was enough evidence for a tentative guess that these Indians were a small people, no bigger than the Tapirapés, and probably rather smaller. (Legend credited the Chavantes with a towering stature; but Queiroz, who had seen their tracks in the sand after a Caraja massacre in 1929, said that this was false.)

The Vestiges made things much more amusing. We applied with gusto the methods of Sherlock Holmes to the data of Robinson Crusoe. We knew now that somewhere up the river, not so very far ahead of us, little dark men were flitting through the trees, padding on naked feet in and out of the still pools of sunlight. Perhaps they had halted and were camped on the next bend of the river. Perhaps they had seen our smoke, and were coming back to investigate. Perhaps another party was coming downstream towards us. ... At any rate, it was just worth-while, when you stood still for a moment, listening for footfalls in the brittle silence of those parched, crackling places, where nothing could stir without making a disproportionate noise: just worth-while trying to reduce the volume of sound created by your own passage: just worth-while examining the praias for footprints which you never found. For it took your mind off your own exertions, and these were considerable enough to make that a valued service.

Early in the afternoon, the jungle cleared on the north bank; here was a place where the campo came down to the river. We recrossed the river and again fired the tall grass with a view to another back bearing. Then we sat down up wind and ate a little food, while the breeze took the flames and stripped the hindering grass from the beginning of the next stage of our journey. We hoped to get an answer to the smoke.

The heat was intense that afternoon. We trudged on through thick wasted grass between clumps of trees. A house agent with unusual self-control might have described the country as park-like. We came on a veado feeding by the corner of one of these clumps. She looked up, more in curiosity than in alarm, and I took a quick shot, hitting her too far behind the heart. As she made off, a sick beast, I hit her again, and at the end of a brief pursuit we found her lying dead. It was a satisfactory, though not a brilliant performance by the .22, which was by rights too weak a weapon for an animal of this size. We took the liver and a bit of meat off the haunch. (Our meat had to be carried skewered on a stick over somebody's shoulder. In thick jungle it was always being caught and dragged off by the vegetation. When the time came to cook it, it presented a sorry and unhygienic spectacle.)

Two hours before nightfall we decided that it was time to make for the river. The campo here no longer skirted the bank. Once more there was a wall of jungle between us and the essential water: once more we had to enter it at hazard, hoping to strike a convex and not a concave curve in the river's course. This was always the limiting factor on our sallies across the campo: the fact that we never knew whether we were ten minutes or two hours from water. We had to assume (though the assumption was by no means warranted) that the general direction of the channel was roughly parallel to, and not very far away from, the outer edge of the jungle; the impossibility

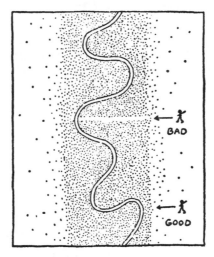

of selecting the best point to penetrate it is best explained by a diagram. There was never, of course, any particular reason why the river should not have slanted away in an entirely new direction, leaving us to seek blindly for a goal which we could never reach.

We guessed badly that evening. For two hours we kicked and butted and hacked in cover which was as nearly impassable as makes no odds. It was a fearful place. Only the imperative necessity of getting through it saved us from being beaten. Bleeding, furious, and, for the last hour, secretly convinced that we should not see the river that night, we struggled in those dense and jagged thickets with a horrible feeling of impotence, as wasps must struggle in marmalade. Roger was very good indeed. He is absurdly tall, and there was a good six inches more of him than of me for the jungle's tentacles to oppose. But he had the lead most of the time and used his knife indomitably and his compass with discretion. Reading the compass was a trying business in those circumstances. If you held it in your hand the ironmongery about you corrupted the truth in the needle. You had to stoop, and set it carefully on the ground, and stand back, and take your reading, then stoop again, and pick it up, and pick up also the rifle and facão which you had thrown down, and go ahead. It sounds and is, a trifling, not an arduous business. But under a heavy load, with your endurance tautly stretched, to repeat it at intervals is tiring.

But luck was with us in the end. As on the night before, we had an undeserved eleventh hour delivery from despair. It was nearly dark when we stumbled on the river. The place where we struck it was of a peculiar beauty. Between two long deep pools a little rocky promontory narrowed the channel; the water slipped between boulders with a soothing noise. In the passage large handsome fish forged slowly up, or flashed swiftly down, from one pool to the other. Under the opposite bank two mutuns paraded the water's edge. To come at the end of fierce struggles to such a place was heaven.

We camped on a rocky platform above the promontory and boiled the deer's liver and some farinha and gorged ourselves. We were extraordinarily happy. We had slipped out of the world into a detached, precarious existence. Our goal, our ostensible goal, was virtually unattainable; in our hearts we knew that we had insufficient excuse for doing a wild and unprofitable thing. But we were living now under the most satisfactory conditions — conditions in which the mere prolongation of life is all the business and all the pleasure you require. We were troubled by no extraneous hopes and fears. That day we had travelled a certain distance: had filled our stomachs: and were now in a place of great beauty. Night fell on what one might have been pardoned for mistaking for Paradise.

But I suspect that there are no mosquitoes in Paradise. They were very bad that night. They, more than anything else, brought home to us the full meaning of the phrase 'irreducible minimum' when it is applied to one's personal possessions. We had just enough odds and ends with us to devise some sort of protection for the parts of our bodies which our clothing left exposed. Roger slept in a hat, and we both had mosquito netting to cover our faces. I bound a handkerchief round the gaping hole in the knee of my breeches, and we both put socks on our hands. But that night Roger had a stroke of bad luck. He was trying to dry the sweat out of his shirt when it caught fire, and a large hole was burnt in the front of it. Thereafter he had to fasten across his bosom an elaborate and insecure chest-protector, in the shape of a handkerchief, before he went to sleep. By night we were strangely muffled figures.

It was an instructive experience, which even the worst provided, the most destitute member of a civilized community can hardly appreciate in imagination, to find yourself in a situation where your desperate need for a piece of string or a rag could in no circumstances be satisfied: where your well-being could be seriously affected by the loss of one old sock. We were indeed, in Roger's phrase, 'riding on the rims'.

Roger and I discussed the advisability of keeping a watch at night. Not that there could be any two opinions about it, as a matter of theory. There were Vestiges on both banks of the river here, and it looked as if the boulders in the narrow channel beside which we were camped marked a regular crossing place. There was also the question of jaguars. These are normally cowardly; man runs little danger from them unless they are wounded or at bay. But there is a popular and plausible theory that in very remote places — such as this — where human beings are a rarity, they are more likely to look on you as a meal than as a menace: especially if you smell — as we did — different from any biped they have ever smelt before. We decided that some pretence must be made of taking elementary precautions; but we had only had two hours' sleep the night before, and it was purely as a matter of form that we drew up a schedule of watches which we knew it would not be humanly possible to keep. In the end, however, what with the mosquitoes, and the recurrent necessity of fetching wood for the fire to keep ourselves warm, one or other of us was awake during most of the night. But there were no Indians, no jaguars. We saw nothing more formidable than a toad, detected in the act of climbing into my trouser pocket as I slept. If I knew my job, I should say it was a man-eating toad; but I cannot slander so trustful a creature.

Night in these jungles had a curious rhythm to it. It was as though one was in some nightmare engine-room, a vast place working quietly to some predestined purpose. There was a permanent regulated background of noises, as there is when you are in the presence of machines. The cicadas and the frogs laid measured strips of sound across the silence — monotonous, impersonal strips of sound, with no end and no beginning, such as are produced by pressing a button. You could not define or comprehend the elusive tempo of these sounds; nor did you try to. Yet it clearly had some abstruse significance, just as the sequence of purrs, clangs, thuds, and hisses coming from a powerful and elaborate machine has for those who control it familiar, tell-tale connotations. For the layman it was too complicated, a thing beyond his curiosity: a cue for wonder only.

There, then, was this machine, throbbing methodically in the blackness. You lay there, not listening, but hearing. Every now and then the cry, the movement in the branches, of some big bird, would come from close at hand, immediate and obtrusive: a throaty, confidential cry, a soft, a careful movement. It was as though these were the masters of that machine, the engineers: speaking in the dark without raising their voices, certain that their laconic utterance would be understood. Against the steady background of sound their voices stood out with a dominating, muted urgency. You imagined that the darkness all round you, the hard, strong earth beneath you, pulsed to their command. The uninitiated stars looked down incuriously; the river ran hushed. The cold hours crept on towards the dawn.

We were stiff and numb when we woke. But the mosquitoes had vanished with the darkness, and the river looked lovelier than ever in the soft expectant light. Queiroz made some tea, and we opened fire on the big fish in the shallows with the little rifle. But the puny bullets were deflected by the water; we cursed, not for the first time, our lack of a fish-hook, and Roger began carving one out of a bone. It never came to much, though.

While we drank the tea we held a council of war. It seemed to me both unprofitable and dangerous to go on travelling as we had travelled so far: exploiting good going whenever we found it and relying entirely on luck to keep us within striking distance of the river. The slap-dash opportunism of those tactics had already met with more than the success it deserved; we could not trade much longer on our luck. Moreover, those tactics entailed beginning and ending the day with an attack on the jungle which might have to be sustained, with all due ferocity, for two hours or more at a stretch; and we could not afford to let ourselves in for much more of this sort of thing. Although we were all three in good condition, we were carrying as much as we could manage, and perhaps rather more; we were short of sleep, and not very well fed. To conserve our staying power sufficiently to make any progress at all we should have to reduce drastically the amount of time and energy wasted in getting from the river to the campo and vice versa.

There was only one way of doing this. We took off our boots and breeches, slung them round our necks, and got into the river.

# CHAPTER VII

# MAINLY AMPHIBIOUS

ALL day we waded up the river. If we had felt top-heavy on dry land, we felt more than ever top-heavy in the water. In the sandy, swift-running shallows you could see what your feet were doing; but in the deeper, nearly stagnant stretches the water was dark, and in the tracks of whoever passed ahead of you clouds of grey mud rose and spread slowly, billowing. Balanced unsteadily on one bare foot, we groped for snags with the other; and usually found them. Thorns which had not yet rotted in the slime made us lurch sharply, clutching for support at the overhanging vegetation: this, as often as not, had thorns in it too. Sometimes a dense tangle, reaching out from the bank into midstream, drove us ashore, and we picked our way with oaths through thickets which would have seemed formidable even if we had not been naked from the waist down. But this happened comparatively seldom, and our unorthodox choice of route was surprisingly successful.

Roger, as usual, had the worst of it. The river grew desperately tortuous; straight stretches became rarer, and were at the best only 200 yards long. Every two minutes he had to stop, taking a bearing, gauge the distance to the next bend, observe the time, and make a note of all this. It was a tiresome business. Figures were a burden and an impertinence in the scramble up this magical, inconsequent stream; there were enough preoccupations in its beauties and its difficulties without adding to them the need, the unfortunately vital need, for accumulating statistics at frequent intervals. Nor was there anything very reassuring in the results they showed. The channel was wriggling feverishly, and we knew that for every mile we waded the crow (that depressing and ubiquitous bird) had probably flown only about 600 yards.

We floundered on for several hours, It was hard work for the body but a holiday for the spirit. There was something protective about the river. It had shouldered the graver half of my responsibilities. To-day there were no alternative routes, no alternative plans, to present themselves as each fresh obstacle arose, to be discussed, and to be adopted or rejected at hazard. I no longer had to pass off a guess as a decision. Our chief danger (to which we had already perhaps been closer than we admitted) was getting cut off from the river and dying of thirst: this was now absent. The river, for all its disadvantages as a highway, gave us an intoxicating sense of liberation and security. I felt elated all day. It was as though we had stolen a march on the jungle.

About noon Queiroz, who was leading, committed himself too far and too fast to a pool which deepened suddenly. He is a small man, and the sack of food on his shoulders was soaked by the time he had scrambled into the shallows again. This was bad luck — though it was bound to happen sooner or later — for farinha becomes unfit for consumption when it is wet; we had lost the nucleus of our food supply at a single blow.

It sounds a grave misfortune, but we did not take it very seriously then. It was indeed impossible to take anything to do with this enterprise very seriously; and unless you remember this you cannot appreciate my account of it. We had already burnt so many of our boats that the loss of any further shipping could affect us only negligibly. The margin by which the hand-to-mouth element in our existence˙could be increased was unimportant.

We halted on a tongue of dazzling sand. It was time for a meal, and Roger (who had had a much worse time with last night's mosquitoes than I had) badly needed some sleep. We spread out our sodden and coagulating belongings to dry in the sun and bathed and put some meat on the fire to boil. Roger went into a torpor, and Queiroz into a kind of trance, induced by smoking damp tobacco on an empty stomach. I was left to my own devices.

For some reason, I remember that hot bright noon as being full of a curious delight. I was in that psychological state always described by the characters in Mr. Ernest Hemingway's novels as 'feeling good'. My perceptions were sharper than usual, my power to appreciate had suddenly expanded. All the things I saw seemed to me exactly right; I read their meaning so easily, so instinctively, that there was for once no need to try and define it. I had that uncritical exhilaration, that clear conviction that this was a good day in a good world, which one has known so seldom since childhood, when snow overnight would evoke it, or permission to bathe before breakfast, or the crackle of brown paper on a Christmas morning.

It was very quiet. A wet log in the fire hissed in a sing-song, meditative way. Among the wreckage of our rations a few big flies buzzed drowsily. An unseen pigeon cooed in a gigantic tree, placating, confidential. Fish broke the water round a scrap of silver paper floating on the dark pool; a square corner of the paper stood up at an angle, like the sail of a junk heeling to the wind. On a branch hanging low over the water sat a kingfisher, a tiny kingfisher, a bird so small that it seemed impossible that it should exercise the functions of a kingfisher. It was smaller than a sparrow. It had a sharp black beak and sharp black eyes, surely too small to be of any service. Its markings were gay, distinct, and contrasting, like the colours of a toy. An orange chest: dark-green back and wings, very lustrous: a black head and a neat white ring round its neck. It looked very compact and proud, and at the same time rather absurd: like a medieval page in a new and splendid livery.

As I watched, it plunged suddenly, wounding the surface of the water hardly more than a falling leaf. Then it went back to the branch, having missed its prey, and sat glaring and fussing the water out of its feathers. Failure rankled. It registered a microscopic indignation.

At this rate, I thought, we shall have the butterflies hawking for fish.

And indeed the only butterfly in sight, which was electric blue and had wings four inches wide, seemed to have much more substance, to be much more capable of wresting a living from the river, than this puny upstart creature. The butterfly, which was of the sort called morpho, came slowly past me from upstream, loitering resplendent, aimlessly quartering the channel, as though in vanity desiring to keep as close as it might to its image in the water. When it left the river it floated through the trees close to the ground, like a delicate sliver flaked from the blue roof of the world, unable to rest on earth: an unreal homeless thing, disowned by all the elements.

I watched it disappear. The silver paper had gone too by this time, floating downstream to disappoint more fish: an erratic vagrant, travelling light and at the mercy of circumstance. If it has luck, I thought, there is in theory no reason why it should not reach the Amazon; just as if we have luck there is in theory no reason why we should not reach the place where Fawcett was killed. But I knew that in practice neither of these goals would be attained; our demands on fortune were exorbitant.

Roger and Queiroz lay like the dead beside the sun-dimmed fire. I took the little rifle and crawled across a fallen tree which spanned the river. The jungle here was easy going. There was a network of dried up lagoons: the beds of them were clear of undergrowth, and the arching trees made of each a dim cool tunnel. I wandered at hazard up the nearest.

There was silence and a pleasant mystery here. I had not gone far before the mystery became all at once specific and tangible. The place was full of Vestiges: more Vestiges, newer Vestiges, than I had seen before. Not only along the river bank, but up several of the tunnels, trails of broken twigs led unobtrusively. The dry and unrevealing ground was still not marked by feet. But the place was frequented; there could be no doubt of that. There was a strange fascination in following up the marks, in gauging the strength needed to break the branches by hand, in trying to judge with what sort of stroke and what sort of implement the ragged blazes had been made. Everybody enjoys the conviction that he would make a good detective.

I had gone, on a zigzag course, perhaps three quarters of a mile inland when I heard a noise: the sharp isolated noise of a twig snapping. It came from a clump of trees on a bank above me; it was not more than twenty yards away. I stood quite still. It occurred to me for the first time that people who read their *Wide World Magazine* have really no excuse for penetrating unknown jungle equipped only with a pair of boots, a wrist-watch, and a rook rifle. For an encounter with savages tradition prescribed full evening dress; shorts and an Old Etonian tie would have done at a pinch. In only a wrist-watch I knew that I was under-dressed.

But the reader — familiar by this time, poor wretch, with the miasma of anti-climax which hung about our enterprise — will have guessed that no encounter with savages took place; and he will have guessed correctly. Very cautiously turning my head, I met the large troubled eyes of a little deer, standing, sun-dappled, among the trees and watching me with mild perplexity. I freely admit that this was a relief. I raised the rifle. The deer still stared. I shot it through the neck, and it fell dead where it stood.

It was a slice of luck getting meat so close to the river. This was the only time I saw a deer except out on the campo. I went back for a knife, and Queiroz and I cut off what we wanted. I showed Queiroz the Vestiges, and he said he thought they had been made by Chavantes: an unencouraging but a more or less arbitrary conclusion, in which he appeared to find no cause for alarm. He was a person not easily intimidated.

We went back to the river and ate a meal and strapped on once more our complicated loads. We went on through the afternoon, lurching and splashing up the river-bed. It narrowed and grew shallower, and the current swifter. There were fewer obstacles below, but more above the surface of the water. More and more frequently the jungle choked the stream. At almost every turn we had to hack a passage through blowsy, overbearing vegetation which came sprawling down the banks and laid a lacerating barrier across our path. Our hands were in a bad state, and our legs none too good.

There was a queer thing you saw quite often there. From the underside of a fallen tree, disturbed by your rough and blasphemous passage, a family of little bats would detach themselves — fifteen or twenty of them — and go hastily flitting on to another log. They were the smallest and flimsiest creatures imaginable, so grey, so silent, so altogether negative, that you could hardly be certain that you had seen them at all. They existed only in flight. Before you dislodged them, and after they had come once more to rest, the eye was not aware of them. They clung, flattened and undistinguishable among the bark and lichen. They disappeared when they settled, and though you knew where they were you could only pretend to discern them: as you might pretend to read a printed page at fifty yards, knowing it already by heart. In the air they kept close together, flitting urgently through the alien sunlight in a little grey cloud with no more substance to it than a puff of vapour: apologetic fugitives, a troop of small evasive ghosts. I do not know what they are called.

Towards evening it became obvious that we should not camp in comfort that night. Praias were non-existent in these strangled reaches. We pressed on, hoping to find a place where the campo touched the river, so that we could sleep in the open, away from the insect-haunted trees. But at last, with only an hour to go before sunset, the quest seemed hopeless;

we chose a place where the floor of the jungle had more sand in it than mud, and where the mosquitoes would, theoretically, be fewer. Leaving Queiroz to cook a meal, Roger and I, mercifully relieved of our burdens, went on up the river-bed to reconnoitre.

It was our ambition to get a fish. You would have understood this ambition if you had seen what we had seen that day. There had been fish in sight all the time. Little fish, big fish: fish that fled away gleaming in shoals, solitary fish that slipped morosely under logs at our approach: fish with eccentric whiskers, fish with disproportionate teeth, all kinds of fish. Some of their names I have forgotten, some I never knew. The commonest were the piranhas, and they were very common indeed — even the black piranhas, whose reputation both for savagery and succulence stands higher than the ordinary variety's. All day we had waded among them. Like beggars flattening their noses against the windows of a restaurant (not that I have ever seen a beggar's nose thus flattened, except on the films), we were tantalized by this smooth glittering parade of food just beyond our reach.

We derived what comfort we could from the belief that we were exposing a fallacy; we were debunking the piranha. We remembered all that we had read, all that we had been told, about the rapacity, the vindictiveness of these fish: how a shoal of them, if you ventured into waters which they infested, would tear the flesh from your bones before you could scramble ashore again: how because of them a man could not safely immerse so much as a finger in the rivers of Central Brazil: how those cruel and undeniably imposing teeth could cut you to ribbons in a trice: how the blood-lust of the piranha was so keen that it would not hesitate an instant before attacking. . . .

We remembered all this, and much more. The memory lent a certain irony to the sight of the man-eating shoals which slipped past in the narrow channel within a few feet of our unprotected thighs. We could not but admire the rigid self-control with which they ruled their blood-lust. We noted the ascetic, indeed the almost apprehensive glances which they cast at out tempting calves. Sometimes, if we stood still, a small shoal, a kind of deputation, would approach and hang diffidently suspended in the translucent water, staring at our legs with a wistful, perhaps a slightly covetous awe: as shop-girls gaze at the sentries outside Buckingham Palace. But they never attacked us; these tigerish creatures might have been poultry for all the harm we took from walking among them.

I cannot explain their policy of non-aggression. There is no doubt that, although we never had any trouble with piranhas on the Araguaya, they were a very real danger there. The Carajas treated them with respect and made us treat them with respect too. Their ferocity, and their power, by attacking furiously in large numbers, to disable men and animals, are established facts: not legends. Our immunity cannot be ascribed altogether to luck. Perhaps it was that the piranhas in the Tapirapé were unusually well-fed: or that the extremities of human beings were so rare an item of their diet that among the shoals a lack of unanimity prevailed on the question of our value as food: or that piranhas actually never do attack unless they smell blood in the water. Probably a combination of all three reasons would account for our escape, with the emphasis on the last. If any of us had gone into the water with a sore, or a bad cut, on his legs, he might have looked for trouble.

We dragged tired legs lackadaisically through the current, plunging carelessly — now that we carried nothing worth keeping dry — through the middle of deep pools. Maddened by the sight of fish, and yet more fish, Roger cut a stake and sharpened the end.

We were strange anglers. It is probable that no one, in all his life, has such good fishing as the sticklebacks gave him in his childhood, capriciously hovering round the mouth of a glass jar full of crumbs, while he lay, quivering with excitement, ready to jerk it to the surface. The more primitive, the more improbably successful your methods, the more keenly you savour their results. Ours were at first noticeably unproductive. I wounded one or two big fish with the little rifle; but the thinnest layer of water spent the force of its bullets, and for the first time we really missed the Mannlicher, which could deal death at a depth of half a fathom. Roger with the stake tilted furiously at fish which, believing themselves cornered, tried to double past him downstream; but this was chancy harpooning, when the target was past you like a flash, and Roger's luck was out. We floundered on, vengeful but empty-handed.

Presently we saw a barbado, a big one: a spotted fish with a wide malignant mouth, about which fleshy whiskers whelked and waved, like the horns on Edgar's trumped-up fiend. I was ahead and had passed it. It lay in shallow water, so I turned and tried a shot. The small bullet must have grazed it. It was off downstream like lightning, ridging the surface of the water with a belated turbulence such as a seal leaves, quitting a bay in panic for the open sea. Roger lunged savagely across the channel; and spitted it. That was a magnificent stroke. To stab at right angles a five-pound fish travelling at full speed is always good; and it is always good to get an excellent dinner unexpectedly. To do both at once is to know (as we did then) the keenest kind of triumph.

We got back to camp with this noble and nourishing fish and an encouraging report of fairly open country about a mile upstream on the north bank. We could tell from the little charred flecks which came floating down between the trees to settle on the water that there was a big fire quite close to us. When night came down we placed it. Above the dishevelled silhouette of the jungle on the opposite bank the darkness was lurid; a huge stretch of campo must be burning beyond that belt of trees. The fire was coming up towards us from the south, with a breeze behind it. By the time we had eaten and were ready to sleep the vanguard of the flames was within a quarter of a mile of us. We could hear them raging impotently at the non-combustible wall of jungle on the other side of the river; a kind of harsh dry guzzling sound rose and fell as the flames ran on from thicket to thicket. Birds called in terror. Small glowing particles alighted on the river with a hiss. The little intimate stage lit by our fire was set before a highly melodramatic back-cloth.

We wondered how far away the Indians who had lit the fire were sleeping. We hoped they were sleeping.

# CHAPTER VIII

# THE LAST FLING

THE next day we changed once more our plan of operations. And here I must disgress to explain one of the difficulties which beset our enterprise, and which I have not so far mentioned.

It was a linguistic one. Roger and I had arrived in Brazil knowing no word of Portuguese, though I had a little bookish and erratic Spanish. On the way up country we had picked up a little of the language, and coming down the Araguaya we had perfected a kind of rudimentary patois, sufficient for the purposes of badinage with the men. The prop and mainstay of this dialect was the word *Tem*, which corresponds (at least I think it does) to the French *Il y a* and the Spanish *Hay*. This was almost our only verb, and on it devolved the onerous duty of vitalizing an extensive though inaccurate vocabulary of nouns; it bore the burden of all the persons and all the tenses. On the part of the natives it required a great deal of intuition to set the Tems on fire with meaning.

Our patois was adequate for the simple contingencies of camp life. But when it came to discussing the merits of some elaborate and not easily definable plan of action, and comparing them with the merits of two or three alternative plans, its deficiencies were painfully evident. Queiroz was a rapid talker and only a fairly good guesser; and at our councils of war we could never be certain whether we had interpreted his wishes rightly, or he ours. So many of the factors which helped to form our plans were imponderable — there was so much supposition and guesswork, so many combinations of possibility — that in the absence of an effective *lingua franca* generalship was a difficult business. Queiroz's opinions, though not those of an expert, were at least based on a wider experience than ours; unfortunately, we were rarely able to make the most of them. Our ignorance of Portuguese, like our lack of a fish-hook, was a constant source of irritation.

Though it was possible to outline a course of action to Queiroz, we could not explain our reasons for adopting it, or elicit his views on its potential modification. There was a sense of frustration, of incompleteness, about our discussions: just as there would be about the intercourse of two deaf men trying to expound to each other the theory of relativity in the middle of Piccadilly.

Anyhow, this is how we changed our plans on the day after we had waded up the river.

It was obvious that we should not make much more progress up the river bed itself, for it was getting more and more over-grown, with deep pools between the tangles; we had exhausted the benefits of amphibianism. The open country which Roger and I had spied the day before looked promising; but I was still determined not to lose touch with the river by striking away from it at a venture. Moreover, we were now in, or at least very near, Indian territory; to cover distance was no longer our first concern, the crow's flight no longer the sole criterion of our efforts. For it was idle to pretend that we should get much further towards the Kuluene without guides and fresh supplies; even barring accidents (a bit of grit in the action of the .22 would have crippled us altogether), I knew that we should have to acknowledge defeat at any moment. Our only hope of post-poning that moment lay in getting in touch with these invisible Indians and finding (a) that they were friendly, (b) that they had with them more food than they needed, and (c) that they would come with us towards the Kuluene. It would have been difficult to find three more remote contingencies than (a), (b), and (c).

All the same, it was worth trying, if we could only find out how to try it. I decided to take all our gear to the edge of the open country, a mile upstream; to leave it there in charge of

Queiroz; and to make an unburdened reconnaissance with Roger. Apart from keeping a look out for Indians, we would aim at finding an easily accessible camping ground further up the river; if we did, we would return to Queiroz, bring up the stuff along our tracks, and make camp before nightfall. The advantage of this scheme, theoretically, was that it left Roger and me active and mobile without our packs, which by this time were reducing us to the the level of oxen, able merely to plod forward, without enterprise, without curiosity, hoping only for a valid excuse to lie down. I looked forward to a certain amount of the eagle eye business.

An hour later we were saying good-bye to Queiroz on the edge of the jungle. He fired the scrub there, to make a landmark for us, and went back to our base, 400 yards away on the river bank. Roger and I struck across the campo in a westerly direction.

It was a hot, bright morning. The country looked somehow more exciting, promised more, than usual. Perhaps it was the knowledge that we were close to Indians, that at any moment a string of little black figures might debouch across the blank yellow grass between two distant clumps of trees. Perhaps it was the lie of the land, the disposition of the solitary or clustered trees which picketed its desolation, that lent it a fortuitous attraction: just as, at a shoot where all the covers are new to you, one irrationally arouses higher hopes than the others. But I think that really it was I, and not that immutable plateau, who was different on that blazing morning, still acrid with last night's smoke.

Hitherto my imagination had not been fired by the thought that we were in a place never before visited by white men. There were several reasons for this. I abhor labels, and I am not impressed by records. If you tell me that a thing is the largest, or the oldest, or the newest of its kind in the world, I feel no awe: I am not conscious of that sense of privilege which the mere fact of being in its presence ought by rights to arouse in me. I am, if anything, rather prejudiced against it. For by that braggart and fortuitous superlative the thing seems to me to be laying claim to a respect which has nothing to do with its essential qualities. The phrase 'to go one better' has come to be very loosely used; it is too often forgotten that to exceed is not necessarily to excel.

In my mind the thought of the word Untrodden aroused some shadow of this prejudice. I looked at those plumed expanses, aching in the heat, at the inviolable murmurous reaches of our river, and I did my very best to feel like stout Cortés. But it was no good. Common sense strangled at birth the delights of discovery, showing them to be no more than an unusually artificial brand of snobbery.

After all, common sense pointed out, the things you see would look exactly the same if you were not the first but the twenty-first white man to see them. You know perfectly well that there is for practical purposes no difference between a place to which no one has been and a place to which hardly anyone has been. Moreover it is quite clear that your visit is going to be entirely valueless; for all the useful data you are capable of bringing back the Great Unknown will be the Great Unknown still. You will have made a negligible reduction in that area of the earth's surface which may be said to be Untrodden; that is all. On your return you will write a book in which you will define at some length the indefinable sensations experienced on entering territory never entered before by a white man; but you know perfectly well that these sensations are no more than the joint product of your imagination and literary precedent — that at the time you were feeling only tired and hungry, and were in fact altogether impervious to whatever spurious attractions the epithet Untrodden is supposed to confer on a locality.

So far common sense had had things all its own way. But on this fiery golden morning, plodding across those decorative and enigmatic wastes, I became suddenly converted to the irrational, the romantic point of view. I felt all at once lordly and exclusive. After all, nobody *had* been here before. Even if we found the spoor of no prehistoric monsters, even if we brought back no curious treasures and only rather boring tales, even if we were unable to give more than the vaguest geographical indication of where exactly it was that we had been — even if these and many other circumstances branded our venture as the sheerest anti-climax — Roger and I would have done a thing which it is becoming increasingly difficult to do — would have broken new ground on this overcrowded planet. As an achievement it was quaint rather than impressive: like being married in an aeroplane, or ringing up Golder's Green from San Francisco. But as long as one recognized it as freakish rather than creditable, as long as one never forgot how little it was really worth, it would be to one for ever a source of rather amused satisfaction.

In this comfortable though childish frame of mind I stumbled through the long grass beside Roger. We were making for a distant clump of very tall trees, which was as good a goal as our aimless purpose required, and a better landmark than most of the scenery on this empty stage provided. We were expecting — at this date, so long after disillusionment, it is odd to remember how confidently we were expecting — to sight at any moment a range of mountains: the Serra do Roncador, no less, the Snoring Mountains. Hardly a map of those which we had seen — from the most cautiously non-committal to the most recklessly chimerical — but had stamped those words across the country before us, the country between the Araguaya and the Xingu. But our horizon remained empty; we might as well have searched it for the Angels of Mons. The Serra do Roncador does not exist; or exists elsewhere. One of the first things I read on my return to London was the statement of Mr. Petrullo, of the Pennsylvania University Expedition, who flew over some of the Kuluene country, that 'the supposed range of mountains does not exist'.

But we could not know this at the time. We could not know

that the Serra do Roncador was a figment of the fevered imagination of Brazilian cartographers, a stage property in the un-
authenticated legends of Indians. Somewhere at the far end
of the shimmering, unnumbered miles in front of us we looked
for mountains.

We came at last to the clump of very tall trees. We passed
the cordon of indolent palms which fringed it. We crossed the
hard cracked bed of a dried up pool which had given the trees
their extra cubits. On the far side we found one which looked
as if it could be climbed. We piled our equipment at its roots
and went up.

Climbing trees made us realize how far we were from being
in the best of condition. The last few days had geared us for
solid unrelenting endurance: not for frantic acrobatics, which
told on us more than they should have. In physical emergencies
we discovered alarming weakness.

All the same, we followed the branches as far as they would
take us and clung, sweating, to the last tapering forks, sixty or
seventy feet above the ground. All round us the heads of palms
nodded in gracious, slightly ironical condescension. We had a
magnificent view of the Great Unknown.

To us it looked familiar. Open country, quilted with the tops
of close-set clumps of trees, stretched as far as the eye could
reach: and doubtless farther. We cursed the visibility, which
was bad; last night's smoke lingered as a tenuous haze. We
had hoped from here to see those mountains.

It is always pleasant to be higher than one's surroundings;
sky-scrapers have contributed materially to American self-
confidence. We hung there, cooling, as our tree swung slowly
to and fro. I ran my eyes along the river's carapace of jungle,
searching for a break.

Then something happened that changed all the values of that
spacious but unresponsive scene. From beyond the river's
guardian belt of trees — here at its narrowest — a yellowish
club-shaped cloud of smoke rose slowly and began to spread.

We watched it. We were too far away to hear the ravening of the flames. We could see only the smoke, a sudden, bulbous, and significant growth above the green wall of trees less than a mile away: laborious but dramatic in its rise, like the beanstalk in a pantomime. We were indeed close to Indians; and they knew it.

Looking back along the way we had come, we saw the smoke from Queiroz's fire, a diffuse brackish stain across the blue sky. It was being answered.

'Come on,' said Roger.

We were both rather excited. We swarmed down the tree, to the ominous but unregarded sound of tearing. Then we picked up our equipment and the rook rifle and made for the jungle.

For once, the jungle did us a good turn (though we did not feel like that about it at the time). It tripped us up on the threshold of what would probably have been disaster. Forced to scramble and make detours, cut off by the enclosing trees from the irresistible beckoning of that pillar of smoke, our forlorn hope lost impetus. By the time we reached the river, sanity, sponsored by exhaustion, had returned; and the smoke had thinned and spread, so that you could no longer trace its original source. Moreover, the river was deep here, too deep to be crossed without stripping: a thing we were loath to do while we stood a good chance of being attacked. Also the jungle on the further bank was inordinately thick; it would be folly to cut our way through it when our only hope lay in silence.

We were disappointed. Anti-climax, as usual. Our high hopes withered. Our excitement, like the smoke, was dissipated. We began to drop downstream along the river, searching for a clearing on the opposite bank. Vestiges were plentiful. I wondered if the Indians had marked us down, or if they thought of us as being out on the campo, near our smoke.

We had only the river bank to march by, and that led us on a twisting course. It was a long time before we found the place we wanted: a good and strategically strong camping ground, with only a thin fringe of trees on the opposite, the Indian bank, between the river and the campo.

But it was past noon. If we were to get back to Queiroz and bring up the gear before nightfall we had no time to reconnoitre the opposite bank now. We marked the place and went on working our way down-stream.

The going was bad, but we hesitated to strike back on to the campo, where it was better. Queiroz's fire, lit with such forethought for our guidance, had exceeded its terms of reference, spreading swiftly over a huge tract of country and making a holocaust of all our landmarks. It was better to play for safety and stick to the river bank, which must eventually lead us back to our base, by however maddeningly tortuous a route. We had a strenuous, groping afternoon.

Queiroz received the news that Indians had answered our smoke with his usual impassivity. We ate a partridge which I had shot, a particularly well-knit bird, and shouldered our loads. We got back to the chosen camping ground with an hour to spare before nightfall. It was a good place, sandy and secret and backed by thick cover which made the distant possibilities of night attack even more remote. The river here had altogether changed its nature. It was no longer swift and shallow and much overgrown, but ran in a deep and very nearly stagnant channel between steep and sometimes rocky banks. Though we were a stage nearer its source it seemed to have grown rather than diminished.

There was some talk of crossing to the other bank after dark and taking compass bearings on anything that looked like a camp fire, so that in to-morrow's reconnaissance we should have some clue to work on. I wanted to have a look at the lie of the land; so while Queiroz was making a fire I stripped and tied a pair of trousers round my head and waded across. The water came up to my neck; the river was deeper here than we had known it since we had left São Domingo.

As usual, the open country on the other side was less open than it looked. The scattered trees and the tall grass made a screen which the eye could not penetrate to any great depth. About 400 yards inland there was a thickish belt of low scrub, and on the edge of it stood a tree with a broad but curiously twisted trunk. This I climbed.

I stayed up it for half an hour, and in that half hour the world below me changed. A wind began to sing in the sparse leaves round my observation post. The sky darkened. Massed black cohorts of clouds assembled in the west and came up across the sky under streaming pennons. The wind rose till its voice was a scream; great weals appeared in the upstanding grass, and in the straining thickets the undersides of leaves showed pale and quivering in panic. My tree groaned and bent and trembled. The sky grew darker still.

The earth was ablaze. That fire which the Indians had lit raced forward under the trampling clouds, and behind me, on the other side of the river, a long battle-line of flames was leaping out across the campo we had fired that morning. Huge clouds of smoke charged down the wind, twisting tormented plumes of yellow and black and grey. The air was full of fleeting shreds of burnt stuff. The fall of sparks threw out little skirmishing fires before the main body of the flames. A dead tree close beside me went up with a roar while the fire was still half a mile away.

There was something malevolent in its swift advance. The light thickened and grew yellow; the threatening sky was scorched and lurid. If there could be hell on earth, I thought, this is what it would look like. I remembered with a curious distinctness a picture which had made a great impression on me as a child: a crude, old-fashioned picture of a prairie fire in a book of adventure. Swung to and fro among the gesturing branches of my tree, I saw again in memory every detail of that picture: the long grass flattened in the wind, the fierce and over-stated glare of the approaching fire: and in the foreground a herd of wild horses in panic flight. I remembered that they were led — inevitably — by a grey: that a black horse in the right hand corner of the picture had fallen and would be trampled to death. I even recalled the place and time when I had first seen this picture: the dark winter afternoon, the nursery in which I was recovering from illness, the smooth brass rail on top of the high fender gleaming in the firelight, the shape of the little tree outside the window where half a coconut always hung for the tits. I realized with surprise how near the distant image in that picture had been to the reality now before me, and how curiously the fascination exerted by the image had foreshadowed the fascination exerted by the reality.

There was indeed a kind of horrible beauty in the scene. A fury had fallen upon the world. All the sounds, all the colours, expressed daemonic anger. The ponderous and inky clouds, the flames stampeding wantonly, the ungovernable screaming of the wind, the murky yellow light — all these combined to create an atmosphere of monstrous, elemental crisis. The world would split, the sky would fall; things could never be the same after this.

The fire was almost on me now, but my retreat to the river was open and secure. Flames flattened and straining in the wind licked into the belt of scrub beside my tree; great gusts of heat came up from below and struck me. Little birds — why so tardily, I wondered — fled crying to the trees on the river bank. Two big kites warily quartered the frontiers of the fire, though I never saw either stoop. Presently one of them came and sat on a branch below me, so close that I could have hit him with a stick. He stayed there brooding majestically, with his proud eyes, over the work of desolation. Every now and then he shrugged himself and fluffed his feathers: for fear, I suppose, that he might entertain a spark unawares. I felt oddly friendly towards him, as one might to a coastguard in a storm; his imperturbability, his air of having seen a good deal of this sort of thing in his time, were comforting. But a spark stung my naked back,

and I swore. The kite looked at me in a deprecating way and
dropped downwind to the next tree.

Then the storm broke. It opened first a random fire of huge
and icy drops. I saw that we were in for worse and scrambled
down the tree: not without regret, for I had seen a fine and
curious sight and would willingly have watched for longer, the
cataclysmic evening having gone a little to my head. But shelter
of a sort was essential, and I found the best available under the
trees on the river bank.

On the opposite side Roger and Queiroz had bundled our
belongings into a hole between the roots of a tree and were
sitting on them, to keep them dry. It was a hopeless task, though.
There began such rain as I had never seen before. It fell in
sheets and with ferocity. It was ice-cold. It beat the placid river
into a convulsive stew. The world darkened; thunder leapt and
volleyed in the sky. From time to time lightning would drain
the colour and the substance from our surroundings, leaving us
to blink timidly at masses of vegetation which had been suddenly shown up as pale elaborate silhouettes, unearthly,
ephemeral, and doomed. The rain beat land and water till they
roared. The thunder made such noise in heaven as would
shortly crack the fabric of the universe. The turmoil was almost too great to intimidate. It could not be with us that Nature
had picked so grandiose a quarrel; her strife was internecine.
Dwarfed into a safe irrelevance, dwarfed so that we seemed no
longer to exist, we had no part in these upheavals. Roger and I
smiled at each other across the loud waters with stiff and frozen
faces.

The thunder drew slowly off. The rain fell still, but no longer
with intolerable force. I slipped into the river, on my way across,
and found it so warm that I wished that I had gone to it for
shelter from the numbing rain.

The trees had done something to protect our fire, but it was
almost out. Shivering like pointers, Roger and I knelt over
it in curious heraldic attitudes; our bodies sheltered the last

dispirited embers and kept the fire alive. We were so cold that we could hardly speak.

But presently the rain stopped, and the fire was coaxed out of its negative frame of mind into a brisk assertiveness. We thawed, and began to cook a meal and to review the situation. It was not so much a situation as a predicament. Everything we had with us was soaked. It is true that in this circumstance there was no cause for immediate alarm. We should no doubt survive a night spent in clothes which were after all not much wetter with the rain than they normally were with our sweat. The little that was left of our food was not in a form which could be spoilt even by what corresponded to total and prolonged immersion. As for the films and cameras, their ruin would not prejudice our chances of survival. As far as our possessions were concerned, the storm had left us virtually unscathed.

There were, it is true, our weapons: the little rifle and the revolver. We depended on the one for food, and we might have to depend on the other for defence. Both were wet; they were rusting before our eyes, for lack of a dry stitch to wipe them with. Their never very reliable mechanism would be in a horrible condition by the morning.

But there was more to it than the certainty of an uncomfortable night and the danger of a partial disarmament. We had good reason to feel daunted as well as draggled. For we could not afford to look on this storm as an isolated phenomenon, an unlucky fluke, a source only of easily bearable inconvenience. We had to admit that it looked very much as if we had seen the beginning of the rains.

We knew what it meant if we had. We should have to turn tail and run for it, guzzling quinine as we went; even if all turned out for the best there were at least five hard weeks of travel between us and the nearest roof. If this was really the rains, we should be lucky if we all three got down to Pará with our skins.

The worst of it was, there was every reason to suppose that

it was the rains, or at any rate that they were almost upon us. Local opinion set their advent for early September; and these were the last days of August. The two storms in the last week were the first rain we had seen in Brazil.

All through the night the sky was threatening. It was too cold to sleep very much; Roger and I, huddled over the hissing fire, drowsily debated the merits of retreat and advance. In the end we put off a decision till the morning.

In the morning the sun was reinstated. The sky was bland and blue, pretending that it had never been anything else. But the ground steamed; as birds moved in the branches there was a staccato patter of drips. Our clothes were still wet. The little rifle was red with rust. We set about facing the facts.

Lacking the gift of prophecy, or a meteorological flair, we decided to ignore for the moment the relation between last night's storm and the approaching rains, and to assume for the purposes of argument that we had several weeks in hand before they broke.

In the light of this unwarrantable assumption we examined the situation. Our total food supply was now as follows:

> One half pound tin of Quaker Oats.
> One and a half hunks of rapadura.
> Two ounces of Horlick's Malted Milk Powder.
> One ounce of tea.
> A quantity of salt, estimated by Roger (who carried it) at a ton or slightly over.
> Half a pound (approximately) of sediment at the bottom of the sack, comprising farinha, chocolate, biscuit crumbs, toilet paper, ants, blood, sweat, and tobacco. (But in the process of taking the inventory most of this got eaten.)

This sounds as if we were on the verge of starvation. Actually we were very far from it, as long as the little deer continued accommodating and plentiful, and the .22 did not let us down. But it will be clear to the discerning reader that our reserves of food were too limited to permit of any protracted operations in the field: unless, of course, we could supplement them.

Our chances of doing this were problematical. We were close to Indians, who in the absence of evidence to the contrary must be assumed to be hostile. We should certainly not meet them unless they wanted to meet us; and though clearly aware of our presence it looked as if they belonged to that class of persons (happily almost extinct in the civilized world) who are said to keep themselves to themselves. Besides, even if we did meet them, and they did prove friendly, there was little likelihood of their having with them enough food to put our commissariat on its feet again: I remembered those exiguous bundles of mandioca, those few poor heads of maize, which were all the Tapirapés took with them on the march.

In short, we had at that moment just enough food to see us through the journey back to São Domingo. Were we justified in chancing our luck and using that food for a further advance of two or three days, relying on our digestions and the .22 to get us home on a purely meat diet?

We decided that we were not. I know that this decision was theoretically sound; and in practice, as things turned out, it was extraordinary lucky that we took it, for when we got back to São Domingo, as you shall hear, the supplies we had left there had disappeared and our iron rations had to last us until we got back to the Araguaya. But it went against the grain to turn back on that clear and lovely morning. We were certainly within a hundred miles of the place where Fawcett met his death, and the distance may have been considerably less if he made good progress on those days when the Kalapalos were watching his fires. Provided the rains held off, we could very easily have kept going for two or three days more until we ran completely out of food. But we should have had a bad time of it on the way back, and I hardly think we should have done much good. If one of us had gone lame, or if anything had happened to the .22, it is improbable that we should have got out at all.

But I felt very sorry to be giving up this ridiculous scramble; it had been great fun. As we strapped on our still sodden loads an enormous alligator, the biggest I have ever seen, came quietly gliding up the narrow channel opposite our camp (I wondered where it had been when I waded the river the night before). Here was a chance to work off some of our resentment against unkind circumstances; and as it drew level I took a careful shot with the .22 and got it in the eye.

That was probably the most phenomenal result ever produced with a rook rifle. The peaceful river boiled. The alligator thrashed its head from side to side in agony. Then, as the tiny bullet touched (I suppose) its brain, it reared itself out upon the further bank and lay there, killed with a crumb of lead.

There was no time to strip off my load and wade across to measure it: though I should have liked to do this, for it really was a very big one. We left it sprawling there, to mark the futile end, reached with much difficulty, of a hopeless quest. If those secret Indians came to our camp after we had gone (as I expect they did) I hope they were suitably impressed by a monster so mysteriously dead.

# CHAPTER IX

# WHAT HAPPENED TO FAWCETT

I HAVE called ours a hopeless quest; but only circumstances made it so. A small, resolute, and properly organized expedition could, I am convinced, make the cross-country journey from the headwaters of the Tapirapé to the Kuluene, and thence, after getting into touch with the Kalapalos, go back over the last lap of Fawcett's trail to the place where the Indians saw the smoke from his last fire. They would need to start much earlier than we did — probably in May, at the beginning of the dry season. What they would find when they reached their objective it is impossible to say: not very much, certainly. After all these years it is too much to hope for bones; but if they could establish contact with the Arumás or the Suyás (one or both of whom probably had to do with Fawcett's disappearance, or at any rate knew something about it) they ought to be able to get the information they need, and it would be surprising if they did not find articles of the expedition's equipment in the Indians' possession. After completing their investigations they could either return across country over their own tracks, or else they could buy canoes from the Kalapalos and go on down the Xingú to the Amazon.

But I fancy that the future of the exploration of these regions lies in the air. They are not, as is popularly supposed, covered with dense jungle; a box of matches and a slight breeze is all you need to make an excellent landing field. The campo is as flat and as hard as a billiard table, and it might even be possible to do a lot of good work with an ordinary Ford car, if you could get it to your jumping-off point.

The difficulty with aeroplanes would of course be your petrol supply. Even in the inhabited parts of the interior petrol is very

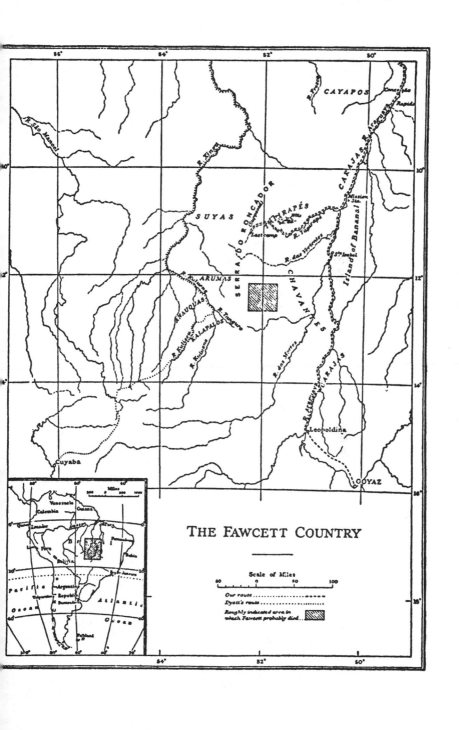

THE FAWCETT COUNTRY

Scale of Miles

Our route ....................
Dyott's route ....................
Roughly indicated area in
which Fawcett probably died...

scarce and prohibitively dear. Probably the simplest solution would be to bring a launch up the Araguaya during the rains, when the river is high, and make a dump somewhere. (You could take the petrol up the Tapirapé by canoe, if you wanted to, and establish your base at São Domingo; but this would only gain you a hundred odd miles, and you would be better off on the banks of the Araguaya.) From there you could make an aerial survey of the enormous tracts of unknown country to the west; until this is done, however superficially, all exploration of these regions on foot will be a groping, hit-or-miss business; and all the better for that.

Our abortive march towards the Kuluene accomplished nothing at all. But in so far as it gave us an idea of — and indeed almost exactly reproduced — the conditions under which Fawcett was travelling when he disappeared, it helped to confirm our tentative conclusions with regard to what happened to him. These conclusions may be summarized as follows:

In Chapter II I have said that the evidence collected by Dyott in 1928 indicates that Fawcett's party was massacred, probably by Suyá Indians, at a spot four or five days' march east of the Kuluene. In Chapter VIII Murika's story, mysteriously produced by Major Pingle, gave general support to this theory, modifying it in that Murika claimed to have seen the smoke, not for five, but for eleven days, and laid on Arumá Indians responsibility for the outrage. On my return to London I found independent confirmation for these closely similar conclusions in the statement by Mr. Petrullo, archæologist and ethnologist to the Pennsylvania University Expedition which visited the Kuluene in 1931. Mr. Petrullo elicited from the Kalapalos substantially the same story as they had given to Dyott three years before; smoke had been seen for five days, but this time the Indians were less specific with regard to the fate of the party, saying only that the cessation of the smoke meant that they had disappeared into dense jungle. Little importance, however, can be attached to Mr. Petrullo's statement that, while flying over the country east of the Kuluene (the expedition had an amphibian plane with them) he was able to 'confirm the smoke incident of the story'; for after six years all traces of Fawcett's burns, however extensive they may have been, would have vanished wholly; any charred patches which Mr. Petrullo may have seen must have been the more recent work of Indians. At the time of writing, these three stories represent the only reliable body of evidence with regard to Fawcett's fate. Taken in conjunction, they establish almost (but not quite) beyond doubt that the expedition perished in 1925 at some spot not less than five, and not more than eleven, days' march east or northeast of a Kalapalos village situated on the Kuluene south of the small tributary called the Tanguro. As a rider to this I would add that Murika's figure, eleven, is open to suspicion for two reasons. First, because the Brazilian aboriginal is not a great arithmetician, and should never be pinned down to any statistical statement involving a number larger than five. (We heard of one Indian woman who, although born with six fingers on one hand, was never in any intellectual sense aware of her singularity.) Secondly, because — unless there is high ground near the banks of the Kuluene, which is extremely unlikely — I doubt the ability of even the hawk-eyed Indians to see smoke eleven days' march away: though it is, of course, likely that Fawcett was travelling very slowly indeed, and may have been compelled by the obstacles he encountered to follow a tortuous course.

It is probable, but by no means certain, that the party was massacred. By no means certain, because it is not necessary to postulate the hostility of Indians to account for the end of that wild and gallant enterprise. In the last few chapters I have described in some detail an attempt by three white men, carrying their own provisions and equipment, to make a journey through the country which lay ahead of Fawcett when he crossed the Kuluene; and you can judge for yourselves from that description how precarious is the position of such a party.

It is, of course, considerably less precarious if the party is led by a man of wide experience in these matters, and not by a literary editor. But against this you must set the following considerations:

Fawcett's party, when it crossed the Kuluene, was not (as we were when we left São Domingo) comparatively fresh. They had already endured a long and arduous journey down the Kuliseu. The two young men, Rimell and Jack Fawcett, were lame and — if the Kalapalos are to be believed — reluctant to go further. It is by no means certain whether they had any firearms with them, and they could not, by this time, have been carrying a large supply of ammunition. Moreover they were not, as we were, following the course of a river, but striking into a region considerable tracts of which are probably entirely waterless. Finally, the Kalapalos say that one of the young men could only move slowly, and was being forced to lag some way behind his companions.

In the circumstances, hunger, thirst, and exhaustion must have greatly weakened, if they did not at last combine to destroy, the little party. I do not think the Indians would have attacked an expedition, however small, that kept together and was in good shape physically. If they did, as the evidence suggests, perpetrate a massacre, they merely anticipated a result which they could have achieved, slowly but surely, simply by withholding their good offices. It is virtually certain that the Fawcett expedition could not have survived for many days after crossing the Kuluene; but probably we shall never know whether to bring in a verdict of murder or suicide.

For all this, however, there still remains an infinitesimal, a million to one chance that Fawcett is still alive. If he is, we must assume that he is in some way mentally deranged. Suppose one of the young men broke down, an Indian tribe proved friendly, and the explorers had no choice but to stay in their village and recuperate. Suppose again that they were not fit to move before the rains began, and had to face those incredibly unhealthy months in miserable huts, eating miserable food. The young men, being ordinary mortals, could never have survived this long-drawn-out ordeal. And if they had, they would certainly have made their way back to civilization at the first opportunity; I find it impossible to believe that, if the white men were healthy, any tribe could have held them (or even one of them) captive, over a period of years, in an area where they would never have been more than one hundred miles away from friendly Indians.

The young men, then, must have died, if they were not killed. Fawcett, whose powers of endurance and immunity to disease were extraordinary, might have lived through the rains. He might conceivably have elected to stay with this tribe, or with other tribes, for a year: perhaps for two years. But not for eight. There is nothing to keep him there. Even if he could have endured the terribly primitive life of the Indians, he would hardly have given the last years of his life (he was sixty when he disappeared) to a study of it — a study of which the results would never be made known. His quest led him to no Lost City; even the mountains on which it was to have stood were missing. No, there is nothing to keep him there of his own accord for so long; and, as I say, I do not think he could have been kept there against his will.

So if he is still alive he is mad or he has lost his memory. There are no other circumstances in which it is conceivable that he would deliberately choose to end his days in an existence which at its best, in the dry season, is on a level with the life of beasts.

I repeat: everything points to the whole expedition having perished in the summer of 1925, probably at the hands of Indians.

# PART THREE

THE RACE TO THE AMAZON

# CHAPTER I

# IRON RATIONS

EVENTUALLY we got back to São Domingo.

It was the least spectacular of home-comings. We struck the path a mile from the port, and for this last lap whipped up the semblance of a swagger. We were tired and ridiculously hungry, and we knew that it was not our fault that we had not lost our way altogether. But we did our best to look nonchalant and undefeated, lounging along the path at a good steady pace, trying to give the impression that our forlorn hope had been after all no more than a whim. Had we not said that we should be gone only a few days? Well, those few days were up, and here we were.

But there was no one to impress. The clearings were peopled by little save memories. There was no one there to see through our truculence to the disappointment and exhaustion which it was intended to conceal. Almost everyone had gone away. Only half a dozen of the Tapirapés were left, and the missionary, and Robin Hood, the man with the muzzle-loader.

For this we were not sorry. But there was a nasty shock in store for us. The missionary gave me a letter from Neville, in which he described the horrors of his journey back to São Domingo with the two captains: they had lost their way, they had broken their only gourd of water, they had wounded a puma and lost that, they had had a terrible time. And it appeared that we were in for a terrible time too; there had been a muddle, and the river party had inadvertently allowed Chico to take downstream with him all the supplies and equipment which we had left at São Domingo. This meant that we were still without all those luxuries (only our pride denied them the

status of necessities) to which we had been so desperately looking forward: blankets, mosquito nets, a change of clothes, extra
food.

But it couldn't be helped; there was nothing to be done
about it. We washed in the river, and put on our sticky clothes
again, and paid Robin Hood with .44 cartridges for the privilege of distending ourselves with his rice, and fell into a heavy
sleep beside the fire. We were too tired to feel the cold; we slept
like swine, with our faces in the dust. The next morning we
started home.

We started home . . . It sounded rather grand when you put
it that way. As we bailed the canoe and threw in our few belongings, we felt a faint stirring of excitement at the thought
that we were now definitely on our way back. Henceforward
we should have an objective which was not only attainable but
well worth attaining. In the past few days we had had no
inclination, and very little time, to think about home; but now
we began to remember that it was in many respects a most
attractive place. We were facing it for the first time, and in our
imaginations it loomed up very clear and close.

Then all at once it receded, dwindled, became blurred and
irretrievable, like a bright coin dropped by accident into deep
water. There was a moment when I had the sudden stabbing
conviction that we should never get back, that we were altogether too far away and too ill-provided.

I was plugging a leak in the bottom of the canoe, pushing a
bit of Queiroz's shirt into a little crack with the blade of my
knife. It was a familiar job and I did it with care. But the canoe
was old; many years of scraping had worn the shell to the thin-
ness of cardboard, and at the pressure of the knife a large slice
leapt out of the bottom of the boat and the water rushed in.

We jumped overboard and dragged her nose out on to the
bank and remembered that it would take us at least six weeks
to reach the Amazon and that there was no other canoe on the
Tapirapé. It was a bad moment.

But we survived it. We cut up a biscuit tin, and found some old nails of the missionary's, and put a neat but precarious patch over the hole on the inside, and finished it off with some more of Queiroz's shirt. The canoe floated. We had to bail her out every half hour, but she floated. We pushed off from São Domingo and paddled downstream.

We did the journey down to the Araguaya in four days, which was a good time for amateurs. There is not much to tell about those days.

It was hard work, though Queiroz did more than either of us. We paddled all the time, balanced on tormenting perches made by jamming two short stout sticks between the gunwales. These sticks were always working loose and required constant re-adjustment. The current was too weak to help us much, and we renewed acquaintance with the shallows on the old un-friendly terms. By day we went naked, for it was very hot and we were always having to jump overboard and drag the boat. But at night we put on all our clothes against the cold and bandaged the rents in them against the mosquitoes. Neither of these precautions were very efficacious; we would have given anything in the world for a couple of blankets and a few feet of gauze, and we cursed the incompetence which had robbed us of these things.

We had very little food, and we felt terribly the need for something with fat in it; the rice, of which we had a certain amount, left us bloated but unsatisfied. However, we were lucky with the game, necessity lending a phenomenal accuracy to our aim. We got duck, and pigeons, and a plaintive but delicious water hen, and once a huge clutch of turtle's eggs, which are very meaty and sustaining. We were always hungry; but never, until the last day, seriously short of food.

I do not remember that we were conscious of any strain, but I think that perhaps we were more tired than we knew. I can-not otherwise explain the policy of *laissez-faire* and non-aggres-sion which we adopted on discovering that there was a *sucurý* —

an anaconda — in a hollow tree on the praia where we had camped. We could not see it, but a sound between a moan and a hiss issued rhythmically from the trunk, and we knew that it was there. There were any number of things we could have done; if it had proved impossible to cut open the tree we could have lit a fire underneath it and killed the snake when it came out. But a curious kind of indifference had come upon us, probably the result of weakness and lack of sleep; and we contented ourselves with emptying a revolver lackadaisically into the tree, which quickened the tempo of the moaning hiss but produced no other result.

What else do I remember about those days? Two tapirs which swam across the river just ahead of us and waded up through the shallows into the jungle, looking unexpectedly equine: a very long shot, a fluke, which brought a pigeon out of a distant tree when we were desperate for food: the clouds of little butterflies — white, and pale yellow, and very pale green — which haunted the patches of mud along the shore, lovely and incongruous decorations of the slime for which they forswore all cleanlier resting places: Roger's humour in the small hours, when we were too cold to sleep: the taste of coarse farinha, with handfuls of which we bridged the long gaps between our meals ... They were good days, on the whole.

The last of them, the day before we reached the mouth of the Tapirapé, was a hard one. We ate the last of our food at breakfast. We had fifteen hours in the canoe. The last three of them were in darkness. We knew that the river party was not far ahead of us, for we had been travelling much faster than they; we were fairly sure that they would have camped on a praia at the river's mouth. But we could not be certain of this; nor did we know, until the very last moment, whether we could reach the mouth ourselves that night.

The lower waters of the Tapirapé, before it joins the Araguaya, are a network of lagoons. The current there is negligible, and the channel, to which so many promising alternatives constantly offer themselves, is difficult enough to follow in daylight. By night it is a maze which you must thread blindfolded. Queiroz did extraordinarily well in getting us through, for he knew it no better than we did and was going on guesswork as much as memory.

There was no moon. We had never paddled at night before, and at first it was amusing. But the novelty wore off quickly, and was replaced by a vivid feeling of impotence. The water was grey, the land was black. The stars looked down, impersonal, unhelpful, and very far away. With aching arms we dug our paddles into the water; and nothing happened. Or nothing seemed to happen. The canoe, as far as we could judge, floated motionless on that grey and irreducible expanse. We could see no reassuring arrowhead of ripples at our bow; on the thick black walls between which we strove so sullenly there was nothing by which we could gauge our progress. Advance was not registered perceptibly in that obscure world.

It was difficult to judge our distance from the bank. The trees whose tops scolloped the teeming stars cast shadows as dense as their own substance. Only a thin and intermittent hem of phosphorus along the water's edge offered a landmark, told you where the river ended and the jungle began, bisected the black wall, dividing reality from reflection.

The sky-line played cunning and incalculable tricks. Trees twenty yards away would suddenly suggest a low range of hills in the middle distance; fireflies, and some unknown insect larger and more luminous than they, would counterfeit the lighted windows of houses on those hills. Nothing was certain. My eyes ached with staring. I paddled with a languid, ineffectual desperation, as one runs through sand in a nightmare. It seemed to all of us that we had missed the channel, that we were struggling slowly up some interminable lagoon, that we should get no food or rest that night. There was altogether too much darkness and silence in this unfamiliar world.

Presently, while we rested on our paddles, Queiroz admitted that he was to all intents and purposes lost: that he *thought* the mouth of the river was just round the next corner, but . . . Then, all at once, we heard that least romantic of all sounds, the lowing of a cow; and thereby knew that we were close to the Caraja village at the mouth of the Tapirapé. I never knew there was such music in a cow.

> 'No nightingale did ever chant
> More welcome notes to weary band
> Of travellers in some shady haunt
> Among Arabian sands.
>
> 'A voice more thrilling ne'er[1] was heard
> In springtime from the cuckoo bird
> Breaking the silence of the seas
> Among the farthest Hebrides.'

Our paddles became lighter and stabbed the water triumphantly. Roger yodelled, and we raised the ban on talking about food. We forgot that our bodies, after all this crouching, appeared to have been tied in not very workmanlike knots which we should have some difficulty in undoing. The first stage of the journey home was almost over, and we had done it in record time.

Soon the black walls melted away in front of us. The jungle dwindled to an insignificant margin along a wide expanse of grey. The world was lighter and less confusing. We were back on the Araguaya. A fire was burning on a praia in the middle of the mouth, and our hail was answered by a sleepy and sarcastic cry of 'Dr. Livingstone, I presume'.

The expedition was reunited.

---

[1] Wordsworth is sometimes a little obvious. There are no cuckoos in the farthest Hebrides.

# CHAPTER 11

# THE GLOVES ARE OFF

It was the afternoon of the next day, and it was full of the stimulating atmosphere of suspense.

We stood beside our beached canoes on the praia below the Bananal Mission Station, five leagues downstream from the mouth of the Tapirapé. Our men embraced with fervour their comrades who had been left behind with the baggage. But there was a certain constraint abroad, and among those who welcomed us a tendency to giggle, to cast oblique and mischievous glances at the truants, to go in fact through all the motions proper to the anticipation of a first class row. Major Pingle was nowhere to be seen.

The sun beat down on familiar bags and boxes, and there was a strong, familiar smell. The green tarpaulin, stretched on poles, projected its little rectangle of shade. In the sand round the fire flies crawled dreamily over rich deposits of fish bones. In the lee of Major Pingle's personal gear a number of empty brandy bottles sprawled raffishly; it was news to me that the expedition had once possessed a cellar.

José Tiburce, a nice man and a good cook, came up to me.

'Oh, Senhor Pedro,' he said, 'Major Pingle is very angry with you. I have never seen anyone so angry, so *zangado*. When Chico brought your letter he became quite wild with anger.'

The other men joined in. 'Oh, zangado!' they cried. 'Zangado com Senhor Pedro! Oh, Senhor *Pedro!*' They grimaced with burlesque terror and chortled with glee, exactly as small boys do when one of their number has been sent for by the Headmaster. But they were at heart sympathetic to me, which pleased me.

I asked where Major Pingle was, and they said he was up at

the mission. So we all trooped across the praia and climbed the bluff and came to a little white one-story building standing under a clump of palms. This was the headquarters of the mission.

The missionaries were very good to us. We were shown into a low cool room and given stools to sit on and promised tea. There ensued a scene which I found funny and enjoyable.

The six of us sat there, with one eye, literally or metaphorically, on the door through which Major Pingle was expected to appear. With the missionaries, on their hospitable comings and goings, we made desultory conversation, and this in itself was a source of humour, for the ennobling effect notoriously produced on the character by first hand contact with Nature had not, I am sorry to say, permeated to our vocabulary, and these good people were so very mild and soft-voiced and unobtrusive that it was sometimes difficult to detect, or at any rate to acknowledge, their presence. Time and again an unforgivable and quite superfluous oath blighted our courteous trivialities, leaving its horrid echoes to spread across the ensuing silence, as a wine stain spreads over a white cloth. We realized with a certain surprise that we were disqualified by more than our appearances from polite society. Feverishly and sycophantically we tried to make amends; but always, in the middle of some halting eulogy of missionary ideals, those unfortunate oaths would reappear. . . .

So there was comedy in our idle talk and drama in our thoughts, which were full of doubt and curiosity and the anticipation of conflict. And on top of all this we were presented with a queer, symbolic, and quite irrelevant dumb-show. The missionary from São Domingo had arrived a few hours before us, and he brought with him a convert. This convert kept on skipping in and out of the room: a Tapirapé boy, naked, with long black hair, bright, rather malicious eyes, and a bird-like gait. When Roger and I had seen him on the way downstream, he had been homesick and full of misgivings; his was not, by

the look of him, a profoundly spiritual nature, and we strongly
suspected that it was the love of adventure and the hope of gain
which had landed him in the missionary's canoe, from which he
had seen so many and such splendid presents brought ashore.
At any rate, the further he got from his people the more doleful
he looked; his eyes were stubborn and frightened, like those of
a rebellious little boy going to school for the first time. His
Ticantós had a wistful and perfunctory ring, and sitting in the
canoe behind the missionary he was a small, huddled, and un-
happy figure. His long black hair hung down over his narrow
shoulders, so that from behind it looked as if the missionary had
chosen for himself what is usually referred to as a Dusky Mate.

But all his misgivings had vanished now. That bold, acquisi-
tive and enquiring spirit which had so effectively supplied the
place of a religious impulse was very much alive in him. He
stepped on tiptoe through his brave new world, trembling with
excitement as he fingered door-handles and picture-frames and
unprecedented panes of glass. 'Ticantó' he crooned at us, beaming. But his manner was a trifle abstracted; among so much
novelty he had no time to spare for old acquaintances. Sometimes he would stand quite still in the middle of the room, gazing
at its simple furnishings in an ecstasy of wonder: one hand
rapturously caressed the polished surface of that strange
phenomenon, a table, the other fingered the only outward and
visible sign of his conversion, a spruce little reticule made of
flowered chintz which hung from the string tied round his waist.
The joy and awe in his face, if they were not particularly holy,
were very real. 'So this is Christianity!' he seemed to be saying.

His was an odd intrusion into that tense, abnormal scene,
rich enough already in interest of its own. It was as though
someone had wheeled a Punch and Judy show out of the
pavilion during a Test Match, I thought: or as if . . .

But just then Major Pingle came in, and I gave up my
academic pursuit of analogies.

Major Pingle was smoking a cigar, a thing we had not seen

for weeks, a jaunty relic from another life. But his face was white, his eyes hostile and uncertain; his whole appearance suggested either a poor state of health or a considerable depth of emotion. I found the sight of him depressing. He did not look at me.

Nor at Roger, nor at Neville. He spoke in a thick angry voice, on trivial subjects, to the others; but the three members who had resigned he studiously ignored. This was his first mistake, for it takes two to respect an artificial convention like that, and we were at the time in no mood for artificiality. We countered by employing that allusive technique of insult which the nursery adopts when someone has decided to sulk. Major Pingle had taken up a position from which he could not retaliate to this.

But it was almost the only thing he could not retaliate to. We slept that night on the praia, and in the morning received a message that Major Pingle was coming down for a talk. As I watched that gawky figure plodding over the white-hot sand towards us I reflected that we were wholly at his mercy. He had all the money, and controlled the remains of the supplies, which he had taken no steps to supplement at Bananal. His power was undeniable. What was he going to do with it?

It was clear that he meant business. He had spent the best part of three weeks alone with his thoughts and some inferior brandy; and in the middle of this period his feelings had been further exacerbated by my letter of resignation. Our absence could hardly have been calculated to make his heart grow fonder; it must have been a bad time for him. He had disliked me when we parted; I knew that he hated me now.

It would be difficult, I thought, to avoid being humiliated; to forgive and to forget would form no part of Major Pingle's policy. Our relations would be strained; but I did not anticipate that Major Pingle would sever them altogether. I had always understood, from the *Wide World Magazine* and other authorities, that in the Great Open Spaces this sort of thing was never done, however much you wanted it; there was a thing called the Unwritten Law which prevented you from doing it. So I did not seriously contemplate the possibility of Major Pingle withholding from us not only his society but his assistance, and not only his assistance but our own funds, on the long and rather difficult journey down to Pará.

But Major Pingle, it turned out, had never even heard of the Unwritten Law.

'Good morning, Major Pingle!' we cried effusively, as he stumped into camp. 'How are you this morning, Major Pingle?' we enquired with lively solicitude. '*Dear* Major Pingle!' said Roger, with some emotion. Our plight was too desperate to be damaged by this baiting; we had nothing to lose.

But Major Pingle was not to be drawn. He sat down sullenly on a box, and we sat round him, an expectant and a really very ridiculous semicircle.

'Well,' said Major Pingle, who appeared to be in rather lower spirits than we were, 'first of all you'd better read this.'

He handed me a letter addressed to the three of us who had resigned. It is a document which I shall always prize. It begins as follows:

'In answer to your letter dated 25.8.32. Please note as each of you signed an agreement in which you agreed to abide by my decision as leader, I have nothing further to say at present other than I consider you three to be not worthy of further consideration.

'Paragraph, referring to your passage money. You can take your three passages out of the £200 (two hundred pounds) owing to me. . . .

'The new bataloã will be left for you, so if you need funds you can sell same.

Yours truly,<br>Major G. L. Pingle.'

I read this letter with interest and amusement. Nobody

owed Major Pingle two hundred pounds; indeed the statement was so preposterous that I regarded the whole thing as a ramp, a try-on, an attempt to put the wind up me and bring me to heel by showing what might have happened to us if we had arrived twenty-four hours later than we had — if we had not caught up the others before the whole party started downstream towards the Amazon.

'But, Major Pingle,' I said, 'nobody owes you two hundred pounds.'

'That's as may be,' replied Major Pingle, with unwonted accuracy. 'So much the worse for you if they don't. You won't get any other money out of me.'

Still I thought that he was only keeping up the bluff; and I believed that I could call it.

'Well, what's going to happen now?' I said.

'Happen?' cried Major Pingle vehemently; and embarked on a most remarkable harangue. The first thing that was going to happen was that he and anyone who still acknowledged his leadership (and had not already resigned) would start downstream that day. After about a week they would reach Conceição, the first village, where there was a wireless station. 'From Conceição,' exclaimed Major Pingle, with flashing eyes, 'I shall tell Brazil and the world that the expedition has been dissolved, due to the indiscreet conduct of certain members, and through no fault of mine.' (This was a very moving passage, and we often used to quote it to each other afterwards.) As for the three members who had resigned, they could have — as stated in his letter — one of the batalōas and make the best of their way home in that. If they wanted funds, they could sell the batalōa. It was not made clear how they were to continue their journey after doing so.

Thus far the speech went well, though Roger and I, who were perhaps rather fine-drawn after the events of the last three weeks, were for some reason in fits of uncontrollable laughter. But now Major Pingle made his first important mistake. He revealed the fact that he had intercepted my mail. Postal facilities on the Araguaya are of a modest nature. They are neither punctual nor regular. Flashy achievements they disdain; to guarantee you a delivery every three months — that is not their way. The men who man the official canoe take their time. Everything depends on the will of God, the state of the river, and the number of saints days and relations encountered en route.

But it so happened that the post had passed Bananal, going downstream, while we were up the Tapirapé, and my mail should have caught this post. Major Pingle, however, had frustrated this by the simple process of commandeering the mail and locking it up in his suit-case. It consisted of two large envelopes, which between them contained about a dozen letters which Roger and I had written home during our journey down the Araguaya, and one despatch to *The Times*, winding up the expedition from São Domingo; this despatch had been read and approved by all the members who had gone up the Tapirapé.

But both envelopes were addressed to the manager of a cable company in Pará, with whom *The Times* had arranged special cabling facilities for me, and to whom I had written asking them to mail any letters for home which the expedition sent downstream. Major Pingle knew about this arrangement; but the name of the cable company on the envelopes conjured up his pet bogy, the Press. He was firmly convinced that he held in his hands several ounces of libellous matter, that those envelopes were full of front page stuff, none of it redounding to his credit. To release them, he believed, would be to blazon an exaggerated account of his activities across the breakfast tables of Great Britain. So, very naturally, he stuck to them; and they missed the post.

I do not altogether blame him. During his three weeks' vigil at Bananal I dare say that his mind had dwelt overmuch on the past history of our comic expedition; and perhaps the various miscalculations into which his good nature had led him had acquired in his thoughts a disproportionate and ominous importance — had shown themselves to be capable of an altogether more sinister interpretation than any which I wish the reader to put on them. Major Pingle had had a wide experience of a society with a rather elastic code of honour; he had learnt in a hard school. Accordingly it seemed to him only natural that I, having been in some respects disappointed in his conduct, should take the first opportunity of showing up that conduct in the most unfavourable light possible. When he assured me that he had not as yet opened my envelopes it was easy to see that for him such forbearance marked a noble, a magnanimous gesture.

All the same, this commandeering of my mail was a bad tactical error, the first of many; and from the moment he admitted it my respect for him began to wane, and he became a less formidable adversary. For it put him definitely in the wrong and he gained nothing by it. When I demanded the letters back, he refused to give them up, saying that they would be opened in the presence of the British Consul at Pará. He was acting, of course, on the assumption that they contained those libellous despatches, and he would not accept my word for it that they contained nothing of the sort. This created what is known as a Strong Situation. We withdrew to consider it, leaving Major Pingle sitting on his box, looking malignant and rather forlorn.

He need not have felt forlorn. Two of us, we discovered, were still prepared to acknowledge his leadership and travel downstream with him. At the time I was surprised at this; but I see now that it was a natural and a prudent decision. It looked on the face of it, as if allegiance to Major Pingle represented the only chance any of us had of getting back to England before the end of the year. And when it comes to a choice between being stranded without any mony 1000 miles from the coast on the eve of the rainy season, and travelling home in comparative comfort with the man who holds the purse-strings, there can be very little doubt which is the sensible thing to do. Two of us, at any rate, talked a good deal about loyalty to our original leader and began to pack.

I felt rather guilty. If it had not been for me, I knew that the rest of us — Roger and Neville and Bob — would never have been involved in a situation which we should be forced — once its extravagance had worn off — to recognize as uncomfortable and perhaps disastrous. I approached the two loyalists and persuaded them without any difficulty at all to represent to Major Pingle that by leaving us in the heart of Brazil in a state of complete destitution he was going to lengths which he might afterwards have cause to regret, and that he ought to give us at least enough money to start us on the way home. This they did, and it answered well. Major Pingle — who, as we discovered later, had expeditionary funds amounting to a very considerable sum in hand — did what in this sort of story is called the Big Thing. He gave us 550 milreis, which is roughly the equivalent of ten pounds. Almost without a murmur, too.

At noon his bataloa was loaded. The two loyalists took their seats beside him with alacrity, and the order was given to push off. Our parting, I am sorry to say, was not without acrimony. I was really very angry about those letters. I was not prepared to bet on their being posted, and some of them were important — particularly if (as seemed possible) we were going to remain out of touch for another three or four months. So I waded out to the boat and demanded them for the last time, and for the last time Major Pingle refused to give them up, and there was very nearly an ugly scene. Very nearly, but not quite. That far-seeing man, we discovered, had borrowed our revolvers.

The flagship of the expedition dropped downstream, the target of invective only.

# CHAPTER III

# THE RACE BEGINS

The four of us reviewed the situation. We came to the conclusion that things might have looked blacker than they did; but not much blacker.

We were short (one so often is) of capital. Cash in hand amounted to six hundred odd milreis (a milrei is worth about fourpence) and 80 rounds of .44 ammunition. (One cartridge is worth 800 reis, or four-fifths of a milreis, on the upper reaches of the river; as you get nearer civilization its value declines gradually to 400 reis.) We had also the batalõa, a good one, and a certain amount of junk which we might be able to sell, and food for four or five days. Our greatest asset was Queiroz, at that moment scouring the purlieus of the mission for a brace of oarsmen; he had rather touchingly elected to stay with us at a wage of five milreis a day. When you came to think of it, we might have been a lot worse off.

But equally, when you came to think of it, we might have had a very much shorter and easier journey before us. All we knew about this journey was that in about a week we ought to reach the village called Conceição. When the river was high launches came up as far as this, and for part of the season there was a regular service. I knew that Major Pingle expected — or gave out that he expected — to be able to hire a launch there; if he did, the rest of the journey to Pará should take him less than a fortnight. But I had my doubts about that launch, for the river was very low, and below Conceição the rapids were said to get really bad; very likely nothing bigger than a batalõa could get through them at present.

In any case we could not possibly hire a launch, or even afford passages on one which might be going downstream already. We should have to hire a crew to take us down through the rapids to Marabá, said to be three weeks' journey further north by canoe. The rest of the run had to be made in a series of launches, and if you were lucky it took only a week; but as according to even the most optimistic calculations we should have exhausted all our money by the time we got to Marabá, it was prudent to allow a somewhat longer period.

Then there was the question of the revolution. Rumours current at the Mission Station said that this was raging in the northern states and, more specifically, that the young men of Conceição were being pressed into military service. How much truth there was in this we could not tell; but the rumours seriously affected our chances of getting a crew to take us down there, nobody in the district appearing particularly anxious for either death or glory. Moreover, if the revolution really was in full blast, things might be awkward for us, since all the papers, passes, and credentials which had brought us safely up country from São Paulo were in the possession of Major Pingle.

The missionaries were kindly but not very reassuring. They did not expect us to get farther than Conceição. 'We shall see you back before very long,' they said. 'You're always welcome.' They knew there had been some sort of a row, and I think they were faintly appalled; they were gentle people. 'You'll all camp on the same praia and make up your differences,' they predicted. We grinned in a tough way, and said we should see about that.

An hour after the others had left Queiroz turned up with a crew. It consisted of one Caraja, a tall man with long, rather histrionic black hair and a patient, enduring face, ravaged by deep lines, and a young negro who worked for the missionaries. The negro's name was Casimiro; he had liquid eyes like a spaniel's and a startlingly musical voice. He was very much afraid of being press-ganged at Conceição, but we offered him a good wage, and a pair of pyjamas as a bonus, and he conquered his qualms. Both these men worked wonderfully for us, and we liked them.

It had been a rapid, violent morning. Personally I enjoy almost any crisis as long as it lasts, and the very nearly hopeless situation which was the legacy of this one had not been in force long enough to produce in any of us a due despondency. Now, unexpectedly, we were in a position to get under weigh on the heels of the others. Eventually we must meet delay, annoyance, perhaps disaster; but for the moment those things were too far away to bother about. We started in the highest of spirits.

That same evening we overhauled and passed Major Pingle. It was a triumphant moment.

His batalõa was lighter than ours, and he had a two hours' start. He had counted on our losing at least a day, and probably more, before we found a crew; he had counted on reaching Conceição well ahead of us; he had counted on finding a launch there which would get him to Pará anything from three weeks to three months before us. He could count on nothing now — until he caught us up again.

We sighted his party an hour before nightfall. They had been taking things easy and were camped, early, on a comfortable praia on the Bananal side. We paddled past them, 100 yards away, in silence; there was no need to underline with derision the shock they had received. When we first came in sight we saw them standing still, looking blank; but by the time we were close they were very busy feeding the surviving otter, all bending over it, very absorbed, now and then laughing heartily: like a group of people to whom someone has said: 'Now, don't look up. Stay just as you are while I take a snap.' We went smoothly by, feeling absurdly elated.

We camped where night caught us, two miles further downstream. From the highest point on our praia we could see their fire, a small petulant flicker in the gloom. The race — a very long and in the end a very close race — had begun.

It had never occurred to us that we might pass Major Pingle: by both sides it had been tacitly, and with good reason, assumed that we should not meet again until we reached Pará — if then. Now that we had passed him we began to discover unsuspected implications in that delightful circumstance. We remembered that a good deal of the expeditionary funds in Major Pingle's possession were in the form of cheques on which — if we got to Pará ahead of, or even soon after, him and had money left to cable with — we could stop payment. We remembered also Major Pingle's threat to 'tell Brazil and the world' that our indiscreet conduct had wrecked the expedition, and we realized that he would confidently expect us to do the same by him, if we got the chance to do it first. And then there was always the possibility that we might somehow manage to commandeer the only launch at Conceição. Yes; Major Pingle stood to lose — or at least he thought he stood to lose — a great deal by letting us get ahead. And though it still looked as if in the end he must be first past the post at the mouth of the Amazon, with us a very bad second, we knew that we had given him an anxious moment. We hoped devoutly that we should be able to prolong it.

The next day I woke everyone an hour before dawn. Major Pingle's fire was already alight, and we were delighted to think that he and the loyalists — none of them keen early risers — had felt impelled to make a flying start. While Queiroz made a hot drink called *agua doce* by boiling a lump of rapadura (this was the nearest thing we had to a substitute for tea or coffee) the rest of us cut loose and threw overboard the thatched awning which made a little cabin in the stern of the batalõa. It was perhaps rash to jettison our only protection against sun and rain; but at this time of year a stiffish north wind, called *banzeira*, blows with invariable perversity upstream through the middle hours of every day; and the little cabin, offering resistance to this, delayed our progress. From now on, speed counted for everything; we should get plenty of comfort when the race was over.

We were off while it was still dark, going as hard as we could;

a two-mile lead is not much when the course is a thousand miles and the rules ill-defined. Queiroz and the Caraja rowed, Casimiro steered, and we four paddled in two shifts, taking alternate hours. The blue and gold macaw, which Neville had bought from Indians at the mouth of the Tapirapé, sat on the roof-pole of the vanished cabin and did nothing at all. Nothing very helpful, that is. She ate with an air of abstraction such articles of clothing or equipment as hung on the pole within her reach. Every stroke of the oars made the clumsy boat rock slightly, and every single stroke she greeted with a short, distressful cry. Every single stroke, every day, for several weeks. I can hear her now; I shall hear her still twenty years from now.

Her name, curiously enough, was Polly. It turned out afterwards she was a male.

# CHAPTER IV

# THE FIRST RAPIDS

Six days later we were eating the last of our rice, squatting in the shade of great trees on the east bank of the Araguaya. We ate with determination, but without relish; we needed a change of diet.

We were just going to get one. On the opposite bank, half a league downstream, the top of a square tower broke the knobbly sky-line on the jungle, defiantly symmetrical among so much casual confusion. We were in sight of Conceição; the tower was the tower of a Dominican monastery. The rest of the village was out of sight.

As we ate, we looked with curiosity at that comforting landmark. I thought more kindly than I usually do of that civilization of which it was the fantastically advanced post, recalling almost with emotion things like policemen, and telephone directories, and being polite, and publishers' advertisements, and the smell of petrol, and week-ends — details, not in themselves very admirable, in a background for which I now for the first time began to feel a vague nostalgia. We discussed with animation the sort of meal we might expect to be eating in a few hours' time, and indulged in largely academic speculation on our chances of finding a launch at Conceição. From time to time we remembered — as one remembers to touch wood — to look back upstream; but the wide river was always empty, and we did not seriously fear to find it otherwise. We were confident that we had increased our lead on Major Pingle.

It had been a successful run, so far, and as swift as we could make it by rising ridiculously early, and paddling for thirteen or fourteen hours a day, and bolting our food at the midday halt. Not that there was much temptation to do anything but bolt it. Our diet was simple. When we left Bananal we had with us, besides a certain amount of rice and farinha, and a little rapadura, a large slab of dried meat, or *carne seca*. This was about the size of the top of a card-table, over which — in the matter of food-value — it did not at first appear to us to possess any very obvious advantages. It lay about the boat, looking like the charred wing of a dragon who had made a forced landing in the Everlasting Fire, and emitting a powerful but unattractive smell. The chips which we whittled off and cooked with the rice provided good exercise, but poor eating; we masticated with a sense of frustration.

On the second day after leaving Bananal our suspicions were aroused by the appearance on this meat of a number of small, well-knit grubs, of a whitish colour. Built on the lines of a caterpillar, they closely resembled those little livid creatures which are often to be observed roaming unhappily about your place after you have been so ill-advised as to order Camembert cheese at one of those picturesque country hotels — resorts whose cuisine fosters, among foreign visitors, the belief that the Englishman's capacity for enduring hardship without complaint is as great to-day as it ever was. When we saw these grubs, which appeared to be of a home-loving disposition and could only with difficulty be evicted from their burrows in our precious meat, we were at first filled with misgiving. 'By God,' said some of us, 'anyone who touches any more of that meat is a damned fool.'

Queiroz, however, was not perturbed. Whenever a grub appeared on the meat he was cutting up, he flicked it away; but he had no qualms about eating its favourite haunts, and we very soon forgot ours, arguing, for the sake of form, that if it did not hurt the men it would not hurt us. This was just as well, for there was nothing else to eat.

Actually there was nothing irregular in the presence of these little creatures. The method of manufacturing *carne seca* (which I believe to be much the same thing as *xarque*, or jerked beef) is as follows: You cut the fresh meat into thin slices, salt it, and spread it in the sun. After three or four days, it is dried. Theoretically, the salt should have kept the insects away while it was drying; but in practice this has not been so. Long before the meat is hard and stiff like a board, hundreds of flies have laid their eggs in it, and the white grubs are established in force. The meat is accordingly hung up and severely beaten with long sticks; the grubs fall out of it and carpet the ground like snow. Not all of them, however, do this; in the folds and crinkles of the meat a skeleton staff remains to carry on the business of eating it. It was these gallant survivors who obliged us now to examine each mouthful more attentively than, in the normal course of events, we should have cared to examine it.

We did all we could to vary the menu. Once we brought off a coup by buying up all the bananas in a Caraja village (most of them had no fruit of any kind) and these tasted all the better for the knowledge that we had left none for Major Pingle's party. Once a man sold us 150 oranges for threepence. Once I found and boiled some gull's eggs, which unhappily turned out to be bad. But mostly we lived on rice.

Almost every day we passed a hut, or a cluster of huts, where a family, in which the Portuguese, the negro, and the Indian strains were inextricably mixed, lived in unimaginable, un-resented poverty, I never quite got used to such startling, such easily avoidable indigence. There is a saying, 'No one can starve in Brazil.' But I think it was coined by someone who had never been to the interior, who had never had his illusions about the jungle dispelled, who believed all he had heard about the fruits and the roots and the nuts which grow with such proverbial luxuriance in the equatorial forests. Alas, that railway poster, that Swiss-Family-Robinson conception of these regions is all wrong: you will find — in the dry season, at any rate — nothing to eat in this jungle except what you take there. No, not so much as a berry.

On the other hand, the soil is fertile and the climate good.

Anything will grow there, they say; and I think they are right, though I don't know how they can tell, since cultivation is never seriously attempted.   In any case, it is hardly conceivable that anyone could be content to live with so narrow a margin of subsistence as those peasants do on the banks of the Araguaya.

A thatched roof shows among the trees at the water's edge. This is Barreira de Santa Something, of which we have been talking for the last forty-eight hours. 'Here we shall get rice,' the men have been saying, 'and meat and rapadura: milk, fruit, cheese: yes, and perhaps coffee. Here they have everything.' 'Garantido!' they add, seeing my scepticism, 'Garantido, Senhor Pedro!'  In their confidence they become almost plaintive.

So we land, full of hopes but otherwise empty, and scramble up the bank.

In a clearing on top of the bank we find two or three mud huts, each consisting largely of a kind of veranda with a room behind it in which the women live, and which no man is allowed to enter.  The veranda, with its floor of hard dry mud, is the living-room, the dining-room, and the kitchen; and at night most of the men sleep there, slinging their hammocks from the beams.  The furniture consists of a few stools and boxes; but the bareness of the place is concealed by a litter of saddles, lariats, facões, paddles, cooking pots, and sometimes a very old Winchester rifle.  The people of the house sit listlessly, and with an air of resignation, doing nothing at all.  Life for them seems to be no more than keeping an appointment with death, and they wear a faint air of disgust, as if their instinct tells them that death is going to be unpardonably late.  Only the children — unaware, as yet, of what kind of a sentence it is that they are serving — move with joy and vigour in the sunlit world, warring eternally with mangy dogs and pigs and poultry, passionately embracing kittens, tumbling in the dust with tears and laughter.

In the trees on the edge of the clearing sit a dozen urubús nuzzling for ticks in their noisome feathers; when they flap their heavy wings there is a dull, nasty, hollow sound, and the air seems full of doom and decay.

When we come into sight the people of the house look at us without interest; the men are genuinely incurious, the women pretend to be. Across an elaborate barrier of reserve we exchange greetings, all the while eyeing the hens in a calculating manner and reading in the piles of cow-dung a promise of milk and meat. As quickly as is decent we approach the business in hand.

'Have you any rice to sell us?'

'Or meat?'

'Or eggs?'

'Or milk?'

'Or rapadura?'

'Or cheese?'

'Or bananas?'

On tenterhooks we await the answer.

They gaze at us with lack-lustre eyes. The less dejected of the two girls giggles. Her mother looks up slowly and says in a silvery unapologetic voice:

'Não tem. Aqui tem nada. We have nothing here to sell. There is enough only to feed ourselves.'

She drops her eyes. The interview is closed.

It is useless to expostulate. What she says is true. A little rice, a little farinha: that is all they have. This evening one of the boys will catch some fish, and in the morning there will be milk for the children. Existence will be prolonged; there is no need to look ahead.

I hope they never do look ahead, these people. They are inured to the emptiness of the present; and no doubt for them, as for most of us, the past always manages to seem as if it had not been empty. But the knowledge that the future too will be a blank, a vacuum, would surely shake the sour equanimity with which they keep their appointment with death.

So our shopping was never very successful, and when we re-embarked we would rag the men for believing so firmly, as all Brazilians do, in Promised Lands where experience ought to have taught them that the milk and honey were never in fact on tap.

At only one place were we not disappointed. This was Santa María, a tiny village standing on a bluff, which we approached through luminous whorls of mist while the sun was still low. Here we found, bought, and consumed two bottles of beer, our first for many weeks. It was a solemn moment. The beer was warm and extremely nasty, not at all the sort of thing to break one's fast with after three hours' paddling. But we enjoyed it, because we so obviously ought to have enjoyed it; and its vile taste made it easy to form good resolutions about not wasting any more money on useless luxuries.

After the beer we had breakfast with the Municipal Prefect, a charming man. He gave us coffee and milk and sugar and little sweet cakes made of farinha. Poor man, he might as well have tried to entertain a troupe of sea-lions with a single tin of sardines. Almost before he had pulled up his own chair the little cakes were gone; we drank all his milk and all his coffee, and when he left the room to fetch more we ate up all his sugar with a spoon. We had, I fear, no shame. Afterwards we reeled off elaborate thanks and apologies in bad Portuguese, and I took a photograph of him standing in his front door, with a wide-eyed grandchild in full military uniform beside him. We had an awful business getting the child to look pleasant; all through breakfast he had been teaching jiu-jitsu to a small pig underneath the table, and he was full of indignation at being interrupted in this enjoyable and health-giving pursuit. This was the first of many occasions on which I repaid debts of hospitality by taking photographs of our hosts; we had no other means of repaying them.

Santa María was a success. We were not only refreshed but enriched. The .44, that disgraceful weapon, we had oiled and polished till it shone, and at Santa María we sold it, on its lustre, to a man of extravagantly villainous appearance; he gave us sixty milreis for it, and bought thirty rounds of ammunition as well. After that we pushed off hastily and paddled hard. We wanted to be out of range before he tested it; he had not the air of a good loser.

Since the moment when we passed them we had seen Major Pingle's party only once. This was on the evening of the second day. We were on shore, bartering bullets for cheese in a fazenda one degree less miserable than most. The opposition paddled slowly past, hugging the other bank, looking for a place to camp. The river here was wide, and they did not recognize our batalõa, newly stripped of its palm leaf cabin and looking quite a different shape from when they saw it last. We let them pass, and then cut down under the lea of a long island out of their sight, and camped downstream of them. That night we toyed with the idea of raiding their camp and stealing their cooking pot, which would have brought upon them inconvenience, ignominy, and delay. In the end we abandoned the project: a thing I shall always regret.

After that we had not seen them again; our backward glances grew steadily rarer and more perfunctory. We had good reason — especially during the last two days — to believe that our lead had been substantially increased. Two days ago we had struck the first of the rapids, and for a variety of reasons we were fairly certain that we had made better going here than the others had.

We had rounded a bend, to find that a long low line of rock was ruled across the river in front of us; from beyond it came a steady muttering sound, which grew as we came nearer into a roar. At first there was something unnatural about this, and I realized with surprise how completely we had come to expect silence from the river. In all these weeks it had never once been vocal, so that we hardly thought of it as running water at all; for many hundreds of miles it had slid away before us without making a sound.

Presently gaps appeared in the barrier of rock, and through them we could see a series of similar barriers, interspersed with little outcrops and islands; between all these the water was white and dancing or else humped itself up in smooth dark green cushions, curiously veined and dimpled, which gave you a great sense of tortuous, ulterior power.

We picked a gap where the channel looked promising and was not too ominously flecked with white. We went at it bald-headed, the oars and paddles going like mad, for to dodge the sudden rocks you need plenty of steerage way. Our boat, that unresponsive hulk, gathered speed as the current caught her and plunged in among the rocks like a mad thing. Though these first rapids were a small matter compared with what we were to meet further downstream, we were filled — because we had been travelling so slowly for so long — with the best sort of exhilaration that can be found in speed. We yelled like demons as the rocks fled past and the banks of the river, hitherto so drearily static, streamed astern. At this unheard of rate, we should be home in no time. In a quarter of an hour we had doubled our mileage for the morning.

I think we were lucky to get through unscathed. (Major Pingle's boat, we heard later, was stove in on a rock; they lost half a day repairing it.) None of us knew which of a dozen channels was the right one, and to guess it, with the river as low as this and white danger signals everywhere, was not easy. Queiroz fancied himself at the helm and insisted on steering; but since he lacked one eye and all local knowledge, he was not really the man for the job. He gave us our only bad moment by impaling the bows on a rock in the middle of a fast, steep run. We were overboard at once, balancing painfully on sharp ledges in the fierce current and trying to lift the boat free. In this we succeeded; but the stern swung giddily round and knocked Bob off his perch. He disappeared. Clinging to the painter, we let the straining boat drop gradually downstream, scanning the waters with some anxiety and coining obituaries. But Bob reappeared under the stern, looking surprised and rather offended. His topee was still on his head, his pipe still in his mouth. We were not an explorer short, after all. Miraculously, he was not even hurt.

There was one very bad place, where our slapdash tactics had to be modified. In the mouth of the rapid we landed on a rock and surveyed, not without misgivings, a long stretch of roaring broken water, steeper and more turbulent than usual. We had not a chance of getting through this at full tilt.

We covered up the gear and supplies as best we could, and divided into two parties. One, swearing and staggering as the current tugged at their bodies and the rocks cut their feet, established themselves as firmly as they could in the mouth of the rapid and hung on to the painter, paying it out a little at a time. The others, clinging to the gunwales, were carried slowly down alongside the boat and manhandled her over the rocks on which she went aground. It was a tricky enough business, working in opposition to so great and so swift a volume of water, and when it was over, with no damage done and hardly any water shipped, we felt very pleased with ourselves. Basking luxuriously on a sandbank, with the batalõa floating at peace before us, we stood ourselves an extra ration of rapadura and speculated maliciously as to how Major Pingle's party would overcome the difficulties in store for them. We knew how little an amphibious hurly-burly would appeal to them.

So we felt that we had put six good days behind us, as we gazed across the river at that square stone tower standing up out of the welter of green. The first stage of our journey down to the Amazon was over, and at the end of it we were better off than we had ever expected to be: for we were still ahead of the others. But the first stage had been straightforward going, the easiest part of the whole journey. If we were going to have troubles, I reflected, it was now that they were going to begin.

# CHAPTER V

# THREE FRIENDS AND TWO MONKS

DOMINATED by the now familiar tower, a huddle of houses showed among the trees. On the foreshore tiny figures moved slowly in bright clothes, and we remembered that to-day was Sunday. Shipping was represented by one launch, derelict and eviscerated, lying on its side in the mud; Major Pingle's hopes of being wafted to Pará in speed and comfort were dashed.

We left Casimiro in charge of the batalõa and invaded the village. No money, we kept on telling each other, must be spent on luxuries; but one of the booths in the market was open, and almost before we knew what had happened we found that we had indulged in a swift, horrible orgy of bananas and biscuits and beer. Distended to the limit of our capacity, we warned each other remorsefully that this must not occur again.

The next thing that happened was the sudden appearance of the Paulistas. The Paulistas really deserve a chapter to themselves.

There were three young men of good birth from São Paulo: Herman (26), Oscar (22), and Cassio (21). They had left the city in June, over a month before the revolution broke out, and we had first come across them at Piedade, half way between Leopoldina and the mouth of the Tapirapé. They were travelling downstream, with no men and very few supplies: doing their own cooking and taking their time. They had a number of vague but rather dashing plans, each of which they abandoned in turn. They were going up the Rio das Mortes: they were going up the Tapirapé: they were going to look for diamonds: they were going to stay in the interior through the rainy season. Each project fired their imagination for a time, and each was eventually dropped and forgotten. In point of fact, they did not much mind what they did and they had no particular qualifications for doing anything at all, except travel, under the best sort of rough conditions, through a part of Brazil which very few of their countrymen, and none of their class, had ever dreamed of visiting. They were cheerful, aimless vagabonds, full of an enterprise which was none the less admirable for being ill co-ordinated.

Below Piedade they used often to camp on our praias and stroll across at nightfall for a better meal than they could have given themselves. I was always glad to see them, for they were charming and intelligent people, full of stimulating though inaccurate information about the country; their invariable good humour and their boundless romanticism were a welcome contrast to the strained relations and the more or less obligatory cynicism which prevailed in our small, cramped world.

Major Pingle, however, did not like them. He always treated them politely, for their families were influential in Brazil. But to us he confided dark suspicions of their motives. He thought, or pretended to think, that they were envoys of his favourite bugbear, the Press. For him they were spies, and cunning spies; in their artless, friendly conversation he contrived to discern a series of deep-laid traps, against which he never tired of warning us.

'Don't tell them anything,' he would mutter urgently, as their long black canoe slid across the twilit water towards our camp. 'They're out to pump you. Don't you see how close they're sticking to us?' And he would ramble off into a foolish, growling tirade against the unscrupulous Press.

It was useless to point out to him that, even if he would not accept their own statement that none of them was connected with any newspaper, they had gone out of touch with civilization before we had left London, and long before any information about the expedition had been made public in Brazil: and that in any case they had no swifter or surer means of sending news down to the coast than we had. He refused to be influenced by these considerations. 'They're spies,' he repeated sullenly. 'I know those newspapers. . . .'

So by degrees the poor Paulistas, with their high spirits and their courtesy, their easily stirred sensibility, and their quick enthusiasms, acquired in the eyes of our more impressionable members a sinister glamour, and were treated by some as Countesses of foreign extraction are (or ought to be) treated by King's Messengers. They were very far from deserving this.

Herman, the eldest, was fair and extremely good-looking: much more like a Scandinavian than a South American. He was the most confirmed romantic of the three. In him you had that rare thing — a man born to wander and be a vagabond, who recognizes this need in his nature, and who can talk about it without making you feel sick. It is true that his ideas on the subject, and the words in which he clothed them, were painfully conventional, and derived from the lowest schools of thought and literature. But what on another man's lips would have seemed trite and intolerable patter about Romance and Adventure and the Great Open Spaces was on Herman's real and true and easily acceptable. Here at last was that mythical figure, the Adventurer; it was the world's fault, and not his, that the phrases in which he revealed himself were hollow and hackneyed and stank of the Sunday papers during the hiking season. His simple and impetuous nature shone through them and redeemed them, so that one forgot the many base and foolish uses to which they had been put, and saw in them only accurate and deeply felt self-analysis. I saw much less of Herman, as you shall hear, than of the other two, and I wish I had seen more. He was an attractive person.

Cassio was dark, and handsome in a pleasant boyish way; he looked much the youngest of the three. He too was a romantic; but his stock-in-trade was action, not — like Herman's — dreams. His spiritual home was Zenda. Inheriting from his family (his father had been governor of São Paulo in 1924) that instinctive passion for politics which is the ruin of Brazil, he saw himself against a background of barricades and *coups d'état*, machine-guns and manifestoes. He was an idealist; but for him (though he did not know it) the chief attraction of Utopia was the fact that it could only be attained by these violent and dramatic means. He had more gaiety and intelligence than the other two, and though his culture was not deep he was an easy person to talk to; his nature made up in spontaneity what it lacked in profundity, and he was very *sympathique*. He had a capacity — rare in Brazil — for restlessness, and on this I used to trade when the more lethargic Oscar was sunk in despair; for in the next month we often needed their help in the long, hopeless struggle against the forces of incompetence and delay. Taking him all round you will not find many nicer young men than Cassio in South America: or anywhere else, for that matter.

Then there was Oscar. The thing that struck you most about Oscar was how old-fashioned he looked; it hit you in the eye every time you saw him. That full beard: those great, solemn, liquid eyes; that black hair *en brosse*; that large awkward body, tending to corpulence: those fleshy thighs, so tightly encased in their breeches: those brown boots: that air of rueful and dyspeptic piety, of sorrowful surprise — these were all surely out of some dim photograph in some nineteenth-century explorer's memoirs. Even his clothes, once white, had taken on the yellowish, obsolescent tinge peculiar to a faded photographic print. He seemed to belong altogether to the day before yesterday.

Oscar spoke English, in a deep, remorseful voice. Once he had studied law in Manchester, and he used to tell us wild stories of his student days, which usually ended up; 'But my frien' was very dronk, you see, Peter: so I said I would not go with him any more that night.' Oscar's wild oats were a stunted, wistful crop. He was a kind, solid, ineffectual person, almost unbelievably amiable. He had more ballast than Cassio, to whom he acted as a kind of anchor, cancelling out his impulsiveness: so that if you left those two to themselves they never got anything done at all, in the end.

Oscar's digestion was always letting him down and deepening his air of melancholy. 'I think perhaps it is better that I do not eat to-day, Peter,' he would say, looking at me like a wounded stag; and I would agree emphatically. But his good resolutions shrivelled and died in the smell of cooking, and he would be seen devouring a mountain of rice and dubious meat. 'Cassio says perhaps it is better if I eat a little,' he would explain apologetically. And within the hour there would be stifled groans, and a voice full of self-reproach would announce: 'Oh, Peter, I 'ave a bloody stomach-ache, you know.'

To the end Oscar remained something of a mystery to me. What was he here for? And what was he getting out of it? Cassio and Herman had tastes and temperaments which explained their presence; they were in some sense native to the Back of Beyond. But Oscar — that huge, rather pathetic figure, with a literal mind and a serious outlook: Oscar, who so clearly ought to have been working, unhappily and without success, for examinations, and then suddenly marrying a very pretty girl — what was Oscar doing on this hazardous wild-goose chase, which had never even got as far as picking its bird? I never found the answer to this question. One day, sitting among us in the crowded batalõa, he was observed to be hard at work with a knife on the seat in front of him. When he had finished, and had sadly, tidily swept away the chips with his enormous hand, we saw that he had been carving a girl's name: YVONNE. There it stood, in large regular letters, a challenge to our curiosity. Oscar folded up his knife and went to sleep. No reference to the name was ever made in his hearing by anyone.

It was, however, responsible for the theory that Some Woman had Driven him to This; and this theory may have been correct. But I hardly think so. Oscar's romanticism, like his beard, was an occasional growth. I believe the true explanation was simpler and less exciting: Cassio had dragged his anchor.

We had passed Herman, paddling a light canoe single-handed three or four days above Conceição. The smell of revolution in the air had aggravated Cassio's restlessness and split the party:

Herman had been left to his own vague and lackadaisical devices, which he did not mind in the least, while the other two hurried on downstream. Their anxiety to get back to civilization was understandable, for they had both left their families in São Paulo, from which rumour now said (falsely) that the foreign residents were being evacuated, prior to its bombardment by the President's troops. So we found Oscar and Cassio in Conceição.

They had been held up there for twelve days, and were both fatter than when we had seen them last, over a month ago. They exclaimed at my emaciated appearance, of which, lacking a mirror, I had been unaware till now. They themselves had no batalõa, and although they had several times been promised a lift downstream in someone else's, there had always, at the last moment, been something to prevent the boat from starting. They feared, with some reason, that the people here suspected their political motives; for we were now in the state of Pará, which, like all the other Brazilian states except one, was backing the Federal Government against São Paulo. They were sick of delay, and longing to get away from Conceição.

We were delighted to see them, and after some discussion it was arranged that they should come downstream as our passengers, paying a third of the expenses of the journey. There were many advantages in this, chief among them the fact that, since six could travel almost as cheaply as four, it increased our slender capital. Moreover, Oscar would be useful as an interpreter; I was the only one of our party who could speak Portuguese with any approach to fluency, and it was not a very near approach. The drawbacks were two: first, overcrowding would make the boat even more uncomfortable than it was already, and secondly, there was a danger that we might be involved in the Paulistas' political troubles. But on the whole it looked like a very satisfactory arrangement; and so it proved to be.

There was much to be done. Between Conceicão and

Marabá, where we might hope for a launch, the rapids were a serious matter, and expert pilots were scarce and dear. But Queiroz, working with admirable and un-Brazilian despatch, found a pilot, and the pilot found three men to row for him, and we engaged the lot at a surprisingly reasonable wage: 100 milreis for the pilot, and sixty each for the men. We now had eleven mouths to feed, not counting the parrot, and in a frantic hurry we set about buying supplies, the bill for which came in the end to about 150 milreis. Even in Conceição we could not get all we wanted, and we knew that we should have to make more purchases before we reached Marabá.

It is the etiquette of the river that when you pay off a crew you must give them enough money to cover their passage back to the place where you hired them, and you must also make arrangements for their return journey. So altogether Casimiro and the Caraja cost us about eighty milreis and a good deal of time spent in rushing about and interviewing people who were said to be going upstream to Bananal in the near future. Not that we grudged it, for they had both worked splendidly.

But by this time our financial position had begun to look extremely unsound. We calculated that, even if all went well, the journey from the Mission Station to Marabá was going to cost us at the very least 750 milreis; and we had started with only about 650. However, we had got ninety milreis for that rifle and ammunition at Santa María, and the Paulistas' share of the expenses came to 130 milreis. As things stood at present, we should be just solvent when we reached Marabá.

But Marabá was less than half way to Pará, and from Marabá onwards travel would be a much more expensive business. It was necessary to be a good deal more than just solvent if we wanted to get any nearer home than Marabá. Our only hope lay in judicious gun-running.

The people in Conceição were excessively poor. A respectable-looking woman stopped me as I was walking along the street and asked me if I had heard anything of a young man (she told me his name and described him) who had gone upstream seven years ago to the diamond-fields at Registro. I said that I was sorry, but I couldn't help her: I had been no higher up the river than Leopoldina. She thanked me, apologized for troubling me, and then, as if it was the most normal thing in the world, asked me if I hadn't got a few reis to give her. . . . And this was no professional mendicant, but a woman belonging to the better class of villager, in a country where pride plays an important part in determining conduct.

Considering how poor they all were, and considering that we were only in Conceição for a day, we did remarkably well. The armaments market was unhappily not as brisk as it is in more civilized parts of the world, but we sold a Luger automatic for 200 milreis to the lieutenant who was the government's principal representative. Forty per cent of the inhabitants were said to be down with malaria, and we got rid of a lot of fever tablets (we let them have these cheap) and also two snake-bite syringes. For some unearthly reason, dark glasses were in keen demand, and we sold several pairs of these, which hardly any of us ever wore. Altogether we cleared about 300 milreis in Conceição, and prospects looked brighter.

It was not a very attractive place. The three or four streets swarmed with goats and poultry and naked children. The miserable one-story houses were built of wood and plaster, and sometimes painted an unfortunate shade of pink or light blue. From many of them came the wailing of fever-stricken infants, and from all of them came a powerful smell. The people in their cheap soiled clothes looked very dingy after the naked Indians. It only needed contact with civilization to remind us forcibly of its disadvantages.

But Conceição had one redeeming and endearing feature: the Dominicans. The village is the headquarters of the Dominican mission on the Araguaya. Towards the end of the last century the Dominicans opened up the river to the forces of enlightenment, and it was in large part due to their influence that the rather questionable policy of shooting all unknown Indians on sight was abandoned by the traders and prospectors who passed occasionally up and down the river. Everything I heard about the Dominicans inclined me to respect their work. They were the first white men to visit the Tapirapés: they have done a great deal to improve the manners of the Cayapos, an inordinately warlike tribe who live in the country behind Conceição; they have, as far as I could see, earned the respect and liking of everyone on the river: and their bishop (who was away when we passed through) has been under fire from arrows on several occasions — a pleasing trait in any bishop.

Only two of the Brothers were in residence at the time of our visit. They treated us with a kindness which I found rather affecting; one had somehow forgotten that people were quite often nice and helpful. They owned a house in the village, where the Paulistas were already living free of charge, and now they put the rest of it at our disposal. They did all they could to help us, and on the morning of our departure gave us a breakfast to which, in the days to come, we looked back as slum children are said to look back to a visit to the sea. We could do nothing in return, except photograph them again and again.

The elder of the two, Frère André, was French, a grey, ungainly man, with an upper lip stained by the taking of snuff. He had been out here for thirty-five years, in all that time returning to France only once. That had been during the War, and he had been suspected as a spy because of his curious accent. What he had seen in his country then had made him very sad; he was not sure now whether he would like to go back again. By all accounts, Europe was mad in these days.

The other Dominican, Frère Luiz, was a young Brazilian of about thirty. He came and talked to Roger and me for a long time about the Cayapos. Half the tribe is *manso*[1] now,

---

[1] Manso (tame) and bravo (fierce) are the Portuguese terms for 'good' and 'bad' Indians. Thus the Tapirapés are manso, the Chavantes bravo.

thanks to the Dominicans. But a lot of them are *bravo* still, and had indeed recently carried out a particularly brutal massacre at a tiny settlement farther downstream. (A few days later we passed the place, than which I have never seen a lovelier. Tall palms hung their heads in mourning over three huts; the roof of one of the huts had fallen in. An egret sat on the gunwale of a water-logged canoe. There was no wind; everything seemed abnormally quiet and still, frozen in regret. It was in truth no place for death.) The Cayapos shave the front and top of their scalps with sharpened slivers of bamboo, letting the rest of their hair hang down like a mane; this gives them a grotesque and rather daemonic appearance.

Frère Luiz insisted on our accepting as a gift three axe-heads of the Gorutiré tribe, whom he believed to be the especial enemies of the Tapirapés. (These are now in the British Museum with the rest of our trophies.) He also told us of a map which someone had found, torn to pieces, at a little village on the Rio Fresco, a tributary of the Xingú; it was said to have been left there by an Englishman, and was eventually brought to the bishop at Conceição. The bishop pieced it together, and saw that it was a map of the Indian territories on the head-waters of the Xingú, with notes on it in English. It was in the monastery even now, locked up in the bishop's room.

When we heard this we stiffened mentally like pointers. We had almost forgotten about Fawcett; but here once more was a whiff of that elusive scent which we had come out from England to pick up, with so notable a lack of success. If what Frère Luiz said was true, the map covered the district in which Fawcett disappeared.

I got hold of Oscar, and with his help concocted an un-believably flowery letter in Portuguese asking the bishop, when he returned, to send a copy of the map to me in London. This he very kindly did; I received it three months after I got back. But alas, the map was more inaccurate than anything which Fawcett, a Founder's Medallist of the Royal Geographical

Society, could have made, and the spelling of the tribal names of it differed markedly from his usage. All the same, it was the work of a man who knew something of his subject, and who had been in, or near, places which hardly anyone else has visited. I still wonder who he was.

We had reached Conceição about two o'clock in the afternoon. By dusk the same evening it was apparent that we should be ready to leave the next day; and anyone who has ever tried to get things done in a hurry in Brazil will realize from that fact how lucky we had been, and how well served.

We ate an enormous meal, and then went round to get a laissez-passer from the local lieutenant. (This was not really necessary, but it might come in useful later on.) The lieutenant had a shifty, overweening face, and made the formalities as long-drawn-out as he could, hoping against hope that some hitch or irregularity would crop up and give him a chance to display his power. But nothing did, and we withdrew to our quarters behind a barrage of compliments.

We had done so well with our sales that I decided that we could afford ten milreis for a radio to Pará, for transmission to *The Times* by cable. The drafting of this was a comic business. One way and another, most of the village had managed to congregate on the veranda where we were going to sleep. I had written out in English what I wanted to say; it was a non-committal message, not for publication, attributing the failure of our Fawcett-hunt to political and climatic conditions, warning them to beware of unauthorized communications, and asking them to pass on the information that we were all safe to our various families, whose telephone numbers I appended. (What strange and irrelevant symbols those telephone numbers seemed as I wrote them down, by the light of a lantern which picked out stray features in a semicircle of dark, outlandish faces, on paper across which fantastic insects crawled uncertainly.)

But I needed help in translating this message, for I knew that anything but Portuguese would get through hopelessly garbled. When I asked Oscar for a word in English, he would pass on my question to Cassio, and Cassio would pass it on to someone else: so that in the end the whole village was offering equivalents — which I had to sift by instinct — to the words, few but pregnant, which I wanted to use. The result looked to me fairly cryptic, but I hoped it would serve its purpose; as far as I knew no one in England — owing to the blockade on São Paulo — had heard anything of us since we left Rio in July.

Few things became us in Conceição like our leaving of it. Bloated with the Dominicans' breakfast, we staggered down to the boat at the appointed hour. The crew was not there. We scattered to search for them, and in time we found them. But we never found them all at once, and we made the fatal mistake of allowing, and even encouraging, the one we had found to go off and look for his fellows. So that in the end the whole party, with the exception of the parrot, chased its tail for two hot and irritable hours.

The loss of those two hours bulked disproportionately large in our minds, and as we stood on the shore beside our boat we kept looking apprehensively upstream, expecting at any moment to sight Major Pingle's batalõa. The great ones of the village watched our preparations with that expression of rather hostile scepticism which the sight of almost any form of activity produces on the face of the average Brazilian. Every now and then they offered an observation on the phenomenal perils which we must expect to encounter in the rapids in a season as dry as this: on the abnormally long period (eighteen days at the very least) which we must allow for the journey to Marabá: or on the imminence of the rains. But at last everything was ready, and Major Pingle was still not in sight. The order to embark was given.

But where was the pilot? Where was the intrepid fellow whose expert knowledge and address were to bring us through the sharp-fanged rocks, the ungovernable whirlpools? We looked about us anxiously.

We had not far to look. There he was — our white hope, our guardian angel — half way up the bank above the beach, sprawling on the turf with a brace of prostitutes who appeared to be undergoing — and willingly undergoing — the preliminary stages of death by strangulation.

'Pilot!' we shouted. 'Vai embora! We're off! Come here, pilot. Come here at once!'

The pilot began to sing.

He was drunk: not ordinarily, but magnificently. Few people can ever have been so drunk. We clambered up the bank and laid hold of him and marched him down to the boat. We got him into the boat. He fell out of the boat. We got him back into the boat, and this time he threw himself overboard and lay face downwards in the shallows, groping vaguely for a pair of dark glasses which had fallen off his nose. We saved him, against his will, from drowning, and made ready to push off.

The ladies on the bank waved. Casimiro and the Caraja came forward and bade us an affectionate farewell, in the attractive Brazilian formula which includes a request — usually all too pertinent — that you will pardon the faults they have committed in your service. (One of us had given the Caraja a white vest and a pair of navy blue bathing drawers. No longer naked, he looked — with his long, disordered hair, his rather horse-like face, and his half-proud, half-sheepish expression — exactly like the victor of a women's cross-country race in a News Reel.)

The ladies waved again. Our men replied with a valedictory broadside of innuendo. The pilot sang. We put our shoulders to the gunwale. The boat stirred, slid down the shingle. The parrot squawked. We scrambled in. The ponderous oars flashed. The boat began to move. Her bows headed once more for the Amazon. We were off.

The pilot fell overboard again.

# CHAPTER VI

# ELEVEN MEN IN A BOAT

WE made little progress that day; home seemed farther away than ever.

Before we had gone half a mile we found that the spare oar had been forgotten. We beached the boat on a long praia which stretched back to the village, and Cardozo, the leader of the crew, was told to go back and get it. He was on the point of starting when the pilot (who for the last ten minutes had been lying, as one dead, in the stern) came suddenly to life, uttered an unearthly cry, bounded out of the boat, and began to run madly back across the glaring sand towards the village. His speed was phenomenal, but his sense of direction let him down; his tracks in the sand swerved wildly this way and that, like the track of a particularly irresolute snake, so that although he travelled nearly twice as fast as Cardozo, he had to cover nearly twice as much ground to reach his objective. In the end Cardozo caught him and brought him back with the oar. We started off again.

His gallop had restored the pilot's professional pride, but not his professional skill. He insisted on taking the helm, and we zig-zagged wildly down the river, cursing and from time to time running violently aground. The oars and the huge clumsy rowlocks and the disposition of the sacks on which the rowers sat needed constant readjustment, and on top of all this the *banzeira* sprang up with such fury out of the north that we had to pull in to the shore and wait for it to drop.

The crew accepted the shortcomings of the pilot philo-sophically. Drink was notoriously the failing of an otherwise attractive character, they said; but they pointed out reassur-ingly that there was nowhere between here and Marabá where he could get any more: long before we reached the rapids he would have recovered from his bout. We found what comfort we could in this.

The crew were a good lot, on the whole: perhaps an exceptionally good lot, as crews go on the Araguaya. The hatred with which, at one time or another, I came to regard each individual member is not, I find, undying. They had their faults as travelling-companions; and it is probable that, if I had once more to pick ten men with whom to spend a fortnight in an open boat twenty feet long, those four would not be on my final list. But they did their best, or something very like it; and in the end they got us to Marabá.

In the interior of Brazil you cannot divide people into white and black, for the racial strains are too deeply and intricately mixed. But Cardozo and the pilot were undoubtedly white-ish, whereas Manoel and Octaviano were definitely on the black side. Cardozo was a man of about fifty, with a bold, square, rather attractive face and highly developed conversational powers; he reminded me of an Irishman. He was a comparatively civilized product for these parts, having seen something of the world as stoker on a line of ships plying between the Amazon and North America. On the other hand, he was not what is called a good citizen, for he had been in jail fifty-five times in the course of his career, and obtained his fifty-sixth conviction (after a knife fight) immediately after being paid off at Marabá. He evidently had some local reputation as a character, and this he bolstered up by the subtle and effective means of always expressing himself in the third person. 'Cardozo will do what he has undertaken to do' had an authoritative, an almost oracular ring, like 'The Editor regrets ...' Professions of good faith (however truthful) are always more convincing in the third person than in the first, because it sounds as if someone else has accepted them already: compare the phrase 'Duggie Never Owes'. Cardozo was always professing his good faith, and with such vehemence, such burning sincerity, that I put him down at once as a rogue and a bluffer. But he was always as good as his word when circumstances permitted; and when they did not he was genuinely upset, however good an excuse they gave him. He never let us down at all badly.

The pilot none of us liked. He was a delicately-made, rather effeminate man, with large, sad, contemptuous eyes and an ungracious manner. Moody, languid, and reserved, he lolled about the place with an air of profound boredom. At first we put this down to the after-effects of drink; but it persisted, and to the end he was unhelpful and aloof, inaccessible even through that code of fatuous and elementary humour with which we bridged the gulf between ourselves and the rest of the crew. He wore an enormous wide-brimmed hat of straw, which was always blowing overboard and having to be picked up, with much delay.

Octaviano was about eight per cent negro. He rowed bow, and had a curious metallic voice, a sense of humour, and a gigantic suppurating sore on one of his legs. He was a likeable boy.

So was Manoel, who cannot have been more than sixteen. He too was negroid, and his distinguishing characteristics were the toothache, a tendency to giggle, and a capacity for going into trances. Like all the rest of the crew except the pilot, he suffered intermittently from fever; luckily they never had it badly, nor all at the same time.

Handling them was a delicate and instructive business. Brazil is a democratic country in more than name, and all these men thought that they were as good as we were, if not better. Among us, their temporary employers, this theory did not command very general acceptance, and some of us found great difficulty in even pretending to subscribe to it. Neville had lived in the Far East and knew all about a Firm Hand with the Natives, of which policy both he and Bob were ardent and consistent advocates.

You cannot, however, take a firm hand with people when you are completely at their mercy. At least, it is no good if you do. On the Araguaya we were not top dogs, or anything like it. If the crew were slack, you travelled slowly; if you ticked them off for being slack, you travelled more slowly still; and if you ticked them off so much that they actively disliked you and found your society tiresome, they would desert you altogether. (They had been paid part of their wages in advance, and they could always wait at some fazenda for a lift back to Conceição.) Everything depended on keeping our relations cordial — not merely because it is better to be on good terms with the people you are sitting next to in an open boat under a tropical sun and sharing a plate with at night: but because if we were not on good terms with them we should get to Marabá either very slowly or not at all.

If they liked you, and you kept them in a good temper, they worked well. But unfortunately they hardly ever looked as if they were working well. Time means nothing to the Brazilian, has no value for him. It is too much to expect him to save it in the parsimonious, methodical way which plays so important a part in practically all modern activities. To the task of rowing us as quickly as possible from lat. 11 south to lat. 5 south our crew brought a happy-go-lucky and ill co-ordinated technique which hardly set off their exertions to the best advantage; and our orthodox minds, full of reverence for the team spirit and faith in the value (here transparently obvious) of pulling together, were always being shocked by the haphazard and not altogether satisfactory tactics employed against delay.

The crew were incapable of realizing that if every oarsman needs a rest of ten minutes in every hour, the distance covered will be considerably greater if all the oarsmen take that rest at the same time. They refused to be rationalized. If anyone felt like stopping to roll a cigarette he did so, regardless of the fact that someone else had held up our progress by doing the same thing a quarter of an hour before. If Roger and I were paddling at the time, we would continue to paddle in a very pointed manner, while the men lolled on their oars and chattered, maddeningly unaware of the self-righteous reproach on our faces. From the stern the Firm Hand party would enquire in tones of disgust what we were stopping for.

It was impossible to dragoon the men into more systematic habits. If we had cursed them for wasting time unnecessarily, they (being unconscious of the fault) would have rowed on woodenly under a sense of injustice and insisted on camping early that night. All goading had to be done with the utmost tact and good humour; only with jokes and bets and facetious challenges could you pare down the margin of delay to a minimum.

Then there was the matter of food. The peoples of this world may be divided into two sorts — the portion-minded, and the non-portion-minded. For my part, I greatly prefer to live among the latter. The United States of America are portion-minded to an almost fanatical degree. When you order a meal from the menu, you get exactly what you ask for: no more, and no less. If you have ordered brussels sprouts, you get brussels sprouts: seven of them, in a little dish. And you are oppressed by the knowledge that everyone else who orders brussels sprouts will get seven of them too, in an identical little dish. If you ask for marmalade they place before you, not a huge jar or butt of this indispensable conserve, but a little niggling pot, containing exactly one and a half tablespoonfuls, which is what they think you ought to find sufficient, and which with your true marmalade-fiend will not survive a couple of bites at a piece of toast. The pleasures of the table ought not to be standardized in this way: it is shameful.

Russia is portion-minded too, at the moment; but one cannot altogether blame them, seeing how little there is to eat there. No one in the Far East is portion-minded; but I am sorry to say that in this respect England is going rapidly to the dogs, or rather to the Lyons. More and more frequently, when you ask for cheese, you are insulted with a single miserable segment encased — by machinery — in silver paper, synthetic and symmetrical, a quantitative as well as a qualitative hint that you must discipline your appetite. And at the end of your meal the lugubrious chant of 'Let me see, sir, how many rolls did you have?' intrudes statistics where statistics are a blasphemous anomaly.

Brazil is very far from being portion-minded. When you order a meal, they put before you all they can, and everyone eats as much as he wants; the charge is the same for all. So the crew's attitude to our not very plentiful supplies was neither self-conscious nor calculating. The theory of rations was almost as far beyond their comprehension as the theory of relativity. Manoel, for instance, usually ate much more than anyone else; but the others did not look on him as being greedy or anti-social. The fact that the pilot had taken four of the last ten bananas did not arouse their indignation. We would look up from the meticulous subdivision of a hunk of rapadura to find that the crew, without authority but in all innocence, had already broached two fresh ones. The Firm Hand party used to get terribly upset about this; but I knew that it was both useless and dangerous to try and impose our own standards in these matters — the more so since the men were not at all greedy, but merely improvident.

Food dominated our lives. Continuous hunger is in many ways a very satisfactory basis for existence. It is, obviously, not the key to contentment; but it is an effective protection against the darker forms of discontent. An empty stomach does not give you confidence in yourself; but it numbs the critical faculties, and puts an end to introspection. Preoccupied with your memories of the last meal and your plans for the next, you have no occasion to indulge those grave doubts with regard to life in general and yourself in particular which would normally fill days as monotonous and unvarying as ours were.

# ELEVEN MEN IN A BOAT

When we got up, we drank a cup of black coffee and thereafter paddled for five or six hours, during all this period thinking only of the midday meal. The consumption of this turned our imaginations from our stomachs, which had been more or less satisfied, to our palates, which had not; and the earlier hours of the afternoon would be devoted to a discussion of the meals we would have when we got home, and to dietetic reminiscences: Brie cheese — alligator pears — the pint-pots at the Trout — cherry jam in the Pyrenees — a woodcock pie in Roger's room at Eton — sausages and mash. Then, as our hunger grew again, our thoughts would wander to more immediate and attainable things: the desirability of cooking that evening's rice with rather less fat, the chances of buying eggs at the Caraja village we should pass the next day. Our musings were markedly sublunary.

In point of fact, we always had enough to eat. But we worked fairly hard (though not nearly so hard as the men) and the food was perhaps not of a very satisfying kind. Our hunger, permanent though mild, was probably a blessing in disguise; for nothing turns you in on yourself so much as the Great Open Spaces. Those slow bright days on a shining river between two ragged intermittent walls of trees should, by rights, have provided an ideal background for meditation. Here, if anywhere, you would have thought, were peace and comprehension to be found. But it was not so. The uncharted immensities imposed on us an almost unbelievably parochial outlook; the empty world between those boundless horizons was like a room of mirrors. From day to day nothing changed; the interests and contacts which made up our normal lives had been in abeyance for months. We were bounded in a nut-shell twenty feet long; and, although we could count ourselves lords of infinite space, it was to that overcrowded nut-shell, with its small troubles and its small triumphs, that our thoughts always returned. Only hunger and paddling kept the minds of its occupants from dwelling too closely on themselves through the slow, hot hours.

# CHAPTER VII

# RUCTIONS

AFTER the first day things went reasonably well. The country began slowly to change; soon we were among hills again as the river dropped off the central plateau into the Amazon valley. We met rapids at frequent intervals, and they were more amusing than the ones above Conceição, which it needed only good luck to negotiate. Down here they were spectacular, almost operatic. The channels, only one of which was passable, plunged roaring into great tilted masses of dark rock. We sped down narrow corridors in the walls of which the furious water had eaten smooth inconsequent cavities, like the holes in a Gruyère cheese. The miles rushed by; the speed did us good, and the risk dispelled our habitual torpor.

There was one notably bad place, the Caxoeira de São Miguel. The pilot climbed a peak of rock in the mouth of the rapids and came down looking more inconsolable than ever. We should have to portage the gear and supplies and go through riding light, he said. So we emptied the boat and carried all the stuff half a mile downstream to the tail of the bad place, tottering under our loads over the sharp rocks. Then we drew lots for the ride, which everyone wanted but only three of us could take; Roger and Neville and I were condemned to a merely photographic activity on the shore. But the sight was worth almost as much as the sensation. The boat went leaping down that boiling staircase like a live thing, riding the humps and whorls of water at a suicidal speed. The pilot, standing braced to his tiller on the stern, was transfigured from a morose obstructionist to a daring and dynamic master of his craft. His yells, muted by the crash of waters to a reedy urgent whimper, came to us faintly. A flight of cormorants swung up from the rocks and fled downstream, dark outrunners to the careering boat.

It was quickly over. We reassembled in a backwater only vaguely troubled by the current tearing past its mouth and reloaded the boat. The next stretch would be fast, but not dangerous. When I congratulated the pilot, he disowned the praise, ascribing our preservation, with a wholly unexpected air of sincerity, to God.

Half an hour later there was another tricky patch, and we resorted to the old dodge of letting the boat down by the painter. But thereafter it was all plain and delightfully fast sailing. In between the rapids the current grew steadily faster the further we got downstream.

Whenever there was a moon, and whenever we had a clear stretch of river in front of us, we travelled by night. The memory of those silent, black and silver hours is curiously vivid. The cool night air on one's naked body: the melancholy fluted calls of birds: the little shower of phosphorus spreading out fanwise from one's lifted paddle-blade: the shape of the rowers' heads against the stars: the muttering of the sleepers huddled in the stern. Paddling at night seemed ten times easier than paddling by day, and I found so real a pleasure in it that I always took the first spell and prolonged it till dawn.

We went forward smoothly. Sometimes the crew would sing, in low, unmusical, reflective voices; sometimes the moon would make them garrulous, and they would tell me legends (in which they implicitly believed) about the river — how this bend was haunted by a monstrous fish, or possibly an eel, which in the year 1926 had swallowed a boatload of eight men on their way up to the diamond fields, and how there were strange carvings on the walls of the rapids we should pass to-morrow which, if they could only be deciphered, gave the clue to the whereabouts of the Minas dos Martyrios, the fabled diamond mines which some say Fawcett was seeking. The moon made us very friendly and confidential, and I used to tell them about shooting in England; they were disappointed to hear that there were no jaguars there.

Two moments in this night-travel stand out in my memory with especial clearness. One was an hour of the most satisfying sleep I have ever had. The stern was fully occupied, so I lay down on the four-inch gunwale alongside the rowers, under Cardozo's oar. At every stroke his elbow shot back to within a few inches of my jaw, and the enormous sore on Octaviano's leg was less than a foot away from my head on the other side. When I woke up I reflected that I should be lucky if I ever slept so well again in such peculiar circumstances.

The other moment came on a night when we had broken camp at 12.30, as soon as the moon rose. Since then we had been going well, but an hour before dawn a mist came up off the river. Speed was no longer desirable, since we could not see where we were going, and the crew went to sleep at their oars. Roger and I were paddling, and now we sat, talking in a low voice, the only conscious creatures in a shrunken world. The mist was a low belt; some moonlight struggled through it, and our pocket in the vaporous darkness was full of a curious pearly light. The four sprawling figures in front of us, the five sprawling figures behind, lay like corpses. Our boat, to which the ungainly stillness of these figures lent a stricken air, drifted in silence through the narrow corridors of mist. The whole universe had suddenly contracted to a patch of black water forty yards across. We were suspended in infinity, and masters of it. The world was ours, to people with our talk of remote things out of another existence; never again would we feel as utterly detached as this. We ate bananas in a strange exhilaration.

Presently the light grew paler still, and we knew that somewhere the sun was advancing all its spears against the mist. In unexpected quarters indistinct shapes loomed up; behind the ill-defined palisade of trees parrots began to chatter, and doves called drowsily. Then the ranks of the mist broke; it trailed across the water in clouds and pillars of fluid and fantastic shape. Through the gaps between them we could see the jungle, ghostly and smoking, a riot of spare or opulent silhouettes staggering to the water's edge. The mist that hung still about their branches gave the trees a ravaged and theatrical look. Dawn had come. We could go on, now. I woke the crew.

The only person who had a bad time during this stage of our journey was Bob, who went down with fever on the second day out of Conceição. We gave him quinine and hoped for the best. Considering the conditions under which we were living, he bore up remarkably well. He had to lie all day in the bottom of the boat (thereby materially reducing the seating accommodation) with no shelter from the sun except the stifling awning of a blanket. At night we carried him ashore and dumped him on the camp-bed with which he alone — providentially sybaritic — had burdened the expedition; and then, if we were travelling by night, we picked him up a few hours later and dumped him in the boat again. He was always being trodden on, and, except when we were able to buy a few eggs, he got very little of the kind of food which his condition demanded. All this he bore without complaint; and although he had an alarming tendency, when delirious, to prosecute an ancient feud with the pilot, his Portuguese and his strength were alike too limited for any irreparable harm to be done.

'I see no end to this journey,' says my diary, half way between Conceição and Marabá; and indeed our progress always seemed to me to be maddeningly slow. But we were forcing the pace as much as we could, and it soon became apparent that we should do this lap in well under eighteen days.

On the evening of the ninth day we reached São Vicente, the only place between Conceição and Marabá which could be described, even by Brazilians, as a village. We camped on the bank opposite it, partly because Octaviano's aunt lived there, and partly because there was no praia to sleep on on the other side.  Our supplies were exhausted and, after some discussion, I decided that, to save time, Queiroz should go across in a borrowed montaría and see what he could pick up that night. With inexcusable thoughtlessness, I allowed him to take Manoel and the pilot with him.

Unaccountably, there were no mosquitoes on the praia where Octaviano's aunt lived, and I slept hoggishly till dawn, having had only two hours' sleep in the last forty-eight.  Queiroz was still away when I woke up.  I was annoyed but not alarmed; I thought he was probably waiting while they pounded the husks off the rice we wanted — no one ever seemed to keep a sufficient quantity of it 'clean'.

But an hour passed, and then another, and still there was no sign of the shopping party.  We became impatient.  Presently a montaría was sighted; the two men in it, who had business on our bank, brought disconcerting news.  There had been a fight in the local brothel overnight, and three men — strangers in the village — had been arrested.  Cardozo and Octaviano cursed bitterly when they heard this.  They did not doubt for a moment that it was Queiroz and his two companions who had got into trouble; and it meant at the least a fine (which we could not pay) and several days' imprisonment.  Although we were said to be within two days of Marabá we could not get there without the pilot.  Things looked very black.  I decided to take the whole outfit across to the village.

To our unspeakable relief, we found our truants on the foreshore; it was not they who had been arrested after all.  Queiroz ran up, full of indignation against his companions; he had bought everything and had the montaría loaded by five o'clock that morning, he said, but the other two had failed at the rendezvous, and he had never succeeded in getting hold of both of them at the same time.  Queiroz spoke with a volubility which I attributed at the time to emotion.

Then I saw the pilot.  The pilot was drunk again.  He was

walking towards us with careful, precise steps; his slender body swayed wildly, as if he was on a tight-rope; his huge hat was on the back of his head, and his face was suffused with an expression of overwhelming benignity. Behind him came Manoel, also drunk. Manoel giggled continuously.

They were both in that condition which is armoured against reproof. The time was not ripe for reprisals. The thing to do was to get them on board and go on down stream at once. I walked past them without even so much as a nasty look.

It had been an anxious morning; we were all in a filthy temper. The pilot's conduct was about as much as the Firm Hand party could stand, and when the pilot, in an ill-timed access of benevolence, attempted to pat the Firm Hand party on the back, the pilot went too far. His gesture, on account of the drink in him, lacked that crisp and manly impetus with which Anglo-Saxons slap each other between the shoulder blades; it might have been, and subsequently was, described — by a word abhorrent wherever the English language is spoken — as 'pawing'. I was startled by the sound of a blow.

Turning, I saw the Firm Hand party squaring up for further mischief. The pilot was reeling back, frightened out of his wits.

'That man is tight,' I said, rather obviously: adding, in a strained but dramatically effective analogy, 'You don't hit your butler, do you?'

The Firm Hand party recollected itself. The pilot scampered erratically to a safe distance and thence lodged a protest.

Several villagers appeared from nowhere and helped him to lodge it. Their fellow-countryman had been struck, and by a foreigner. The pilot thumped his chest (from time to time missing it altogether) and pointed out that he was a Brazilian. The villagers too made repeated references to their nationality. The honour of two countries was at stake, and a pronounced anti-foreign bias was noticeable in the crowd. The situation was developing on international lines.

Their confidence increased by the number of their supporters,

Manoel and the pilot announced that they would accompany us no further, and were applauded for doing so. I told Queiroz (who, I now noticed, was also in liquor) to ask them whether this was their final decision, as we were anxious to engage men to replace them without further delay. They hesitated, thinking of their wages. I went up to the pilot, flattered him in an off-hand and regretful way, and said that I was sorry he was leaving us, for he had worked magnificently.

Thereupon the pilot became suddenly maudlin, protesting over and over again his devotion to myself; in this he was joined by Manoel and Queiroz. The air became embarrassingly loud with votes of confidence, and before I knew what was happening the men had produced a little spotted fawn, no bigger than a hare, which they thrust into my arms. They had bought it for ten milreis, they cried, as a present for me: and a bottle of milk as well, to feed it on, or to give to Roberto who had fever if I preferred. I have never taken part in a more fantastic scene of reconciliation.

Clutching the token of their esteem to my bosom (which it at once proceeded to excoriate with its hoofs) I tried to combine in my speech of thanks the keenest appreciation with the sternest disapproval. The fawn nuzzled my chin, and looked at me with huge surprised eyes, like the child who used to bring husband and wife together in the third act. I took advantage of the rather sickly emotional atmosphere to extort a promise from the men that they would all come on with us; and they took advantage of it to obtain leave of absence for a meal. The meeting broke up.

So in the end we lost another two hours, and Roger and I had to comb the red light quarter for the crew before we got them into the boat. (The red light quarter in São Vicente extends from the northern boundary of the village as far as the church, and again from the church as far as the southern boundary of the village. Or so it seemed to me.) At last we pushed off. To give the pilot his due, he never fell overboard once.

But he steered with his eyes closed, and our course would have done credit to a figure-skater. So I told Queiroz to take over the helm and made the pilot lie down among the rowers. Here he was an endless source of trouble; for every now and then he sat up — or, in the more vivid and anatomical French phrase, *il se dressa sur son séant* — and seized an oar. I was still angry with him, he cried, and he could not bear it; he would row all the way to Marabá to prove his devotion to me. Whereupon he would take perhaps twenty strokes of the utmost violence and fall over backwards after dislocating the rowlock. In England, I told him desperately, the pilots never rowed; and at last he sank into a kind of stupor.

But it was an anxious afternoon. That blow had bred ill-feeling, and the crew, all of whom were in particularly good voice, kept on resting on their oars to discuss the ethics of the case. Even Cardozo had been shocked by it, and, man of the world that he was, he received with a certain scepticism my statement that in England we were always knocking each other about — it meant nothing, it was just our fun. All the same, infected by the wave of hysterical pro-Fleming feeling which had swept the crew off their feet, he came out with several very moving declarations of his personal loyalty: including one to the effect that he wished Senhor Pedro would place the muzzle of a loaded rifle at Cardozo's heart and pull the trigger, for he well knew that God would allow no harm to come to a servant so invincibly loyal. I said that ammunition was too valuable to be wasted on an experiment of whose result I was not for a moment in doubt.

The little spotted fawn accepted with philosophy its position as a stage-property in this misbegotten drama. It played its part with the easy natural dignity of a beast in a medieval legend. Poor little thing, I knew from the first that it was doomed. But it was impossible for diplomatic reasons to leave it behind in safe hands at São Vicente: I had to take it with us. It was a delicate and friendly creature, and in spite of its pathetic fragility it had a composure which we all admired. When I was not paddling it lay wrapped in a sweater in my arms, eternally licking my chest and arms on which, I suppose, it liked the salt taste of sweat. It never quite got the river sized up. It would stand on its little shivering legs, peering over the gunwale at the wide expanse of waters, its ears cocked forward in perplexity. Without ever showing any dissatisfaction with its quarters in the boat, it betrayed a single-minded preference for terra firma, and when we hugged the shore it would stop licking me and sniff the familiar scents of the jungle with an air of wistful appreciation. Once, when I was asleep, it took a flying leap and left us. The puny sound of its impact on the waters was followed immediately by a louder splash. Looking astern, I saw the fawn swimming resolutely and without panic towards the bank, distant by half a mile, and Neville's fair head in hot pursuit. He brought it back, a comical and dripping object, and it settled down quite calmly in my arms, neither contrite nor resentful, with the air of one who realizes that there have been faults on both sides and prefers to regard the incident as closed.

At night it shared my sleeping bag, making querulous apologetic bleats when the air grew cold towards dawn. But, alas, there were only two such nights. The bottle of milk turned sour after a single meal, and the greenstuff with which I tried to tempt it was collected in too catholic a spirit of experiment. The fawn was not yet old enough to know what was good for it and what was not, and something I gave it was poisonous. When we broke camp in the small hours of its third day with us it was clearly ill. Every now and then a tremor passed through its body, and it gave a little retching whimper, very pitiful to hear. I should have shot it then and there, but I hoped that it might perhaps get rid of the poison. It did not. The tremors grew rarer. The huge eyes — philosophic to the end, not reproachful — glazed. At dawn it died. When we landed for breakfast the gentle body in my arms was stiff. The dirty red ribbon round its neck looked more absurdly raffish than ever. It was a funny little beast.

The fawn died on the morning of the last day before we reached Marabá. That day two things of note happened: the rains caught us, and we passed the mouth of the Tocantins.

If you look at the map you will see that from now on we were, officially, quit of the Araguaya; for after these two great rivers join, it is the name of the Tocantins that persists. In passing their point of confluence we had put behind us the most nominal of landmarks. But almost all important geographical landmarks are like that (what could be more nominal than the Equator?) and it was not entirely in a spirit of burlesque that we toasted the occasion in the tepid waters of our new river.

The rains came up with us at the most opportune of moments. For several days past black clouds had been hanging on our rear, and towards noon the sky darkened and the wind rose. But it so happened that we were on one of the rare bends of this tediously straightforward river, and for once the north wind was almost a following one. With feverish haste we lashed our big tarpaulin sheet to two oars and stuck them up in the bows, making a primitive square-rigged sail.

It filled at once. The boat buried her nose with a purposeful air, like a junk, and everyone crowded aft to keep the clumsy rudder in the water. We began to move at what seemed a dizzy speed.

The air was yellow, ominous, and electric, and the water had suddenly turned yellow too. Thunder was rolling down the river after us with a sound of menace. The trees on the bank thrashed and were tormented. The outlines of the praias were blurred by a fine driven cloud of sand which whipped continuously along them, keeping low. Rank upon rank of racing waves, white-topped, overhauled us; but slowly, and with a curious air of deliberation, for we were travelling almost as fast as they were. Our bows cleft the water with a steady and triumphant hiss. A loose corner of the tarpaulin crackled in the wind like musketry. The parrot clung in silence to its perch, dumb with amazement at such headlong progress.

Then it began to rain. The sky belaboured the earth with water. The waves lowered their crests and rolled doggedly forward with all the flourish gone out of them. The rain beat down so viciously on the river that all the surface of its ridge and furrow was obscured by a dancing up-flung froth.

It was torture to bear those spiteful icy lances on our naked backs. We crouched and shivered uncontrollably in the hurtling boat. But the speed was worth all the discomfort, and between the roaring heaven and the drumming earth we filled the air with wild yells of triumph. Our position was in point of fact a delicate one. The wind was now twice as strong as it had been when we set the sail, and in that demented downpour we could see less than fifty yards ahead of us. A rock we might avoid in time, but not a reef; and at this speed the merest touch would split the boat. On the other hand, we dared not take down the sail, for once we lost way the following waves would swamp the boat, which, incidentally, the rain was filling as fast as we could bail it.

How comforting is the knowledge that you must trust to luck — that it is not in your power to lessen the margin of risk! There was so much to enjoy in this blind and desperate career that it was a blessing to be absolved by circumstances from all responsibility, to be able to clutch the groaning gunwale and appreciate with full detachment this charge through a turbulent and unpredictable world. There was nothing for it but to repose in fate that unquestioning confidence which one used to repose in the managements of scenic railways at Wembley; the most we could do for our salvation was to keep our seats. For my part, I was glad that it was like this: though I confess to feeling a certain anxiety about Bob who, being as weak as a kitten and swaddled in many blankets and a British warm, would fare badly in case of disaster.

Wincing, shivering and yelling in the rain, we did nearly half a day's journey in an hour. The sail, that sublime and labour-saving device, miraculously stood the strain; and though in the absence of the tarpaulin all our supplies were ruined and our clothes and bedding soaked we did not grudge the price of such memorable progress. When the rain at last drew off downstream and the wind dropped, we were so cold that we could hardly speak, the boat was half full of water, and camp that night was a miserable affair. But it had been well worth it.

# CHAPTER VIII

# THE DISENCHANTING VILLAGE

IT was noon the next day.

We swung out of the tail of the last rapid with a rush, and Marabá was in sight: a straggling frontage of shoddy little houses lining the top of a steep high bank. We gazed at it with an ardent curiosity. For three weeks its name had been a beacon in our thoughts: impossibly remote, yet infinitely desirable, like the last day of your first term at school. The dingy reality borrowed some of the glamour of that shining, cherished vision. We were very glad indeed to see Marabá. In front of it, several launches rode at their moorings, looking venerable and desolate.

We beached the batalõa on a praia and bathed and combed our hair and put on our more reputable rags. Our bodies were dark brown, our aspect savage, and our clothes wet; we neither looked nor felt qualified for contact with even the very modified form of civilization which Marabá had to offer. From now on we should travel by launch, if we travelled at all; as we rowed gently down to the landing place I reflected that this was the end of my last hour's paddling, and was surprised to find that I was feeling quite sentimental about it. How many thoughts had passed through my head to the rhythm of that dipped blade? How many hundreds of thousands of strokes had I taken in the last five weeks? With maudlin solemnity I counted the last twenty, and laid the paddle down with a real, though transitory, regret.

When we landed they told us a thing that made us momentarily mad with anger. A launch, the first for many weeks, had gone downstream at dawn that morning; we had missed it by a few hours. This was bitter; we had done the journey in the phenomenal time of twelve days, and we felt that we deserved a slice of luck of which only the crew's drunkenness at São Vicente had robbed us.

However, it appeared that another launch was due to start the day after to-morrow; we so cheered up, and twenty minutes later found ourselves in the presence of its owner, Colonel Raimundo Tola. (I should explain that in the interior of Brazil anyone who is anyone is also a Colonel, unless he prefers to be a Doctor. Neither title has any military or academic significance. I could not discover whether they were hereditary.)

The man Tola merits some description, for during the days that followed he held our destinies in the hollow of his hand, and I came to hate him as bitterly as I have ever hated anyone. He had made a fortune during the rubber-boom, which brought a short-lived prosperity to Marabá; and now that rubber's day had passed he still dominated the local Brazil nut trade, a staple industry in those parts. Even in these days of depression he was a wealthy man, and the most powerful thereabouts.

His appearance was mildly repellent. He was what the Victorian humorists used to describe as a Seedy-Looking Individual. He wore the national costume: a frogged pyjama jacket, a straw hat, dirty white trousers, and an umbrella. His face was equine and flabby. His ready smile (in which his eyes played no part) disclosed decaying teeth, and it was apparent after the briefest conversation that not only was he one of those unhappy Four out of Five, but also that he suffered from that malady of which the reticence of your best friends is, according to the advertisements, the surest symptom. He had soft, heavy hands, and his manner towards us was full of a flapping courtesy. He looked, even for a low-class Brazilian, almost incredibly unreliable.

He received us with affability, talking rapidly in a thick, fulsome voice. Yes, it was true that his launch was going downstream the day after to-morrow. He would be very pleased to give us passages on it. The price was fifty milreis a head as far as Alcobaça, where we must get another launch to take us to Pará. . . . No, it was unfortunately impossible for him to start any sooner. After all, we had less than two days to wait; he gave us his word that we should leave at dawn the day after to-morrow. In the meantime there was a house in the village which he would put at our disposal; he would send men at once to bring our luggage up from the boat.

We thanked him and withdrew. The situation looked fairly satisfactory. I knew we could raise the 200 milreis for our four passages, though whether we should have any money left when we got to Alcobaça was another matter. The burning question (a question destined to burn more and more fiercely in the ensuing days) was: How big was our lead over Major Pingle, and would he arrive in time to catch our launch? We had heard or seen nothing of him for over a fortnight: we could only speculate as to the sort of progress he had made. On the whole it seemed likely that we had a lead of just about two days: possibly rather more, certainly not much less: so the chances were that he would miss us by a smallish margin.

Marabá was bigger than Conceição. Its long dusty streets tailed off into scrub and patches of cultivated land on the edge of the jungle. There was a church, and a police station, and quite a lot of shops, and a telegraph-office (not working), and a miniature billiard saloon. The first thing we did was to buy and eat an enormous quantity of bread, our first for two months. It tasted delicious.

The day after to-morrow came; and went. The launch did not start.

Tola excused himself perfunctorily; his affability was on the wane. Yes, it was true that he had given us his word; but circumstances beyond his control had necessitated this delay. We must be patient. After all, we had lost only one day.

In the end we lost five. It became apparent that to base our expectations on the assurances of these Brazilians would have been as idiotic as to allow the number of prune stones on a plate to determine, by the 'Tinker, Tailor' process, one's choice of a career. The Day After To-morrow maintained a lead which we could do nothing to reduce. Departure was postponed again and again.

We were never told that it had been postponed. We would wake up in the morning with the pleasant feeling that twenty-four hours from now we really should be starting; it was inconceivable that there would be further delay. The first doubts were delivered with the milk. This was brought, in two beer bottles, by a boy, a leering and omniscient youth with a fatalistic slouch and a lock of fair hair hanging down over his shrewd, thin face.

'Shall I bring the milk again to-morrow, Senhor Pedro?'

'No. The launch starts at dawn. We shall have no time for milk to-morrow.'

A cynical expression would come over the boy's face, and he would look at me in silence for a moment. 'To-morrow?' he would say, shrugging his shoulders. 'Perhaps: perhaps not.' He would disappear, whistling loudly.

For a moment our minds would darken with misgiving. But, as we strolled along to breakfast in the pensão at the other end of the village, our confidence would be restored by the piles of luggage on the doorsteps of our fellow-passengers. 'Yes, yes,' they would cry. 'To-morrow we start. It is certain. It has been guaranteed.'

But on the way back from breakfast we would find them a shade less confident. 'To-morrow, if God wills' was the formula now; and by noon they would be less categorical still, saying that we should start to-morrow if it was humanly possible, if all the preparations could be made in time. Fuming and fretting, we would seek out Tola. We were, of course, starting to-morrow as he had guaranteed? We asked because there had been rumours —

Tola would become voluble and rather indignant. Every effort was being made — he himself was straining every nerve — if all that remained to be done was finished to-night, why then certainly we should start to-morrow ... We knew then that it was hopeless, that we were as far as ever from escape, that the Day After To-morrow had been reinstated. Disconsolate, maddened by our impotence, we would spend the hours before sunset scanning the river for Major Pingle's batalõa, now momentarily expected. We were not going to win our race, after all.

How we hated Marabá! For me, this was the only stage in our journey where disenchantment got the upper hand. There was nothing to do. Every afternoon it rained. Most of the time we lay on our blankets on the floor, glumly enduring delay. The room in which we lived (it was more of a veranda than a room) was dark and very dirty; the smell in it was vile. We grew terribly restless. We envied (when we did not curse) the ants which marched and counter-marched across the floor, all blissfully preoccupied, all armoured with a purpose: big *sauba* ants, and fire-ants, and many other kinds. The bites of the fire-ants were painful.

The hours passed slowly in that shoddy place. Urubús scavenged in the yard outside with a buffeting of wings. Occasionally a rat ran along the beams in the roof. Bob, with the fever on him, tossed and muttered in a corner; his clothes and blankets were sodden with sweat, and it was difficult to dry them on account of the rains. Roger developed an abscess in his ear and was very nearly speechless with pain; I applied lethally unhygienic compresses and made all the capital I could out of his plight in my interviews with Tola, pointing out, what indeed was true, that we stood in urgent need of a doctor.

Neville had traded a red arara for his sheath-knife with a man in the village, and this, with its blue and gold companion, sidled up and down the window ledge. Both uttered at frequent intervals their characteristic and foolish cry, and Neville attempted to teach them the phrase 'Damn your eyes' by repeating it over and over again in a low, tense voice. This practice we had to ask him to abandon. The new parrot was an exceptionally handsome bird, called Rosa. The inhabitants treated us as a cross between a zoo and a museum. They would present themselves, with a formal bow and a 'Com licença' and sit down on the only stool. It was true that we had guns to sell?

It was indeed, we hastened to assure them, and for a time there would be a great rattling of bolts, a great translating of ranges from yards into metres. In the end, having admired our armoury unreservedly, they would rise and go away, muttering that times were hard, that no one in Marabá had any money.

The market was indeed sluggish. We were in desperate need of money, and it was maddening to have to economize now — to have to think twice before indulging our craving (it came on us about every two hours) for coffee and bananas and little cakes; it seemed unfair that, after these months of mild but continuous privation, our fall into the flesh-pots should be broken like this. But in the end we found customers for most of our wares. A vital spring was missing from the automatic shot-gun, but Neville got one made, and we sold this showy weapon to a rich Syrian for 200 milreis. (There are a lot of Syrians in the interior of Brazil. Some have settled and become prosperous, others are still pedlars; many, I was credibly informed, are dentists, though why this should be I cannot say.) We also sold the tarpaulin for quite a good price, and all our cooking utensils, and finally Queiroz got a hundred milreis for the batalõa. (He swindled us in this matter, and lost face. Though he travelled on with us to Pará, he was no longer in our employ, and our relations were not so cordial as before.)

So in the end we found that, after paying off the crew, we were still about 300 milreis to the good, and we hoped, with a great deal of luck, to be able to get to Pará on that. The crew hung about the village in a state of more or less permanent intoxication, varied in the case of Cardozo with a brief term of imprisonment. Considering that we had paid them a minimum wage, and had been unable to supplement it with presents, they remained on surprisingly good terms with us. In the evenings I used to join the circle of the *élite*, who sat on stools in the street and drank little cups of coffee and talked. God, how they talked. They did it all day and most of the night. They did not make a great noise. Their gestures were not extravagant. They talked with a quiet intensity and with profound conviction. In nine cases out of ten they did not know what they were talking about, and what they said was not worth saying. But one had constantly to remind oneself that this was so, for the technique of Brazilian conversation is curiously impressive and has a hypnotic effect. Nothing ever happens in Marabá, and nobody ever does anything; so I find it hard to imagine what they are talking about to-day, now that the revolution is over and the four mad Englishmen have gone. But I expect they manage somehow.

As the days dragged slowly by it became apparent that we were racing against time as well as against Major Pingle. I had found out in São Paulo that a boat left Pará for England on October 4th. We arrived in Marabá on September 23rd and discovered that the rest of our journey was as follows:

One day's journey below Marabá our launch would reach the Itaboca Rapid, seven leagues long and at present quite impassable. The passengers would be landed and taken overnight by lorry to the tail of the Itaboca, where another launch awaited them; it was only a short day's journey thence to Alcobaça, whence, if one was lucky enough to make connection with a launch going downstream, it took only three days to reach Pará. It will thus be seen that five days was the absolute minimum time for the journey from Marabá to Alcobaça. There were however two points at which that minimum was

THE DISENCHANTING VILLAGE

almost certain to be exceeded. One was at Alcobaça, where it was highly improbable that we should find a launch ready to start: the other was at the Itaboca. His passengers were only a secondary consideration to Tola; the real object of his journey was to take a big cargo of Brazil nuts down to Alcobaça. He swore to me, again and again, that if it proved impossible (as I knew it must) to tranship this cargo from one launch to another without delay, he would take the passengers straight on downstream in the second and leave the cargo for another time. But I did not expect him to keep his word over this; and events proved that my suspicion did him no injustice.

Someone in the village lent us a bundle of month-old papers from Pará, and I spent many hours sifting the information contained in their shipping advertisements. The results were not encouraging. There, indeed, was our boat, the romantically-named *Pancras*; she would sail on October 4th, at 9 a.m., and would carry a few first class passengers. The chances that she would carry us grew more and more remote. The 4th was a Tuesday, the day before it a National Holiday, and the day before that, of course, a Sunday.

We knew that we should have a great deal to do when we got to Pará. First of all, there was our luggage — as we fondly imagined — to collect from the British Consulate: we could not know that it was still blockaded in São Paulo, and that we were destined to arrive in London in the same rags which even in Marabá were an offence against propriety. Then there was the business of drawing money out of the bank; that always, we reminded each other, took time. (Had we only known, it was going to take a good deal more than time; for our instructions to our banks in London to open credits for us in Pará had never left São Paulo.) But we could not, happily, foresee these Parthian shots of the unkind fate which had dogged our enterprise; nor could we guess that Major Pingle, by way of a joke, had further complicated the situation by wiring from Conceição to the British Consul and the Shipping Company, asking them

329

respectively to refuse us visas and passages: a singularly ill-judged step on his part, as it turned out.

Ignorant though we were of all this, it was obvious that if we were going to catch the *Pancras* we must have at least a day in which to transact business before she sailed; and as on the two days immediately preceding her departure the bank and everything else would be shut it looked more than ever as if we were going to miss her.

The most diligent search of the shipping announcements failed to disclose any other boat leaving for Europe in the near future. On the 6th we could sail, if we so wished, for Buenos Aires: on the 9th, for Japan: on the 14th, for New Orleans. But no boat left for England before the end of the month, and the prospect of spending three weeks in Pará was almost too bitter to contemplate: particularly for me, who had guaranteed my employers that I would be back by the middle of October at the latest.

All the same, those stale papers were a blessing, and I read them all from cover to cover, taking in even the advertisements for depilatories, which appeared to represent one of the principal industries of Pará. I tried to discover what had been happening in the revolution, but found this difficult: in Brazil, as in China, the student of politics will find that there are far too many generals, and that they all have far too many names. As far as I could make out, all they had been doing was to send each other telegrams of hysterical congratulation from places whose names meant nothing to me, and for reasons which did not appear. There was however a very stirring account of a naval engagement on the Amazon between four small steamers, two of them manned by Federal troops and two of them by insurgents from Manaos. They had joined battle off Itacoatira (which Mr. Tomlinson describes so well in *The Sea and the Jungle*) and after brisk fighting at close quarters the Federal boats had rammed and sunk the other two. It all sounded very exciting; perhaps those three weeks in Pará would not be so unbearable after all.

# THE DISENCHANTING VILLAGE

But what gave me most pleasure was the discovery that the world had not altered its ways in my absence. People were still taking photographs of Mussolini and Miss Dietrich; Mr. Bernard Shaw was still being unsuccessful in his flight from publicity; the interest in murder and adultery appeared to have been well maintained; Geneva was still full of sound, and the Far East of fury; Professor Piccard (you can't keep a good man down) had once more attempted to pluck bright honour from the vicinity of the pale-faced moon; skirts were going to be longer again, or it may have been shorter. . . . I realized, with surprise, that I had had very nearly enough of the interior of Brazil (the reader will, I think, appreciate this feeling). I was homesick for a greater stage of bigger fools.

In those dreary days there was one moment which, for sheer, blank, numbing despair, exceeded even the moment when my knife had gone through the bottom of our canoe on the headwaters of the Tapirapé.

The loading of the launch had gone forward briskly all day. I had spent most of it in the company of the eight indomitable but undersized men whose business it was to carry sacks of Brazil nuts on their heads from a warehouse in the village to the hold of the launch. By bribes and cajolery and bets I had almost succeeded in getting the whole cargo on board by nightfall; there was still a chance that we might be able to start the next day, rather late. Then, suddenly, an hour before sunset, they discovered that the engine of the launch would not work.

I went at once in search of Neville. Neville is what is known as a handy man. He had shown himself to be expert at skinning things, and sharpening things, and splicing things, and rigging things up; in my memory he is always whittling, with an air of concentration and a very well-kept knife. His skill, his patience, and his ingenuity would have been an invaluable asset to any expedition. Also, he had a mechanical mind.

The aged and recalcitrant engine was no match for the

mechanical mind. Neville worked like a black; masterful and efficient, he dismantled and reassembled a machine which to Roger and me was as baffling as a crossword puzzle in Kurdish. At eleven o'clock it started with a roar. At 11.5 it stopped. Neville's titanic efforts had detached the feed pipe from the petrol tank. I went ashore for some soap and a piece of leather off Bob's suit case with which to patch the tank. This makeshift remedy answered its purpose. By 11.30 the village was once more being deafened; we wanted everyone to know that there was no good reason why we should not start to-morrow, though we had learnt enough to be pretty sure that we should not. It was a splendid bit of work on Neville's part; we went back to our quarters tired, but full of a sense of achievement, for we had removed the only insuperable obstacle to our departure. This time it really would be the Day After To-morrow, at the latest.

I shall be glad to get out of this, I reflected, standing and yawning in the middle of our grimy room. Bob's face showed peaked and ashen. Roger, for all his evasions, I knew to be in agony; I was seriously alarmed about his abscess. I was sick of the whole thing — the smell, the ants, the dirty odds and ends of equipment, the parrot-droppings, the infuriating knowledge that we were at the mercy of these dingy, ineffectual people, the rumours, the postponements, the courtesies, the lies.

'Even if we don't get away to-morrow,' I said, 'there can't be more than thirty-six hours more.' As I said this, I pulled my shirt over my head and began to roll it up. It was then that I realized I had lost my note-case.

It contained all the funds of the expedition, all the proceeds of those tiresome, providential sales. It contained every penny we possessed. And it was lost.

That was a black moment. The note-case had been in my shirt pocket, buttoned up. The only chance it had had of falling out was during my various scrambling and acrobatic passages in a water-logged canoe between the launch and the shore. The chances were ten to one that it was in the river.

I announced the loss calmly. It was indeed so serious, such a complete catastrophe, that one could not help regarding it as rather funny, coming on top of the misfortunes of the last few days. Without any hope at all, Roger and I took a torch and went down to the shore, searching the path thither with mechanical thoroughness. We were reasonably sure that the game was up.

It was not. We found the note-case. We found it lying on the bottom of the river, in the shallows, waiting for the current to get properly underneath it and lift it downstream. We were too dazed to exult. If its loss had been too bad to be true, its discovery was too good. We went back to our quarters bemused but unemotional, like people who have slept through an earthquake.

But it had been a nasty moment, all the same.

# CHAPTER IX

# WE LOSE OUR LEAD

WE started at last. We started on September 28th. We started because they had used up all their excuses for not starting. At one time the supply of these had looked like being inexhaustible. It had taken longer than they expected to float the launch. The cargo could not be loaded on Sunday, because the people were superstitious. We were waiting for some hides which were coming downstream: for an important passenger who was coming upstream: for a telegram which was coming as soon as the telegraph was mended; for a secret political document which the judge was preparing: for an ambush to be laid for the Paulistas at Alcobaça . . . All these excuses, and many others, succeeded each other and were given in the talk of the village the status of realities; people spoke of them as cogent, valid, and interesting. But all the time they knew, and I knew, that behind this shifting, arbitrary cloud of motive there burnt the clear unwavering flame, the sacred little fire, of sheer ineffectiveness: the reluctance to make a decision, the inability to see that certain people carried out certain orders by a certain time.

But at last we really were off, and Major Pingle, miraculously, had not arrived. The launch chugged stertorously, as well it might, beneath a cargo of nuts and hides, twenty passengers, one pig, one turkey, one sheep, four parrots, two dogs, and a turtle. With a look of inexpressible loathing I watched Marabá disappear round a bend in the river. How I hated that place! Even to-day, when my eye is caught by some small item of news from South America, I am filled with a sudden fierce hope (for all the South American news worth printing is bad) that this time it is Marabá: that some civic disaster — bandits, bankruptcy, bubonic plague, I don't care what — has fallen on that beastly place to punish it. But it never has.

We had a good run, through more or less continuous rapids, which the gigantic negro pilot negotiated with assurance and address. The engine, under Neville's supervision, proved unexpectedly reliable. Roger and Bob endured their sufferings in silence on a pile of luggage. Our fellow-passengers, strawhatted to a man, chattered gaily and ate the rapid succession of meals which the cook produced from a brazier in the stern. It almost looked as if our luck had changed.

It had not. We arrived as night was falling at Jacunda, a miserable cluster of huts at the mouth of the Itaboca Rapid, and disembarked. The word went round that we were to stay the night here. It would not be possible to tranship our cargo to the launch at the tail of the rapids, ten miles away, until to-morrow: of the three lorries available for this purpose two were out of commission, and the third had no lights.

I reminded Tola of his promise that the passengers would be taken straight on without waiting for the cargo. It was no good. He must take the cargo with him, he said: we should perhaps be able to start for Alcobaça at noon to-morrow. I knew that we should not.

With the two Paulistas and Queiroz we shared half a very small mud hut. The other half, from which we were separated by a low and perfunctory partition, was the local butcher's shop. Here we passed the night in some discomfort.

The next day was the 29th. We knew that on the 30th a launch belonging to a Syrian was due to leave Marabá; it carried passengers only, and would therefore meet none of the delay in which we were involved. They would reach Alcobaça on the evening of October 1st. It was virtually certain that Major Pingle would catch this launch. Unless disaster had overtaken him, it was inconceivable that he could be more than a week behind us. Very probably he had arrived in Marabá on the day we left it. Yes, Major Pingle would reach Jacunda on the evening of the 30th, Alcobaça on the evening of the 1st. And to-day was the 29th.

To-day was the 29th, and it was very soon obvious that we were not going to leave Jacunda to-day. A crew of six gnome-like boys on the lorry worked furiously, but when evening came there was still a young mountain of Brazil nuts in the shed at Jacunda. I went round the other passengers in the capacity of an *agent provocateur*. They had all been treated by Tola almost as shamefully as we had been: they all claimed to be in a tearing hurry: and they all disliked the squalid lodging and scanty food in Jacunda. Even so, I could not work on their indignation sufficiently to produce effective and united action. The deputation which did finally approach Tola returned to its eternal card-playing quite content with the usual glib guarantee that we should leave the next day without fail.

Neville and I got a lift on the lorry and went down to see how the situation stood at the tail of the rapids.

The lorry-ride was that rare thing, that joy so seldom known to adults — a treat. As we lurched madly along the splashy, twisting road, we relished keenly the familiar roar of the engine, the rush of air on our faces, the speed, the sense of dash and effectiveness. There was something oddly reassuring about that lorry. Our spirits rose. If I learnt nothing else from that long journey in Brazil, it taught me at least how exquisite a satisfaction can, under the right conditions, be found in ordinary, elemental, unregarded things: a drink of water, a bit of bread, the warmth of a fire, a ride on a lorry. By contrast, the pleasures of normal life seem pale and recondite; in civilization one cannot keep one's palate clean for experience.

This was our first direct contact with the equatorial jungle. It was very different from the forests of the Central Plateau: lusher, more opulent and intricate, altogether on a grander scale. Many of the trees were giants, soaring up out of a press of greener, softer, more obviously impenetrable stuff than the brittle drought-sapped thickets through which we had struggled so ineffectually towards Fawcett's grave. This was much more the sort of thing that the *Wide World Magazine* had taught us to expect.

The road ended with the rapids. Here was Jacundazinha, or Little Jacunda: a big shed and a few scattered huts. Our lorry tipped its load into a colossal pile of Brazil nuts on the foreshore and went back.

The only hopeful feature of the loading operations was the fact that they were in charge of the negro pilot, an effective man, and in sympathy with us. But my heart sank when I saw how slow and complicated was the task before him. From the pile on the foreshore the nuts had to be loaded into canoes (for which there were not enough paddles to go round): then ferried half a mile up a land-locked lagoon towards the main channel of the river: then dumped once more on the praia: and finally carried 300 yards across it to the hold of the launch, a boat exactly similar to the one which had brought us from Marabá. (The Syrian's launch was also anchored there. We learnt that she was a faster craft than ours and that all had been made ready for a start the day after to-morrow.)

The pilot was not altogether without hope that he could get our cargo on board in time for us to leave by noon to-morrow and thus arrive in Alcobaça a day before the Syrian and his passengers. He promised to keep his men working all through the night, and when we left gave it as his considered opinion that we should be in Alcobaça by dusk to-morrow. He was a reliable man, and we went home cheered, though we knew better than to be hopeful.

As the lorry roared back through the twilit jungle, rain began to fall in torrents. There was hardly any food available in Jacunda, and the place was a sea of mud. I had lost my only pipe that afternoon, and it was in a state of suppressed fury and in sodden clothes that I crawled into my sleeping bag in that stinking hut and listened to the rain crashing down in the darkness, hour after hour. The crew could never work in such a night as this; the loading of the cargo would have to be left till to-morrow. We had lost another precious day. Our chances of catching that boat were less than infinitesimal now. The comedy was wearing thin.

It rained all night. The pile of nuts on the foreshore at Jacundazinha had no chance to dwindle. After breakfast the postponement of our departure till the morning of the 1st was officially announced.

That day I made a decision which turned out to be a very lucky one. I insisted on taking the other three down to sleep that night at Jacundazinha; they did not want to come, but I felt certain that it was the right thing to do. The Syrian's launch, almost certainly with the loyalists and Major Pingle on board, would arrive at Jacunda that evening. This would strain both the scanty sleeping accommodation and our frayed nerves. By going down to Jacundazinha we would at least postpone the admission of defeat for twelve hours or so: we could not be more uncomfortable than we were already, and I thought that a change of smell might do the invalids good.

So early in the afternoon we scrambled on top of the last load of Brazil nuts and rattled down to the tail of the rapids; our fellow-passengers were to follow at dawn. When we got to Jacundazinha everyone was glad they had come. We were welcomed by a dim, friendly little man, for whom business and pleasure alike appeared to consist of scaring the birds out of his only fruit tree with a catapult. He never hit them, and very rarely frightened them; but although with every unsuccessful shot he tiptoed closer to the tree, panting with excitement, it was a point of honour with him to use no other method save the catapult, even when — as often happened — the birds were pecking away within six feet of his nose. In dead silence he would pour volley after volley at them; and only when he had at last dislodged them from one branch to another on the opposite side of the tree did he permit himself that loud exclamation which, uttered earlier, would have saved him an infinity of pebbles. It was a strange vendetta.

This kindly man placed his hut at our disposal. It had a clean floor, was free from insects, and unaccountably contained a trombone. The crew, who now had the loading well in hand, gave us two good meals, which we needed. Roger's ear was definitely on the mend, and Bob was getting stronger. Before we went to sleep we somehow managed to cheat ourselves into the conviction that Major Pingle had not caught the Syrian's launch: would not overhaul us on the next day: was not at that very moment sleeping within ten miles of us. . . .

But he was. Soon after dawn the lorry, bulging and bristling with passengers, came bumping out of the jungle down to the water's edge. Conspicuous in the huddled mass — as dominant as a dead salmon in a still life study — was Oscar, on whose huge face compassion fought a losing battle with amusement. 'Oh, Peter,' he cried, 'there is bad news for you.'

The world went dark. In vain I pointed out to myself that it didn't really matter in the least, that for all practical purposes it made no difference at all whether we arrived in Pará a day or two ahead of Major Pingle or a day or two behind him. It was no good.

It was nearly a month now since the race had started, since Major Pingle had left us (as he thought) stranded on that hot white praia at Bananal, among the fish-bones and the brandy bottles. For nearly a month, as we crawled down this interminable river, the race had underlain all our agonies and all our exultations; our hopes and our fears, our speculations and our jokes, had had a common origin and a common aim in the really very unimportant and even childish struggle to get down to the Amazon ahead of Major Pingle. It was too late now to laugh the whole thing off. The race had coloured our lives too completely to be reduced — as now, for our comfort's sake, it needed to be reduced — to its true perspective. My sense of proportion, applied like a vacuum cleaner to all that had accumulated on the floor of my mind during the past month, refused its office and made no impression. I felt very bitter. Bitter against fate in general and against the man Tola in particular. It was Tola, that exquisitely dishonourable man, who had done us down: Tola who had cancelled and rendered nugatory all those extra hours of paddling, that feverish yet patient process which had squeezed a few unwarranted leagues out of every day: Tola who, during the last week, had piled on the agonies of anti-climax and made us slowly savour in advance the varied humiliations of defeat. But for Tola we should have been in Pará by now. Because of Tola we were not only going to be beaten, but we were going to miss our boat as well.

At that moment the loathsome creature appeared, flapping his umbrella and urging the passengers into the canoes in the self-righteous tones of a man who has a reputation for punctuality to maintain. I seized the opportunity of being as rude to him as my limited Portuguese vocabulary would allow.

After that I felt better. The lorry had gone back without delay for Major Pingle and the Syrian's other passengers. But it now became apparent that we should leave before they appeared. The admission of defeat was once more narrowly postponed. Our lead (at one time, we realized wistfully, it must have been a week) had been reduced to a matter of an hour or so. But it still existed. We were still, however precariously, ahead. And you never knew what might happen before we all reached Alcobaça.

As the launch chugged out from her backwater towards the turbulent and rock-strewn channel of the river we listened with interest to the Paulistas' fragmentary and second-hand account of Pingle's Odyssey. His party, we gathered, had the air of men who are described in the stronger kind of fiction as having Been Through Hell. They had suffered badly in the rains: their boat had hit a rock in the rapids and sprung a serious leak: at Conceição one of the loyalists had been arrested and fined for bathing naked on the foreshore: and their crew had stood out, successfully, for double the wages we had paid. None of them, the Paulistas said, had been ill, but all appeared dejected, in spite of the fact that they had had the astonishing luck to arrive in Marabá twelve hours before the Syrian's launch left and had thus made an instant connection.

The Paulistas added the disquieting information that the Syrian's launch would probably go straight through to Pará after a night at Alcobaça. It was already crowded; and if there were any passages still available I was reasonably sure that — what with Major Pingle's influence on the one hand and the prior claims of our own fellow-passengers on the other — it would not be we who got them. However, there was nothing to do but wait and see.

The water was very low, and the channel writhed elusively through the rapids, the last and the fastest that we encountered. Anxiety sometimes qualified the good humour on the pilot's broad black face, and a twittering, as of starlings, arose from the straw-hats as we plunged into a boiling passage between steep rocks, already decorated with the bones of a launch which had been lost last year with all hands. But we came through all right, though there was one anxious moment when a valve broke and the engine stopped — luckily in a stretch of comparatively peaceful water. We lost half an hour repairing it; but the Syrian's launch was still behind us when, two hours before sunset, we sighted Alcobaça, a moribund, ramshackle little town, left high and dry by the ebbing fortunes of the rubber trade.

# CHAPTER X

# NOBBLING THE FAVOURITE

THE straw-hats were all positive that there would be a launch at Alcobaça, only awaiting our arrival to start for Pará: a big launch, one of the boats on the regular service. They were cheerfully and dogmatically confident of this, though their confidence was based only on a piece of garbled third-hand information, which itself was based on an out-of-date rumour, and which even so had to be modified and eked out with their own conjectures and deductions to fit the circumstances. The nearer we came to Alcobaça, the stronger grew their certainty, the keener their anticipatory delight. One of them, who knew the boat in question, even claimed to be able to descry her in the little huddle of shipping round the landing-stage, and happy cries of 'Viva!' rang out on the crowded decks on our launch.

But I knew the form. I had too much faith in our own bad luck to believe in that heaven-sent launch, which would waft us to Pará, perhaps just in time to catch our boat. No Brazilian, in my experience, ever betrays surprise, chagrin, or resentment when he is let down by his fellow-men: he has learnt to expect it. It is the same when he is let down by fate. He is so inured to disappointment that he no longer minds being disappointed; and so, against all the lessons of experience, he is an optimist. He has nothing to lose by his optimism. His high hopes, so repeatedly dashed, are resilient in the extreme; and he enjoys having them, it makes him feel good. That premature cheerfulness, for which (he is to discover) there are no grounds at all, was comforting while it lasted; and when it is taken away from him he does not feel, as you or I would, that he is worse off than he was before.

Oscar and Cassio, for instance, always believed the very best about whatever place lay immediately ahead of us, until we got there. Of all the rumours that we heard about it, they gave credence only to the ones they hoped were true: such as that it was only five leagues further on, that we should find meat and eggs and fruit on sale, that there were no mosquitoes on the praia. At first I was amazed at this. I grew impatient of their gullibility, pointing out that we had heard these very things of every place we had passed, and that they had always proved to be wholly without foundation. But they were incapable of scepticism, and would cite against the cream of our local information the roseate assurances of one old dotard in a canoe. When we got to the place, and found that it was ten leagues distant, and not five, and that you could not buy any food there at all, and that the air was grey with mosquitoes, they were neither abashed nor mortified. You cannot disillusion a Brazilian.

And so it happened now, as we sidled across the current towards the landing-stage at Alcobaça, that with the straw-hats who shouted 'Viva!' and assured us that we should catch our boat after all, I betted heavily, in beer, against the good fortune which they so confidently proclaimed; and won. For there was no launch in Alcobaça waiting to take us to Pará. It had left the day before.

We landed at the foot of a steep high bluff, over which the foremost of the crooked wooden houses peered uncertainly. I ran up a flight of almost perpendicular stone steps and plunged into the village. I had a plan.

It was clear that Alcobaça offered, of her own accord, no means of reaching Pará ahead of, or even soon after, the Syrian's launch, on which, for reasons that I have already explained, we had little or no chance of getting passages, and whose tiny crowded decks we were in any case reluctant to share with Major Pingle for two or three days. But would Alcobaça be galvanized into producing a specially commissioned boat by promises to pay an exorbitant price on arrival in Pará? It seemed to me that there was a thousand to one chance that this could be done.

I asked to be directed to the house of Doctor Amyntas. Diligent enquiry among our fellow-passengers had elicited the fact that Doctor Amyntas was to Alcobaça what Henry Ford is to Detroit, what Van Diemen was (one can only suppose) to Van Diemen's land, what Raymundo Tola was to Marabá. Doctor Amyntas was the big noise; in this one horse town he might be said to own the horse. And he possessed at least one fast launch, alleged to be capable of the journey to Pará in thirty-six hours.

I met him strolling down from his house to meet our launch. Doctor Amyntas was a twinkling little man with a sudden, unabashed pot-belly. There was a kind of benevolent authority in his elderly face, a certain honest smugness. His bald head was not unhandsomely shaped, and he spoke in a rich, a rather jaunty voice. He would have been well cast as what is I believe professionally known as a Small Bishop in one of Shakespeare's historical plays. He wore clean white ducks and a felt hat; and of course he carried an umbrella.

I introduced myself rather breathlessly and explained our situation. We were now near enough to civilization for false values to be current again, so for the purposes of my explanation I thought it best to raise Roger to the peerage and to lay a great deal of spurious stress on my own position as correspondent of the most powerful newspaper in the world. Expense, I implied, was no object to us once we reached Pará. Could Doctor Amyntas hire us his fastest launch, C.O.D.?

Doctor Amyntas was amused, as well he might be, and I saw to it that he was flattered as well. He would willingly hire us his launch he said, though the expense would be very great, on account of the price of petrol; but, alas, it was many months since she had been used, and he had no crew — it would take at least two days' preparation, and probably more, to make her ready for the journey. My plan had failed.

But I stuck to Doctor Amyntas. If there was anything that could be done, I felt that it could only be done through him. The little man had revealed in our talk qualities on which I believed I could work to some effect. He had humour, he had a little education, he was what they call in Brazil *delicado*; and if half what was said about him was true he had power in Alcobaça.

We walked together through the village and out on to the bluff above the landing-stage. I had no coat and no hat, both of which are indispensable on even the most informal Brazilian occasions; so I attracted much the same sort of attention as if I had walked collarless down Bond Street with the Prince of Wales. Doctor Amyntas, luckily, was a broad-minded man, and sufficiently well-informed to know that all foreigners are mad.

As we came out on to the bluff the situation underwent a sudden change and hope was reborn in me. Instinctively I had looked upstream, expecting to see the Syrian's launch coughing towards us out of the tail of the rapids. But it was not in sight yet, and when my eyes returned to the little bay below us I saw that it was no longer empty. A big steam launch was working its way in from downstream towards the landing-stage. Scarcely able to believe my eyes, I asked Doctor Amyntas what this might be.

He said that it was a boat that had been expected from Para: it was calling for a cargo of Brazil nuts. As for when it would start downstream again, who could tell? Probably in two or three days, possibly in less. Once she had her cargo on board, she would not delay. It would certainly be worth approaching the commandante and asking whether he could get us to Pará in time to catch our boat: although, seeing that we had not much more than forty-eight hours left, Doctor Amyntas did not expect his answer to be Yes.

I scrambled down the bluff and ran out along a gang-plank to the launch. I found the commandante: a spruce, erect little half-caste, with a quick mind, an incisive voice, and a brusque courtesy. I explained what we wanted of him. Could he do it?

He could not, he said. He was very definite. He had a big cargo to take on board; its loading would occupy the whole of to-morrow. He could not leave Alcobaça before midday on the 3rd, at the earliest. If we travelled with him we should miss our boat.

But I persisted. A strange, a Pentecostal fluency had re-vitalized my halting Portuguese. I drew Doctor Amyntas into the discussion, and the owner of the cargo (a wide-eyed seedy little man like a bedraggled bird) and the foreman of the gang who were to load the nuts. This was a half-caste with Indian blood in him: a proud, reserved, alert person, who walked delicately like a cat. Like most of the Brazilians I met belonging to what may be called the foreman class, this man proved reliable and effective.

All five of us talked at once for quite a long time.

In the end I got what I wanted. An extra crew would be engaged at our expense, and the cargo would be loaded that night; the men would work continuously from now on, and the launch would leave at noon to-morrow. The commandante (who, I began to perceive, not only knew what he was talking about but meant what he said) could not guarantee that we should reach Pará in time to catch our boat. But we should arrive some time on the 4th and he said that it was most unlikely that the *Pancras* would sail until several hours after the advertised time of nine a.m. From what I had seen of shipping organiza-tion in Brazil, I felt that there might be something in his theory. At any rate, we still had a chance; and we should at least not suffer the long-drawn-out ignominy of doing the last lap under Major Pingle's wing. For the moment, it seemed almost too good to be true. I felt very pleased with myself.

The price of the night loading would come to about eighty milreis, and our passages would cost us about forty-five milreis each. We could just do it, though it meant arriving in Pará without a taxi fare. I thanked everyone profusely and hurried up to the village.

As I reached the crest of the bluff, the Syrian's launch came in sight, a dark speck against the foaming background of the rapids. I told the others what I had done, grabbed hold of Oscar, and galloped him off to the telegraph office on the outskirts of the village. Here he helped me to send off two telegrams in Portuguese: one to the Consul, and one to the shipping company, asking them to do all in their power to hold the *Pancras* until our arrival, which would be not later than the evening of the 4th. After this I felt better; it looked as if everything had been done that could be done. But it is perhaps typical of all my, or anybody's else's, efforts on behalf of this comic expedition that neither telegram was delivered until several hours after we had reached Pará.

When I got back I found that the Syrian's launch had docked. All the passengers had come ashore with the exception of Major Pingle's party, who sat, a frigid, meditative, and carefully incurious group, on the deck where they had spent the last two days: they apparently had no wish to risk an encounter. We gazed down on them from the edge of the bluff, feeling — as one always does when one looks down on one's fellow-beings from a height — Olympian and contemptuous. They chose not to recognize us, thereby adopting a position in which they were extremely vulnerable and from which they could not retaliate. We opened an indirect fire of insult of the private school variety; it was perhaps not very dignified, but the temptation was strong.

It was being said on all sides that their launch would leave for Pará at dawn, and almost all Tola's passengers were booking places on her. I was advised to do the same; our steam launch, it was alleged, was not only more expensive but much slower than the Syrian's, and the commandante would find it impossible to keep his guarantee to us about leaving at noon to-morrow.

All this made me nervous. I had been let down so often that

I would not have betted heavily on that guarantee. We were clearly taking a big risk in sticking to the steam launch, and for the sake of what? For the sake of maintaining an entirely valueless independence and avoiding Major Pingle's company on the last stage of our journey, and for the sake of an infinitesimal outside chance of finishing ahead of him. Public opinion thought us mad. The Syrian's launch was a certainty, they said; it could do the journey in well under forty-eight hours.

It could. But would it? I had a short but instructive conversation with the Syrian himself. Yes, he was going to make all the speed he could. How soon he would get to Pará he could not say for certain. There was a great deal still to arrange. . . .

'A great deal still to arrange.' How amazing to find myself deriving comfort from those familiar words! Judicious eavesdropping convinced me of their truth and importance. I discovered that the Syrian lacked a pilot and was short of petrol.

Here was good news indeed, and I took it to the others. Night had fallen, but the opposition was still brooding at its cheerless post on board the launch. We had taken up our position at the head of the steps leading up from the landing stage. Behind us, the open door of Alcobaça's only bar projected on to the darkness a strong glare of light, and we took care that Major Pingle, in the bay below, could always see one or more of our truculent silhouettes against this light. Since he appeared to regard the possibility of an encounter with us as an insuperable obstacle to coming ashore, it was as well to remind him that he could not avoid one if he did; we stood sardonic guardians over the beer and biscuits for which the loyalists must have been pining. Their devotion to their leader, and his command over them, may be gauged from the fact that, although there were no sanitary arrangements of any sort on the launch, they stayed heroically where they were until she left the next day.

We were discussing the Syrian's petrol shortage, a. d someone remarked wistfully what a wonderful coup it would be if we

348

could only corner all the petrol in the village. It was then that I had an inspiration.

I remembered something that Cassio had said about Doctor Amyntas having violently pro-revolutionary sympathies. Oscar and Cassio, in the course of a week spent in talking politics all day with the inhabitants of Marabá, had evolved a number of startling theories about what was going to happen to them when they reached Pará. The only point which all these theories had in common was the belief that they would be arrested as soon as they landed. Cassio, loyal as ever to Zenda and to Hollywood, had confided to us his intention of jumping overboard and swimming ashore under cover of night as soon as we came within striking distance of the city; and he had even gone rather unsuccessfully through the motions of disguising himself as a peasant by buying a suit of sky-blue overalls, which were ten times more conspicuous and respectable than his ordinary clothes.

Now both he and Oscar feared — and I think with some cause — that an enemy in Marabá had drawn up a document revealing their identities, and that this document was now on board the Syrian's launch, on its way to the authorities in Pará. It was this, combined with the fact that Doctor Amyntas had expressed his desire to help the Paulistas in every way he could, that suggested to me a plan for nobbling the opposition on the last lap of our race. In its final form it was as much Cassio's plan as mine; and it was as follows:

Cassio and I would go to Doctor Amyntas; would explain to him about the document on board the Syrian's launch; would point out to him how essential it was that the boat carrying the Paulistas should reach Pará before the boat carrying the document; and would try to persuade Doctor Amyntas, who controlled all the petrol in Alcobaça, to refuse to sell the Syrian any. If we could succeed in this, the Syrian would leave Alcobaça with only enough petrol to take him as far as the next

village; and even if he found in the next village sufficient for
his needs, he would be bound to encounter delay in getting it.
It looked a pretty good plan to us, and we hurried away into
the darkness, childish and fantastic conspirators.

Intrigue is not always delightful. But when it is carried on
behind closed shutters in a remote Brazilian village; when it
aims, by the exploitation of somebody else's political convic-
tions, at reversing in your favour the expected decision of a
thousand mile boat-race which has lasted a month; when it is
lubricated by innumerable bottles of the first iced beer you have
drunk for months; and when, above all, it is crowned with
complete success — in this combination of circumstances (a
comparatively rare one, I admit) there is a great deal to be said
for intrigue. That scene was as near true comedy as anything
else in the whole expedition. I enjoyed it immensely.

We found Doctor Amyntas alone, and he received us affably.
There was an exchange of courtesies, and Cassio and he discussed, with a very authoritative air, the latest crop of manifestoes. (The activities of both sides in the revolution were at
this stage confined almost entirely to the issuing of these stately
but practically meaningless documents.) Gradually we approached the business in hand, and the air grew thick with
flattery as Cassio explained what we wanted. As a personal
favour, and as a contribution to the cause which he theoretically
espoused, would Doctor Amyntas oblige us by refusing the
Syrian his petrol?

When Doctor Amyntas heard our scheme his face lit up, and
he called loudly to his servant for iced beer. He was delighted
with the idea. He had no love for the Syrian, or for anyone
else in Marabá. His sense of humour was tickled, and (above
all) he was flattered by the opportunity of parading his omnipo-
tence. He became radiant, and chuckled almost incessantly.
Of course he would do this for us, he cried. We fell gleefully
on the beer.

Presently two men came in, emissaries from the Syrian. They

sat down, twiddling their hats, and for a time talked politics in obsequious tones. Deviously they approached the object of their errand. The Syrian, they said, was short of petrol for his journey to Pará; he would be very grateful if Doctor Amyntas would sell him a few cases.

A look of profound and almost painfully sincere regret came over the doctor's face. He was desolated, he said, that he could not be of service to these distinguished travellers; but had, alas, barely enough petrol for his own poor needs — he dared not deplete his stock. At this the two men began to mutter together, while Doctor Amyntas winked at us with such vehemence that I feared he would do himself an injury; and presently the emissaries came out with an offer of a price far higher than the ordinary one, which looked as if the Syrian's need was desperate. But Doctor Amyntas was adamant, though seemingly almost in tears; and the two men withdrew with rather perfunctory expressions of mutual esteem. They were both old enemies of mine from Marabá, and I rejoiced to see their discomfiture.

We sat on for a long time, destroying the reputations of generals and consuming bottle after bottle of beer. On two occasions further emissaries appeared, but Doctor Amyntas, revelling in the display of his guile and his power, dismissed them as he had dismissed the first. He and Cassio talked faster and faster; more and more insects circled droning round the naked electric light bulb: more and more beer was consumed; from Doctor Amyntas' gesticulating hands the perspiration splashed upon the floor. . . .

Wrapped in a deep contentment, I went to sleep sitting upright on my stool.

# CHAPTER XI

## STERN CHASE

In the light of day, and of our exclusive knowledge of their predicament, the figures of the opposition, squatting on the launch with their heads together like a covey of partridges on a frosty evening, looked ludicrous and puny. We gloated over them from the top of the bluff. Twenty-four hours ago we had been in despair: now we were full of elation and excitement. In our race the odds were still against us; but they had shortened considerably overnight. We watched with equanimity the Syrian's preparations for departure.

Our own were going forward satisfactorily. Between the sheds in the village and the hold of the steam launch a score of little figures scurried industriously to and fro, carrying on their heads huge baskets of Brazil nuts (a delicacy for which we had come to entertain the most profound repugnance). From time to time I went and photographed them. The foreman said that everything would be ready by noon; and I calculated that we should get away by three o'clock at the latest.

The morning wore on slowly. The Syrian's launch, which was to have started at dawn, remained at anchor. But she was leaving at any minute, we were told; a pilot had been found, and everyone was confident that they would be able to pick up petrol on their way downstream. People began to drift on board with luggage and provisions.

At half-past nine her whistle screamed. The opposition perked up and began to look jaunty. They knew nothing as yet of the petrol situation; they were sure they had us beat. With all due gravity we trooped down to the gang-plank and in a reverent silence took a photograph of them. For some reason, this made them very angry; but we retired in good order, with the air of men who had struck a blow for science.

At 10 o'clock the Syrian went on board, the whistle blew a long, confident blast, and the launch started. Major Pingle was in the lead again.

But the long race was going to have a well-fought finish. As I watched them disappear downstream I tried to assess our respective chances. They had a start of several hours, and probably the faster boat. On the other hand, it was doubtful whether they could travel by night, as we could; their boat was overcrowded, the Syrian was a timid man, and I had heard him express a lack of confidence in his pilot. Moreover, they were bound to lose a certain amount of time replenishing their petrol supply. And I was gratified to observe the presence among their passengers of a number of women; this, in the absence of all sanitary arrangements on board the launch, meant further delay. I decided that we still had a small but respectable chance of beating Major Pingle.

We left at 2 o'clock, four hours behind the other launch. I bade an affectionate farewell to Doctor Amyntas, perhaps the most attractive of the subsidiary characters in this picaresque drama. Our courtesies were interrupted by the red parrot, which seized hold of the string of the siren and lacerated the shimmering midday silence with a ululation of sustained intensity. The launch backed slowly out into the river; then her bows swung round, and we slid downstream after Major Pingle. We had forty odd hours in which to catch the only boat leaving for England that month.

We settled down to what was to prove the most comfortable stage in our journey since we landed at Rio; but it remained, to the very end, painfully exciting.

Half a dozen of the men who had come down with us from Marabá on Tola's launch had elected to back the outsider, and had taken passages on the steam launch in preference to the Syrian's. They were an unattractive lot, and from the first our relations were a little strained, owing to their refusal to pay their share of the extra eighty milreis for night-loading, which I had made a condition of their coming with us. Luckily this did not matter, as we had the money — all except five milreis, which I borrowed from Oscar. (To this day I am not quite clear how we managed to make our original capital of 600 milreis last for four weeks and 1000 miles. We must have been very lucky.) But a tendency to default was not the worst trait in our fellow-passengers; their conduct in other respects, as you shall hear, cruelly reduced our slender chances of success.

The Brazilians are in many ways a likeable people, and although I do not claim to know very much about them, I had first hand experience of three different classes (in so far as classes may be said to exist in that democratic country). First, there was the aristocracy, represented by Oscar and Cassio. It would be hard to find two nicer people anywhere. Their manners and their good humour withstood far better than ours did the occasionally severe tests of that interminable journey. To the last, they were charming, courteous, and unselfish. But they were woefully ineffective. Like children, they would be fired with enthusiasm for some project, would even set about implementing it; and then something would crop up — an obstacle or a diversion — and they would allow themselves to be sidetracked into a complete oblivion of their scheme. They had a kind of irresponsible fatalism; their situation had to be desperate indeed before they took steps to improve it. They had ability, but they wasted themselves; the gulf between ambition and performance was far wider than it need have been.

Then, at the other end of the scale, you had the common people, the labourers: the men who rowed for us, the loaders of nuts, the boys who drove cars or looked after ponies. These were almost all of mixed blood — white and black, or white and Indian, or a combination of all three. They had a tremendous capacity for hard work, though they did not indulge it unless they had to; they were a rough, violent, friendly people, and if they slacked and stole and drank whenever you gave them the opportunity, they did not let you down if they could help it. They belonged to a low type, but they did not have about them that shoddy baseness which distinguished their immediate social superiors.

These were the people of the small shop-keeper class. I saw a great deal of them during the last fortnight of our journey, and found them not at all engaging. They were expansive, facetious, cowardly, and unreliable: grasping, self-important, insular, and dirty. They were full of promises, which they never kept. They did nothing at all except talk; three-quarters of what they said was untrue, and the rest was nonsense. They were altogether in bad taste.

But Brazil is a huge country, and I have no reason to suppose that these generalizations hold good outside that primitive and unimportant part of her interior through which I travelled. They should accordingly be taken seriously only by those who contemplate the descent of the Araguaya-Tocantins. To this minority of my readers they will prove of considerable value.

There were no more rapids ahead of us, and we made a good steady run that day. The little wood-burning launch had no great turn of speed, but the commandante insisted that if we had luck there was a decent chance of our reaching Pará on the morning of the 4th. My confidence in him increased fast, and I remember him with gratitude and affection: he was the only completely reliable man I met in Brazil.

There were no incidents that day, except that we rather unexpectedly met an Archbishop. What he was Archbishop of I am not quite clear; but there he was, a tall, disconsolate man in a long black robe, violet stockings, and a kind of Gothic bowler hat with a sprig of green stuff tucked jauntily into the band.

We thought he looked very queer; God knows what he thought about us. He was going on a tour of his archdiocese in a big double-decker launch; we tied up alongside it at a little landing-stage where we called for wood. It was in many respects one of the most remarkable vessels I have ever seen. The upper deck, which was covered with an awning, was occupied by an altar, several deck chairs and two extraordinarily pretty girls, of a markedly non-episcopal appearance. The lower deck, between the engine-room and the crew's quarters, was heaped high with the gifts of a devout flock: bananas, oranges, coco-nuts, pumpkins, melons, slabs of dried piraracú, maize, honey, a sprinkling of poultry, and one enormous black and white cow, in whose eyes was to be observed that look of rather distrait self-analysis peculiar to those who believe themselves to be good sailors but are not quite sure. Most of our passengers made haste to board this floating Harvest Festival — not, as I at first supposed, to ask for the Archbishop's blessing, but to purchase at an exorbitant price the Archbishop's iced beer. Having no money at all, we were not in a position to enter the market for this commodity.

At dusk we ate a heavy meal, and washed it down with water which, on account of the proximity of the Amazon, was the colour of weak tea: though no one seemed to think any the worse of it for that. The little covered deck was full of pendant Brazilians in their hammocks, so Roger and I lay down to sleep in the bows. This was our last night but one under the stars, and we killed most of it with talk. Somewhere (how far?) ahead of us in the darkness was Major Pingle. Was the Syrian's launch at anchor? Or would he take the risk and run on through the black and silent hours down the ever-widening river? We debated the point at length, but inconclusively.

# CHAPTER XII

# A VERY SHORT HEAD

THERE is something peculiarly satisfying about sleeping on a boat, or in a train. When one wakes up in the morning, and sees the world slipping past, and reflects that it has been slipping past like that all night, one has a vague but gratifying sense of having scored, of having got something for nothing. Progress has been achieved without one's co-operation — that co-operation which, through a long yesterday, one found so tiresome, and which, though it consisted only in sitting still and getting bored and wishing that one was going faster, seemed in some indefinable way essential to the conduct of the journey. Asleep, one has shirked all one's responsibilities, and it has turned out to make no difference at all. One has escaped a penance with impunity.

When we woke on that morning of October 3rd, twenty-four hours before our boat was due to sail, the river was all yellow, and much wider than we had known it. We were very near the Amazon. We plunged at once into frantic speculations. Was the Syrian's launch still ahead of us, or had we passed her, at anchor, during the night? There were no means of telling.

Towards noon I noticed that the current seemed to have turned against us; we were losing speed. The commandante looked troubled, and said something about the tide. Very soon afterwards he put his helm over; we edged in to a little landing-stage and tied up.

At the head of the landing-stage there was a store of sorts, and in the dank oppressive jungle around it a cluster of wooden huts. These all stood on tall piles, so as to be out of reach of the floods, and they were connected by an intricacy of bridges made of rotting duckboards. In the dry season all life was carried on ten feet above the ground level. Huge opalescent butterflies drifted around and underneath this queer suspended world.

The commandante was non-committal and appeared anxious. We might have to wait here a few hours, he said, on account of the tide. I followed him up to the store with trepidation.

The store-keeper was benign, hospitable, and informative. His information was very bitter to hear. The tide was against us now, he said, but that was nothing serious: in an hour or two we should be able to go on. But it would be wrong for us again to-night, and at one crucial point it was liable to hold up our progress for the best part of twelve hours. This point was a narrow channel which branched off from the Tocantins just above its point of confluence with the Amazon, and made a short cut to a smaller river which led directly to Pará. This channel had been made in order to save the seldom very seaworthy shipping of the river from exposure to heavy weather in the great bay of Marajó, which lies between the mouth of the Tocantins and Pará. In the dry season the channel was only passable at high tide; we should reach it at dusk that night, when the water would be low, and we should probably have to wait at this end until the early hours of to-morrow morning before we could get through.

With real regret the commandante explained this new development to me. There was, he said, only the slenderest of chances that we should reach that channel before it became impassable. If we did, we should be in Pará early to-morrow morning; if we did not, we could not arrive before the late afternoon. He was very sorry, but there it was: a slice of bad luck.

I was tired of slices of bad luck. Was there absolutely nothing we could do about it, I asked him? The commandante considered for a moment; then he said, Yes, there was. We could give the channel a miss, go right on down the Tocantins, and round across that stormy bay to Pará; if all went well, we should arrive in the middle of the morning. In such a boat as his, which was not built to face rough weather, there was of course a risk; but he had made this journey several times before, though his owners discouraged him from doing it. To oblige us, he was quite prepared to attempt it now, if the other passengers were willing.

'If the other passengers were willing. . . .' But of course they must be willing, I thought. After all, it was our enterprise and our money which had made this comfortable and expeditious journey possible. Surely there would be no difficulty here. . . . I hurried back to the launch, where everyone was eating a meal, and put the project to them.

They turned it down. They turned it down without hesitation, without shame, without apology. They had no wish to be drowned, they said. It was no business of theirs whether we caught our boat or not. They were not going to risk their lives because four Englishmen were in a hurry; Englishmen were always in a hurry. We must learn to have a little patience. . . .

Loathsome creatures! I appealed to their sympathy, to their pride, to their sporting instincts. I told them that their national honour was at stake: that if they refused this risk I would make the name of Marabá, through the medium of *The Times*, a by-word for cowardice and dishonourable conduct. They laughed. It was no good. I abandoned blackmail in favour of abuse. They went on laughing.

So when at last we were able to go on, our hopes were not so high as they had been, and the element of suspense had been strengthened. We were now virtually certain that we had passed the Syrian's launch last night, for nothing had been seen of her at the various landing-stages where we had called for fuel. But our lead was worth nothing, because the launch, with her shallower draught, could get through that channel whatever the state of the tide. She was gaining on us even now; it seemed likely that she would pass us, impotent and at anchor, while we waited at the mouth of the channel. The race would go to Major Pingle after all.

Just before dusk the tension became acute. We were off the

mouth of the channel now, slanting in haste towards it across a waste of yellow waters. A huge black cloud partly obscured the beginnings of a sprawling amber sunset; the rising wind sang in our scanty and superfluous rigging, flattening the blue plume of wood-smoke at our funnel. A bleak and sickly light heralded the storm's approach. The launch ran for shelter, lurching to the choppy waves.

Suddenly, from behind the last headland we had passed, a boat appeared, and was identified at once as the Syrian's. Like us, she was making for the mouth of the channel with all speed. She was not more than half a mile away. In an hour at most we should be neck and neck.

The commandante was splendid. It was not certain, he said, that the Syrian would attempt the channel that night, though he could get through if he tried. In any case, he would probably call first at a little village at the mouth, in search of local information and perhaps of petrol. The water was low now; but we would push on as fast as we could. If we had luck, we might be able to scramble through before morning. Anyhow, we would go on till we ran aground.

We did. Night fell as we reached the mouth of the channel, a tiny loop-hole in the high black wall of jungle. Very slowly we groped our way on through the darkness, with the engines throttled down. From the bows came the voice, now dreamy, now electric, of a man taking soundings: 'Quatro . . . quatro . . . cinco e meia . . . *tres* . . . quatro . . . cinco . . . *dois e meio* . . . quatro. . . .' The wind had dropped again, and between the close and towering ranks of trees the words had the confidential urgency of words spoken in a small, dark room.

It was ten o'clock before we stuck finally. We manned the poles and raced the engines, but the launch was fast aground and would not budge. We must wait for the tide to turn. I lay down on the roof of the launch, staring into the blackness astern, expecting at any moment to see the light at the Syrian's mast-head crawl cautiously round the last bend towards us. Fireflies glowed and winked deceptively; time and again I could have sworn that a light was coming up the channel behind us, a light intermittently seen through crannies in the solid palisade of trees. My eyes and nerves ached. Presently I fell asleep.

I woke three hours later, and we were under way again, sliding very slowly down a twisting corridor of black water. Only a thin column of stars marched above us between the overhanging trees; the channel was so narrow that two boats could not pass. I stuck my head over the edge of the roof and asked anxiously whether the Syrian had passed us yet. Nothing had passed us, the commandante replied; he thought the Syrian must have tied up for the night at the mouth of the channel.

But at that moment a siren screamed impatiently in the darkness behind us, and a triangle of lights — white at the apex, red and green at the base — stood out suddenly in the night, 400 yards astern. A launch had rounded the bend behind us.

Was it the Syrian's launch? The commandante admitted with reluctance that he thought it was. She came up with us steadily, and as the distance between us lessened the beat of her engines, the dimly seen shape of her bow, confirmed my fears. It was either the Syrian's boat, or her twin. It seemed as if hope was really dead at last. I set about burying mine: a painful business.

Painful, and prolonged. Our pursuer could not pass us here. For an hour we thudded down the narrow channel one behind the other, until I thought that tricolour triangle of lights was stamped for ever on my brain. Occasionally she hooted petulantly, but with the best will in the world we could not have let her by. Major Pingle, I reflected, must be feeling pleased.

At the end of an hour the channel debouched into that other, smaller river which led directly to Pará. Here there was plenty of room to pass, and I prepared once more to admit defeat. The sympathetic commandante crowded on steam; our boat trembled and gathered speed. But the launch behind us gathered more.

Smoothly she overhauled us: drew level, not twenty feet away: and slipped ahead.

She was a boat I had never seen before. She was not the Syrian's launch.

That was a moment of exquisite relief. Amidships, on her covered deck, four men sat round a table playing cards. I can see them now. A hurricane lantern hung over their heads; the glass of it was dirty with smoke, and I remember how the flame inside it trembled to the pulsing of their motor. They all looked across at us and waved, with abrupt, preoccupied gestures: all except the one who sat on the far side, facing us, the one who had only to raise his eyes from his cards to acknowledge our presence, but who did not raise them. He was a thin wolfish-looking man; his cheek-bones stood out sharply in the lamp-light which fell on his head from above.

Very soon the night had swallowed up that stranger boat. There were only three hours to go till dawn. I fell asleep.

It was ten o'clock the next morning. The sun shone hotly on the coloured water. Rich foliage hung heavily along the river's edge. Only the *babassú* palms stood up proudly, refusing to wilt. Pará was in sight.

Pará was in sight. On the horizon a huddle of red and white and grey roofs had somehow slipped in between the eternal river and the eternal forest. The sky-line bristled with masts and funnels. Our journey was at an end.

Or nearly at an end. We should arrive in two hours, at noon. Would the *Pancras* be there? Or had she duly sailed an hour ago?

I am (the observant reader may have guessed as much) an optimist. My instincts told me that she had not; it would be grossly unfair if she had. But I had learnt to know better than my instincts; and to appeal to fate (in Brazil, at any rate) for justice is like appealing to the law of averages for a system at roulette. I pointed out to the others at some length that there would be a great though perverse satisfaction in having missed our boat by so tiny a margin. We prepared assiduously for the worst. To have won our race, we reminded each other, was after all the great thing.

The voracious launch needed a last consignment of fuel. We swerved out of our course and made for one of the familiar landing stages, backed by a store, a bar, and a cluster of huts. We tied up, and Roger and I bounded ashore on the heels of the commandante. We might get news of the *Pancras* at this frequented place.

'I don't believe you,' I said, five minutes later, in a very firm voice.

The commandante smiled and shrugged his shoulders.

'Very well. Read that. It is certain. It is official.' He held out a newspaper, folded with the shipping intelligence uppermost. The newspaper was dated October 4th.

I took it, and read: 'The departure of the *Pancras* has been postponed. She will sail at noon to-morrow (October 5th).'

It was too good to be true. I handed the paper to Roger in silence and stared in a kind of numb ecstasy at a pile of tangerines on the counter of the store. I was dimly aware that our fellow-passengers were embracing each other and ordering drinks with much more than their customary abandon. It was some time before I connected this with the headlines on the front page which announced that the revolution had ended overnight; for it seemed to me only natural that the whole world should be rejoicing at our luck.

We had brought it off, after all. We had struggled for a month to beat Major Pingle and to catch that boat; and now we had done both, with a few hours in hand. It would indeed, I reflected, be hard to find two achievements more intrinsically valueless and more absolutely satisfying. . . .

From now on there was no more need to hurry. One could return to a reasonable life. There would be books, and food, and sheets to sleep in, and decent tobacco, and newspapers: no more uncertainty, no more delay, no more discomfort.

But it had been a good race, all the same. My ecstasy wore off very suddenly. What a minute ago had seemed too good to be true was now too true to be any longer good. It was all over now. The bright world seemed flat and empty and unreal, like something under a glass case. Probably the glass case had been there all along, only we had had no time to notice it. . . .

Roger and I walked back to the launch in silence.

# EPILOGUE

## HOME SWEET HOME

# DOVER

'ANYTHING to declare?'

'No.'

'No spirits, no perfumes, no jewellery?'

'No.'

'No musical instruments . . .?'

'No.'

'No tea, coffee, clocks . . .?'

The official droned on. He was, as they say, exploring every avenue. Or was he perhaps trying to be funny? Before him lay two indescribably filthy linen bags full of old clothes: one rucksack containing the small stage properties of aboriginal life (now on view in the British Museum): and a long, lethal bundle, swathed in puttees, of spears, clubs, and bows and arrows. . . . Musical instruments? *Perfumes?* Come, come, my man. . . .

At last he was satisfied. Chalked crosses sanctioned the import into Great Britain of our battered and outlandish gear. One porter managed the lot with ease. As he swung the dingy, bloodstained sacks over his shoulder I had a momentary vision of that lorry which, five months ago, had panted down to Tilbury with the expedition's impedimenta — the theodolite: the wireless set: the bows with a fifty-two-pound pull and the highly varnished arrows which were to have armed our native guides: the labels bearing the name of the expedition with which everything had been plastered: the automatic shot-guns: the tear-gas bombs: the bull-mastiff. . . . That had been a long time ago. We were travelling lighter now.

Roger and I had left the *Pancras* at Lisbon. Though in many ways a splendid ship, she is none of your Ocean Greyhounds; by finishing our journey overland we had saved several days. We walked now with a certain diffidence among the dapper discharge of the Channel boat. In Pará limited funds and limited time had prevented us from making good the deficiencies in a wardrobe which the non-appearance of our luggage from São Paulo had rendered gravely inadequate to the demands of civilized life. We were hatless. We were clearly the wrong colour. Our clothes bore what the police call Signs of a Struggle. We were regarded on all sides with suspicion.

But there was no denying that it was nice to be back. As we followed our porter through the crowd — an easier task than usual, for those spears had aroused in him, as in his colleagues of Portugal, Spain, and France, something of the long dormant spirit of the medieval tiltyard — we felt an absurd impulse to congratulate everyone who was wearing a bowler hat, or reading the *Daily Express*, or talking about the weather. At the sight of a policeman we could scarce forbear to cheer.

'Well, anyhow,' said Roger, 'we're all right now. We've had all that's coming to us on this journey.'

I agreed. How comforting, how even luxurious it was to feel that we were at last out of reach of delay, annoyance, obstruction. . . .

'Hi!' roared a customs official.

I stopped. Our porter disappeared in the direction of the train.

'What's that?' asked the customs official, suspiciously.

I was carrying in my hand a tapering stick of tobacco from the Amazon, beautifully wrapped in spirals of fibre. It weighed perhaps six ounces.

'It's tobacco,' I said.

'Did you declare it?'

I said it had been placed with the rest of the luggage for examination.

'Where is the rest of your luggage?'

I said that it must be on the train by now.

'It must be brought back here,' said the official, 'and re-examined.

It was. Taken in conjunction with our villainous appearance, those six ounces of tobacco had conjured up in the
official's mind who can say what wild hopes of contraband.
From South America, too! Bombs, drugs, orchids, perhaps
even a couple of diminutive White Slaves, might well be hidden
in those discoloured sacks. Eager hands ransacked them; but
methodically, with deliberation. The boat train whistled. . . .

It was useless to protest our innocence. It was useless to
appeal to their compassion, pointing out that we were pardon-
ably impatient to return to those friends and relations with
whom for five months we had been denied even postal communication. The officials had a duty to perform, and I must
say they performed it thoroughly. Nimble fingers explored the
recesses of old boots thick with mildew. Insanitary relics from
the pockets of malodorous shirts were scrutinized with gallantry
and care. The toucan's bill, the skull and horns of a veado, the
disintegrating copy of *Tom Jones*, the ancient cartridge belt —
all our exotic odds and ends were probed, shaken, held upside
down or turned inside out according to their nature.

The boat train whistled no longer. It had gone.

They said there was another in two hours. Receiving with
an ill grace the cheerful assurances of the officials that they had
found no dutiable article among our personal effects, and that
even on the incriminating tobacco there was nothing to pay,
I wandered off into the town to buy a pipe.

It was late October. The streets were grey and dank. Over
the harbour gulls hovered and incontinently dipped against a
steady wind. Outside little shops the battle-cries of Beaver-
brook and Rothermere rustled in moist unison. A film was
announced on a poster as 'A Jungle Epic. . . .'

A Jungle Epic? Whatever those words may mean, they can
hardly be applied (I reflected) to this journey which is now so
near its end. The spirit of burlesque had been our tutelar deity.
A Jungle Lampoon, perhaps. . . .

As I walked slowly through the bleak autumn streets, memory

paraded for my benefit inconsequent, staccato excerpts from the comedy, like cuttings from a News Reel. I remembered the portentous improbabilities with which we had juggled so confidently in London. I remembered the disillusioned buzz emitted by those stationary bicycles on which we had pedalled across so great a portion of the South Atlantic. I remembered the comic waiter in Rio who over-estimated his command of English and offered us Wild Kidney when he meant Wild Duck. I remembered the sow which had invaded our sleeping quarters on the road up country. I remembered the heat dancing on that barricaded bridge, and the spittoon in the palace of the Interventor of Goyaz, and our first sight of the Araguaya, a crimson sunset river. . . .

These were all isolated pictures. They were succeeded by a jumbled sequence of the small, diurnal things which various stages of our journey had stamped many times upon my mind. The hot sand squeaking as we plodded through it: the plaintive whiffling of the little otters: the cry of a certain bird at night, the very accent of a gentle disillusionment: Roger scowling at the compass: the taste of raw farinha: the smell of Carajas: the familiar play of muscles in the paddlers' backs: the unremitting protests of the parrot: the back of Oscar's head, a study in abstruse contrition: rain on the roof at Marabá: the taste of too many bananas.

It had been great fun, and very funny. Reality is a commodity hard to come by: and, when found, not always easily recognizable. One gropes for it through a fog of preconceptions, misled by other people's labels; the highest authorities have perhaps pondered the subject too deeply to be of service here. No one can say with certainty, 'I found reality at such a place and such a time'; but there are days and circumstances in which, when one looks back on them, it seems as if reality was not so far away as usual. For me, at any rate, some of the days and some of the circumstances which I have described were of that sort, in spite of their strong flavour of the ludicrous and the fantastic.

But I have written down the word reality four times on a page, and that is as much as it will stand. Too many leader-writers, too many shaggy women overheard in small restaurants, too many of the starker authors have sapped the word's vitality. It should be subjected as seldom as possible to the strain of a public appearance.

In the last analysis, it had been comedy that I looked for from Brazil, and comedy had been forthcoming — comedy with a faint but stimulating tang of melodrama. I thought of Major Pingle, and saw again that tall, dilapidated figure furiously decimating its moustache. Poor Major Pingle! I recalled him with gratitude, if not with affection. I had a lot to thank him for. How dull it would all have been without Major Pingle! How drearily those last thousand miles would have passed but for our race with him! Our wide, though perhaps no longer very useful knowledge of the river-folk, our command of a bastard Portuguese, the paddling muscles in our shoulders — all these we owed to Major Pingle's efforts to extricate himself from the delicate position in which his good nature had landed him. The Wicked Uncle had turned out to be the Fairy God-mother in disguise. Poor Major Pingle. . . .

A train whistled. It was time to return to the station, to step back into a former life. The interlude was over. The blue and green scenery must be stored away, the plot condensed to meet the exigencies of conversation. In these demure streets, where regular lamps burnt palely in the dusk, it was all, even now, a little difficult to believe. Soon it would be hard to remember.

A light suddenly turned on in a parlour window projected on to the yellow blind the outline of an aspidistra. I took it as a hint. I said good-bye to the jungle. I bought an evening paper.

# GLOSSARY

# GLOSSARY

*Arara*  A macaw.

*Banzeira*  A local name for the north wind.

*Batalõa*  A four-oared, clinker-built boat, 20 to 30 feet long.

*Boiadeiro*  Cowboy.

*Capivara*  A kind of water guinea-pig, about the size of a sheep.

*Cerva*  A big deer.  I believe their weight runs up to 20 stone, but the heads are poor.

*Facão*  A big knife, like a cutlass, and usually carried in a sheath; similar to, though in my opinion less serviceable than, the machete of Central America, which is heavier and better balanced.

*Farinha*  A coarse flour made from the mandioca root.

*Fazenda*  A farm.

*Feijoa*  Rice and black beans.  The national dish.

*Iguana*  A big lizard.

*Inhuma*  A mysterious bird, bigger than a cock capercailzie, and said to have talons on its wings.  An object of some sort of superstition among the Carajas.

*Jaburú*  A white stork with a black head and a red neck, standing nearly five feet tall.

*Jacaré*  Alligator.

*Jacú*  A foolish, peering, dark-brown bird, which we called a pheasant.

*Jacuba*  A mixture of farinha, rice, and water.

*Mandioca*  The cassava root.  Tastes like a disheartened potato.

*Mareca*  A wild duck something like the canvas-back.

*Mataburro*  A primitive form of bridge.

*Montaría*  A kind of clinker-built canoe.

*Mutum*  The curassow bird: a wild turkey.

*Nada*  Nothing.

*Pato*  The biggest wild duck in the world.  Very handsome in black and white, and excellent eating.

*Pensão*  An inn.

*Pinga*  A spirit made of fermented sugar-cane.

*Piraracú*  Possibly the biggest freshwater fish in the world.

*Praia*  A sandbank.

# GLOSSARY

*Rapadura*  A substance like toffee made from sugar and sold in bricks.

*Sertão*  The Interior. A word with wild and woolly connotations.

*Si Dios quize*  'If God wills.' An indispensable rider to all Brazilian statements about the future.

*Tôldo*  An awning, and hence a cabin on a boat.

*Ubá*  A dug-out canoe.

*Urubú*  A vulture.

*Veado*  A little deer the size of a roe.